# What's in a Poem

*What's*

# in a Poem

John Rylander

*St. Cloud State College*

*and*

Edith Rylander

Dickenson Publishing Company, Inc.
*Encino, California, and Belmont, California*

Library of Congress Catalog Card Number: 71-167902

Printed in the United States of America

ISBN: 0-8221-0003-7

10  9  8  7  6  5  4  3  2  1

# *Acknowledgments*

To Dan, Shireen, and Eric, in partial payment for the time
we stole from them writing this book; to Gary Anderson, for
his research and insights and assistance writing Chapter 4;
to Herb Eschliman of Central Missouri State College, Walker
Gibson of the University of Massachusetts, Robert Griffin
of California State College at Hayward, and all the others
whose suggestions helped us; and to Mike Snell, for years of
encouragement and faith.

The Antioch Review: "Old Man Stuckel Talks to the Hogs"
by Edith Rylander. Reprinted by permission of The
Antioch Review.

Atheneum Publishers, Inc.: "The Dover Bitch" from *The
Hard Hours* by Anthony Hecht. Copyright © 1960 by
Anthony E. Hecht. Reprinted by permission of Atheneum
Publishers. Originally appeared in *Transatlantic Review.*

The Bobbs-Merrill Company, Inc.: "A Poem for Black Hearts"
from *Black Magic Poetry* 1961–1967, copyright © 1969, by
LeRoi Jones, reprinted by permission of the publisher,
The Bobbs-Merrill Company, Inc.

Chatto and Windus Ltd.: "Dulce et Decorum Est" from
*The Collected Poems of Wilfred Owen,* edited by C. Day Lewis.
Reprinted by permission of Chatto and Windus Ltd.

City Lights Books: "American Change," copyright © 1963 by
Allen Ginsberg. Reprinted by perimssion of City Lights Books.

The Clarendon Press: "When First We Met" from *The Poetical Works of Robert Bridges*, 1936. Reprinted by permission of The Clarendon Press, Oxford.

John Ciardi: "My Tribe" from *In Fact* by John Ciardi, © 1962 by Rutgers, The State University. Reprinted by permission of the author.

Cummington Press: "In Defense of Felons" from *The Lovemakers* by Robert Mezey. Reprinted by permission of the Cummington Press and the author.

Curtis Brown, Ltd.: "Song of the Open Road." Copyright © 1932, 1960 by Ogden Nash. Originally appeared in The New Yorker Magazine. "The Private Dining Room." Copyright © 1951 by Ogden Nash. Originally published in The New Yorker Magazine. Both reprinted by permission of Curtis Brown, Ltd.

Delacorte Press: "American Primitive," copyright © 1970 by William Jay Smith. Reprinted from *New and Selected Poems* by William Jay Smith. A Seymour Lawrence Book/Delacorte Press.

J. M. Dent & Sons Ltd.: "Do Not Go Gentle Into That Good Night" and "Fern Hill" from *Collected Poems of Dylan Thomas*. Reprinted by permission of J. M. Dent & Sons Ltd. and the Trustees for the Copyrights of the late Dylan Thomas.

Doubleday & Company, Inc.: "In a Prominent Bar in Secaucus One Day," copyright © 1961 by X. J. Kennedy; "Little Elegy: for a Child Who Skipped Rope," copyright © 1960 by X. J. Kennedy. Both from the book *Nude Descending a Staircase* by X. J. Kennedy. Reprinted by permission of Doubleday & Company, Inc. "Sestina of the Tramp-Royal" from *The Seven Seas* by Rudyard Kipling. Reprinted by permission of Mrs. George Bambridge and Doubleday & Company, Inc. "The Waking," copyright © 1948 by Theodore Roethke. From *The Collected Poems of Theodore Roethke*. Reprinted by permission of Doubleday & Company, Inc.

E. P. Dutton & Co., Inc.: "Rondel for Middle Age" from the book *Collected Poems* by Louise Townsend Nicholl. Copyright 1953 by E. P. Dutton & Co., Inc. and reprinted with their permission.

Norma Millay Ellis: "Counting-Out Rhyme" from *Collected Poems*. Harper & Row, Publishers. Copyright 1928, 1955 by Edna St. Vincent Millay and Norma Millay Ellis. Permission of Norma Millay Ellis.

Farrar, Straus & Giroux, Inc.: "16" and "76" from *77 Dream Songs* by John Berryman, copyright © 1959, 1962, 1963, 1964 by John Berryman. "90 North" reprinted with the permission of Farrar, Straus & Giroux, Inc. from *The Complete Poems* by Randall Jarrell, copyright 1941 by Mrs. Randall Jarrell, copyright renewed 1968 by Mrs. Randall Jarrell.

Harcourt Brace Jovanovich, Inc.: "Ladies and Gentlemen This Little Girl," copyright, 1923, 1951, by E. E. Cummings. Reprinted from his volume, *Poems 1923–1954.* "The Dead in Europe" from *Lord Weary's Castle,* copyright, 1944, 1946, by Robert Lowell. "Juggler," copyright, 1949, by Richard Wilbur. Reprinted from his volume, *Ceremony and Other Poems.* First published in *The New Yorker.* "Junk," copyright, 1961, by Richard Wilbur. Reprinted from his volume, *Advice to a Prophet and Other Poems.* "Splinter" from *Good Morning America,* copyright, 1928, 1956, by Carl Sandburg. All reprinted by permission of Harcourt Brace Jovanovich, Inc.

Harper & Row, Publishers, Inc.: "The Thought Fox" from *The Hawk in the Rain* by Ted Hughes. Copyright © 1957 by Ted Hughes. "Hawk Roosting" from *Lupercal* by Ted Hughes. Copyright © 1959 by Ted Hughes. "My Son, My Executioner" from *The Alligator Bride: Poems New and Selected* by Donald Hall. Copyright © 1954 by Donald Hall. Originally appeared in *The New Yorker* as "First Child." "Those Being Eaten by America" from *The Light Around the Body* by Robert Bly. Copyright © by Robert Bly. "Daddy" from *Ariel* by Sylvia Plath. Copyright © 1963 by Ted Hughes. "A Light and Diplomatic Bird—IV" from *Selected Poems* by Gwendolyn Brooks. Copyright © 1949 by Gwendolyn Brooks Blakely. All reprinted by permission of Harper & Row, Publishers, Inc.

David Higham Associates, Ltd.: "Leviathan" from *Green with Beasts* by W. S. Merwin. Published by Rupert Hart-Davis. Reprinted with the permission of David Higham Associates, Ltd.

Holt, Rinehart and Winston, Inc.: "The Golf Links" from *Portraits and Protests* by Sarah N. Cleghorn. All rights reserved. "Directive," "Dust in the Eyes," and "The Silken Tent" from *The Poetry of Robert Frost* edited by Edward Connery Lathem. Copyright 1928, 1947, © 1969 by Holt, Rinehart and Winston, Inc. Copyright 1942, © 1956 by Robert Frost. Copyright © 1970 by Lesley Frost Ballantine. "Loveliest of Trees" from "A Shropshire Lad"—Authorized

Edition—from *The Collected Poems of A. E. Housman*. Copyright 1939, 1940, © 1959 by Holt, Rinehart and Winston, Inc. Copyright © 1967, 1968 by Robert E. Symons. "When First My Way to Fair I Took" from *The Collected Poems of A. E. Housman*. Copyright 1922 by Holt, Rinehart and Winston, Inc. Copyright 1950 by Barclays Bank Ltd. "Grass" from *Cornhuskers* by Carl Sandburg. Copyright 1918 by Holt, Rinehart and Winston, Inc. Copyright 1946 by Carl Sandburg. "Dover Beach—A Note to That Poem" from *Public Speech* by Archibald MacLeish. Copyright 1936, © 1964 by Archibald MacLeish. All reprinted by permission of Holt, Rinehart and Winston, Inc.

Houghton Mifflin Company: "The Superiority of Music" from *Poetry: Premeditated Art*. Boston: Houghton Mifflin, 1968, pages 313–314. Copyright © 1964 by Judson Jerome. Used by permission. "Patterns" from *The Complete Poetical Works of Amy Lowell*. Copyright, 1955, by Houghton Mifflin Company. Reprinted by permission of the publisher. "The Genius" from *Songs for Eve*. Copyright, 1954, by Archibald MacLeish. Reprinted by permission of the publisher, Houghton Mifflin Company.

Ted Hughes: "Daddy" from *Ariel* by Sylvia Plath. Reprinted by permission of Ted Hughes.

Alfred A. Knopf, Inc.: "Leviathan" from *Green with Beasts*, by W. S. Merwin. Published 1956 by Alfred A. Knopf, Inc. "Iambic Feet Considered as Honorable Scars," as it appeared in *Poetry*. Copyright © 1962 by William Meredith. Reprinted from *The Wreck of the Thresher and Other Poems*. "The Negro Speaks of Rivers" and "Cross," copyright 1926 by Alfred A. Knopf, Inc. and renewed 1954 by Langston Hughes. Reprinted from *Selected Poems*, by Langston Hughes. "Disillusionment of Ten O'Clock" and "Sunday Morning," copyright 1923 and renewed 1951 by Wallace Stevens. Reprinted from *The Collected Poems of Wallace Stevens*. "Winter Ocean," copyright © 1960 by John Updike. Reprinted from *Telephone Poles and Other Poems*, by John Updike. "Janet Waking," copyright 1927 by Alfred A. Knopf, Inc. and renewed 1955 by John Crowe Ransom. Reprinted from *Selected Poems*, 3rd Rev. Ed., by John Crowe Ransom. "Here Lies a Lady," copyright 1924 by Alfred A. Knopf, Inc. and renewed 1952 by John Crowe Ransom. Reprinted from *Selected Poems*, 3rd Rev. Ed., by John Crowe Ransom. All reprinted by permission of Alfred A. Knopf, Inc.

ACKNOWLEDGMENTS

McClelland and Stewart Ltd.: "All There Is to Know About
Adolf Eichmann" from *Selected Poems: 1956–1968* by Leonard
Cohen. Reprinted by permission of McClelland and
Stewart Ltd.

The Macmillan Company: "The U.S. Sailor with the Japanese
Skull" from *Collected Poems* by Winfield Townley Scott.
Copyright 1945 by Winfield Townley Scott. "A Glass of Beer"
from *Collected Poems* by James Stephens. Copyright 1918
by The Macmillan Company, renewed 1946 by James
Stephens. "The Fish" and "To a Steam Roller" from *Collected
Poems* by Marianne Moore. Copyright 1935 by Marianne
Moore, renewed 1963 by Marianne Moore and T. S. Eliot.
"Channel Firing" from *Collected Poems* by Thomas Hardy.
Copyright 1925 by The Macmillan Company. "The Lake Isle
of Innisfree" from *Collected Poems* by William Butler Yeats.
Copyright 1906 by The Macmillan Company, renewed 1934
by William Butler Yeats. "The Dolls" from *Collected Poems* by
William Butler Yeats. Copyright 1916 by The Macmillan
Company, renewed 1944 by Bertha Georgie Yeats. "Among
School Children" from *Collected Poems* by William Butler
Yeats. Copyright 1928 by The Macmillan Company, renewed
1956 by Bertha Georgie Yeats. All reprinted with permission
of The Macmillan Company.

The Macmillan Company of Canada Limited: "The Lake Isle
of Innisfree," "The Dolls," and "Among School Children"
from *Collected Poems of W. B. Yeats* by permission of Michael
Butler Yeats; Macmillan & Co. Ltd., London; and The
Macmillan Company of Canada Limited. "Channel Firing"
from *Collected Poems of Thomas Hardy* by permission of the
Hardy Estate; Macmillan & Co. Ltd. "A Glass of Beer" from
*Collected Poems* by James Stephens, by permission of Mrs.
Iris Wise; Macmillan & Co. Ltd., London, and The Macmillan
Company of Canada Limited.

McNally & Loftin, Publishers: "I Kissed Pa Twice" from
*Little Pansy, a Novel, and Miscellaneous Poetry* by Mattie J.
Peterson. Copyright 1967. Reprinted by permission of
McNally & Loftin, Publishers.

The Marvell Press: "Toads" by Philip Larkin is reprinted
from *The Less Deceived*. © copyright The Marvell Press
1955, 1971 by permission of The Marvell Press, Hessle,
Yorkshire, England.

National Council of Teachers of English: "The Prosodist's
Nightmare: All Quiet on the Metrical Front" by Irving Kreutz

from the February 1970 issue of College English. Reprinted
with the permission of the National Council of Teachers of
English and Irving Kreutz.

New Directions Publishing Corp.: "The Stranger," William
Everson, *The Residual Years.* "Do Not Go Gentle Into That
Good Night" and "Fern Hill," Dylan Thomas, *Collected Poems.*
Copyright 1946 by New Directions Publishing Corporation,
1952 by Dylan Thomas. "The Red Wheelbarrow," William
Carlos Williams, *The Collected Earlier Poems.* Copyright 1938
by William Carlos Williams. "The Dance," William Carlos
Williams, *The Collected Later Poems.* Copyright 1944 by
William Carlos Williams. All reprinted by permission of New
Directions Publishing Corporation. "Let the boy try along
this bayonet-blade" and "Dulce et Decorum Est," Wilfred
Owen, *The Collected Poems of Wilfred Owen.* Copyright
1946, © 1963 by Chatto & Windus, Ltd. Reprinted by
permission of New Directions Publishing Corporation and
Mr. Harold Owen.

Harold Ober Associates: "Evenin' Air Blues" from *Shakespeare
in Harlem* by Langston Hughes. Reprinted by permission of
Harold Ober Associates Incorporated. Copyright 1942 by
Alfred A. Knopf, Inc.

The Peter Pauper Press: Japanese Haiku from *Cherry-
Blossoms: Japanese Haiku, Series III,* translated by Peter
Bielenson. Reprinted by permission of The Peter Pauper Press.

Random House, Inc.: "The Snake" from *Selected Poems, New
and Old: 1923–1966,* by Robert Penn Warren. Copyright
© 1957 by Robert Penn Warren. "The Dirty Word," copyright
1947 by Karl Shapiro. Reprinted from *Selected Poems,* by Karl
Shapiro. "Drug Store," copyright 1941 and renewed 1969
by Karl Shapiro. Reprinted from *Selected Poems,* by Karl
Shapiro. "Shine, Perishing Republic," copyright 1925 and
renewed 1953 by Robinson Jeffers. Reprinted from *The
Selected Poetry of Robinson Jeffers.* All reprinted by
permission of Random House, Inc.

St. Martin's Press: "Toads" from *The Less Deceived* by Philip
Larkin. Reprinted by permission of St. Martin's Press, Inc.

Charles Scribner's Sons: "Night Practice" (Copyright © 1963
May Swenson) from *To Mix With Time* by May Swenson.
"Luke Havergal" from *The Children of the Night* by Edwin
Arlington Robinson (1897). "Jack's Blues" (Copyright © 1960
Robert Creeley) from *For Love* by Robert Creeley. All
reprinted by permission of Charles Scribner's Sons.

ACKNOWLEDGMENTS

The Society of Authors: "Loveliest of Trees" and "When First My Way to Fair I Took" from A. E. Housman's *Collected Poems*. Reprinted by permission of The Society of Authors as the literary representative of the Estate of A. E. Housman, and Jonathan Cape Ltd., publishers.

The Viking Press, Inc.: "All There Is to Know About Adolf Eichmann" from *Selected Poems: 1956–1968* by Leonard Cohen. All rights reserved. "North" from *Letter From a Distant Land* by Philip Booth. Copyright 1954 by Philip Booth. Both reprinted by permission of The Viking Press, Inc.

Wesleyan University Press: "The Bee," copyright © 1966 by James Dickey. Reprinted from *Poems 1957–1967* by James Dickey. "In Bertram's Garden," copyright © 1954 by Donald Justice. Reprinted from *The Summer Anniversaries* by Donald Justice. "Autumn Begins in Martins Ferry, Ohio," copyright © 1962 by James Wright. Reprinted from *The Branch Will Not Break* by James Wright. All reprinted by permission of Wesleyan University Press.

# Contents

## 3  *Rhyme*    *56*

## 4  *Sound and Meaning*    *81*

## 5  *Diction*    *113*

## 9 Free Verse and Self-devised Forms   234

*What's in a Poem*

# Introduction

A friend of ours once said, "Poetry always sounds to me like prose all busted up." This reaction to poetry, phrased in different ways, is not an uncommon one. People often ask, "Why don't poets just say what they mean?"

The student puzzled by the unwillingness of the poet to say what he means, or to whom poetry sounds "like prose all busted up" may, of course, simply be reacting to individual bad poems. But there is a good possibility that his bewilderment springs from a basic misconception of what the poet is trying to do.

Our baffled poetry reader is not too different from a long-time football fan attending his first soccer game. There are certain family resemblances between the games—both are played by men on foot, rather than men on skates or horseback, and both involve the propulsion of a ball down a field and across a goal line. But the differences between the games are many and crucial. If our hypothetical football fan assumes that the way the Green Bay Packers play ball is *the* only way, then obviously those guys in shorts are doing it all wrong. Similarly, an ardent soccer fan would be bewildered and exasperated by his first exposure to the Green Bay Packers, and might well feel that their kind of football was a perversion of his beloved *futbol*. Of course both men would be wrong, for football is not badly played soccer, but a game in its own right, with its own rules, techniques, special skills, and special pleasures for the fan.

And just as football is not soccer, so poetry is not prose. This statement will seem absurdly obvious, but it needs

1

to be made, for readers often approach a poem with the unconscious expectation that they can read it as if it were a newspaper story, a western novel, or even a grocery list. Everybody, even the poet, reads more prose than poetry in our print-deluged age; and almost everybody has to learn to shift his mental gears when he moves from the more customary prose to poetry. This is so not only because poems are rhythmic, or rhymed, or involve a higher degree of language density than is usually encountered in prose. Rather, these differences between prose and poetry reflect the different needs of the poet in pursuing his ends, the novelist or journalist in pursuing his.

The basic aim of most prose is to inform, to tell about. The writer is conveying information or ideas or telling a story. The primary motion of prose tends to be linear—that is, the "this happened, then that happened" pattern of narrative prose, or the "this, therefore that" of logical exposition. The basic purpose of most poetry is intensification of experience. One brief statement which sums up neatly the differences between prose and poetry is this: "Prose attempts communication; poetry attempts communion." What the reader gets out of most prose—the payoff—is quantitative; he knows what he did not know before. But the payoff of poetry is qualitative; the perceptive reader feels, sees, hears, smells, tastes as he never has before.

Obviously this distinction between poetry and prose is not always easy to find in actual practice, since the varieties of written and spoken language are not neat categories, but rather parts of a continuum. One could draw a line on a blackboard, with "pure prose" at one end and "pure poetry" at the other. At the extreme of the prose end of the line, we would find such forms as the maintenance instructions for a bulldozer or an electrical appliance. Moving toward the other end, we would encounter various types of journalism, escape fiction, light drama, serious novels and plays, narrative poems, epic poems, and, finally, the quintessence of lyric poetry. As the diagram suggests, then, the poet is not an entirely different species from the novelist or journalist. But his aim—the intensification of experience— is different enough to warrant close study.

The poems you will be reading in this text come almost exclusively from England and America. We have made this choice partly because giving a broader sampling would have required the use of many translations, and poetry is generally admitted to be very difficult to translate well, and partly because the poet who writes in English writes within the historical tradition of English poetry. This is true even if his own cultural background is not Anglo-Saxon. For language, as we will see, is an integral part of what is said. William Butler Yeats (who was Irish), Dylan Thomas (who was Welsh), and LeRoi Jones (who is a black American) would have written different poems if they had composed them in Gaelic, Welsh, or Swahili.

2

We ought to make clear, however, that poetry does not necessarily have to be Anglo-American, or even written, to be good poetry. If the phrase "American poetry" means poetry by Americans, written in English and published and read, then what happens to the blues, spirituals, and other orally transmitted poetry, to the oral literature of the American Indian, or, for that matter, to the large numbers of Americans who write in Spanish, Yiddish, German, Swedish, and other languages? A somewhat similar situation exists in England, where poetry in the dominant language tends to overshadow the production of Scots dialect poetry, and in Canada, where it overshadows poetry written in French.

Until fairly recently this problem of definition would not have been regarded as important. The literary establishment, while on the whole more humane than some other establishments, tended in England to support the standards of the upper class in the name of "good taste," and in America to support the myth of the "melting pot." The good citizen lost his accent as quickly as he could, and well-bred young Americans interested in writing poetry left Mississippi or Indiana or Harlem and went to London or Shropshire or Paris in search of "tradition." Oral literature was either condemned as lowbrow or patronized as quaint. This state of cultural myopia is changing now, and contemporary American poets are as likely to be influenced by Indian sutras as by the sonnets of Shakespeare. They are also likely to be influenced by the new balladry which the transistor radio, the long-playing record, and television have made almost universally accessible. The new openness to cultural experience is an exciting part of living and writing in twentieth-century America.

Before we can see where we are going, however, we have to have some notion of where we have been and how we got there. The techniques of English poetry which have grown up over the last thousand years are still largely the techniques used by poets writing in English today.

A mistake commonly made in reading and studying poetry is to consider poetic techniques as decorative rather than integral and organic. A fully realized poem fuses form and content, manner and matter, style and substance. There is no waste motion, no pretty but pointless verbalization. Everything works.

We want to demonstrate in this text how poems "work." Our focus will be on both individual poems and on "poemness"—that working interaction of subject matter and technique which results in a poem. Viewed in a different way, "poemness" is the difference between a good prose paraphrase of a poem and the poem itself. What leaks out or evaporates in the transfer from poem to paraphrase is the "poemness" of the poem.

Though any good poem has an organic unity, so that the poem

3

as a verbal instrument is greater than the sum of its parts, nonetheless the greatest understanding and pleasure belong to that reader who knows what the parts are, and can therefore appreciate the whole more completely.

In the following chapters, some of the basic techniques of poetry are discussed and exemplified. The exercises that follow each chapter are designed to let you put yourself in the poet's place—or predicament. To choose as the poet himself did—to make informed, intelligent choices—you will have to discover the principles upon which the poet has been operating.

So we invite you to play a game with us, and with the poets. Poetry, like love, is too serious a game to play haphazardly. But well played, both are enormous fun.

# 1

## Rhythm and Meter

The child on his mother's knees bounces, laughing and crowing, to the familiar rhythm of "HUMP-ty DUMP-ty SAT on a WALL, HUMP-ty DUMP-ty HAD a great FALL." Obviously he is enjoying the physical and social contact with his mother, her laughter, the sound of her voice. But equally obviously—his whole body shows it—he is reacting to the rhythm of her words. He is, in fact, making an early acquaintance with the delights of poetry, especially the delightful possibilities of rhythm.

Rhythmic movement and sound are an integral part of the earliest environment any of us know. Floating in the miniature sea within our mother's body, we are gently rocked back and forth by her movements and, from the time we are capable of sensing or hearing sound, we are aware of her heartbeat. Mothers for thousands of years have soothed fretful babies by rocking and crooning, duplicating the rhythmic motion and soft, repetitive sound of the prenatal environment.

Throughout our lives most of us continue to enjoy rhythm in one form or another. The transistorized teenager responding to the newest pop music group, the elderly gentleman waving a swaying forefinger with the rhythm of a Strauss waltz, the ballet dancer translating music into spins and leaps, the skilled Shakespearean actor utilizing every metrical nuance of "Tomorrow, and tomorrow, and tomorrow/ Creeps in this petty pace from day to day," all are demonstrating in one form or another the abiding human pleasure in rhythmic expression.

Rhythm is more than mere pleasure, more than fun;

5

it is basic to our body's functioning. One of the contributions of modern technology to our lives is an illness which affects air travelers who may cross several time zones in a few hours and find themselves watching the sun set when their bodies tell them it is just about time for lunch. Frequently they suffer some degree of physical and mental disorientation because of this disruption of their personal body clocks. And all of us move constantly to a myriad of personal rhythms, some obvious, like the heartbeat and respiration, others silent but important, like the glandular secretions that move us from childhood to adolescence to adulthood to old age. Any alteration in these rhythms, any change or arrest, can have far-reaching effects, as our language records in such phrases as, "I held my breath," or "My heart stood still."

Very early in his history, man must have discovered the potent effects of rhythm; the right kind of song could cheer him, the right kind of shout could give him courage, the right movements could enhance his sense of oneness with his fellow tribesmen. We still use rhythm today for all these purposes, in forms ranging from the cadenced cheers of the football team's rooting section to the rousing rhythms of a military band, to rhythmically phrased songs such as "The Star-Spangled Banner" and "America." The man who said he cared not who wrote his nation's laws if he could write her songs, must have had in mind the enormous extent to which the group feelings of a people can be summed up in its songs, its poems, and its great orations. So too, early man used chants—rhythmic songs— extensively in his religious rituals, as a stimulus to reverent emotion and perhaps out of a conviction that his gods must find pleasing what he found pleasing. In mass and communion, oratorio and revival meeting, we do the same. Our early ancestors also discovered that rhythm enhanced the telling of tales, helped hold the attention of audiences, and helped in remembering the story itself—an important consideration in the preliterate world, when a bard carried his whole stock-in-trade around in his head.

So in the beginning was the word, and the word was rhythm, and the form of the word was poetry. Prose had to wait for the printing press and mass literacy to become an established literary form.

The earliest literature we know about in any language is poetry, and not necessarily "simple" poetry either, despite the fact that it was carried around for hundreds of years in peoples' memories before somebody wrote it down. The *Iliad* and *Odyssey*, the anonymous ballads of England, the blues and spirituals of black America, all have their own highly developed conventions, relished by poet and hearer alike. These conventions or devices, a number of which we will be discussing in the pages that follow, developed and were modified to

6

suit the purposes of the poet. They were—and are today—not decorative devices but effective ways to move an audience.

As we have suggested, one of the most basic, oldest, and still most effective means of intensifying experience is through the use of *rhythm*. By rhythm, we means a series or sequence of sounds within which the ear detects recurrent, though not necessarily regular, patterns. Most poetry of more than a very few lines in length has a rhythmic pattern, and to the extent that prose attempts to create mood or emotion, it also employs rhythmic patterns. Rhythm captures our attention. Notice the rhythmic patterns (often reinforced by word or phrase repetition and rhyme) in almost every advertisement. Madison Avenue has refined for its own purposes the wandering minstrel with his lute, who prefaced his performances with a ringing, "Listen, lords, in bower and hall." Rhythm also sticks in the memory, as anybody who has lain awake trying to get a song out of his mind can testify. And rhythm appeals to a very broad spectrum of human reactions, from the intellectual pleasure we get out of a complete pattern, to the muscular and visceral pleasure of a good rocking beat. This multiple appeal is one of the poet's most potent weapons in temporarily disarming the reader's customary defense mechanism and fusing his separate mental, sensory, and emotional responses into one entity, one flash of ThinkFeel.

One method of creating rhythm is through the use of *meter*. Meter is the regularized arrangement of stressed and unstressed syllables. Since meter is so pervasive in the body of English-American poetry, some working knowledge of the basic English meters is an essential intellectual tool for an understanding and appreciation of poetry.

When confronted by a list of Greek names and dry-looking definitions, many beginning students of poetry balk. Whether or not they put the question to the instructor, the students may ask, "Is knowing this stuff really necessary?" While an airtight case for the study of *prosody*—the poet's control of the sounds which comprise his poem—is impossible to make, we would at least like to try to answer the question above and some others that are frequently raised.

*"But it's hard to keep all those funny names straight. Do we really have to learn this stuff in order to enjoy poetry?"*

It is quite possible to enjoy poetry by ear, and even to write it by ear, *if* you have a good enough ear. However, as in the appreciation of music or football, some knowledge of basic techniques and conventions can greatly increase the enjoyment of the listener or spectator. No attempt will be made in this text to present an exhaustive survey of all the metrical possibilities of English verse. Only those meters which are common enough to be the bread-and-butter of the poet's art will be discussed.

7

*"Isn't that stuff all outdated? Nobody modern writes anything
but free verse anymore."*

At one time something like a pitched battle went on between the
supporters of free verse and the supporters of traditional verse.
Each side, as in most wars, claimed the possession of all truth, beauty,
and virtue. And, like a good many wars, this one ended in a kind of
informal battlefield truce, though an occasional nonfatal shot is still
fired. However, free verse has certainly not carried the field. Much
traditional metrical verse is still being written. But more importantly,
the modern poet (or at least many of them) feels free to use whatever
form seems appropriate to his subject and mood. He may choose either
traditional or nontraditional forms, or he may elect to combine them.
We could argue, therefore, that a knowledge of traditional prosody
is essential to an understanding of modern poetry.

*"Doesn't the use of meter force the poet to tailor his ideas to
fit the form? Doesn't this make his writing phony?"*

Unskilled poets, it is true, often find it difficult to write a line which
has some resemblance to normal English word order and is acceptable
metrically. But many poets over the years have spoken of the real
pleasure they derive from working within the demands that meter
makes. If a poem is yanked and hacked to meet the movement of the
metrical system, the fault lies not with the meter but with the poet.

None of the above, by the way, should be interpreted to mean
that good free verse (as distinguished from prose "busted up" and
artistically strewn about the page) is easier to write than good metrical
verse. Good free verse has its own demands, which will be dealt with
in a later chapter.

But the question still remains: Does the use of meter really
force the poet into insincerity? Of course people do not usually con-
verse in measured units of stressed and unstressed syllables. In
ordinary prose, whether spoken or written, there are two or three
unstressed syllables to every stressed syllable. In iambic verse, the
most common metrical unit in our poetry, the ratio approximates
one to one, that is, one unstressed to every stressed syllable. Obviously
this is language at a much higher level of concentration and density
than prose. But even in prose, the *stress ratio* sometimes approaches
the one-to-one ratio typical of most poetry. Much advertising copy, for
example, makes use of tight, highly stressed language. The intensely
emotional passages of much fiction, when scanned, reveal a stress ratio
which approaches that of poetry. And even emotional oral language
is likely to be much more heavily stressed than is oral language
intended to be informative or social in nature.

Furthermore, the student who charges poetry with artificiality
and insincerity because "people don't talk like that" is really making a
demand, not only on poetry but on all art, which art is not designed

to satisfy. For art is not life. Art is words on paper, paint on canvas, images on film. This is not to say that there is no relation between art and life, or even that there is no relation between poetry and the way ordinary people talk. Art is always life abstracted, arranged, condensed. One school of writers used the somewhat misleading term, "slice of life." But even the rawest slice of life is always cut from somewhere, and the artist has picked the "somewhere."

> *"Doesn't it destroy the beauty of a poem to take it all to pieces?"*

Like the student who accuses poetry of phoniness, the student who asks this question may have a naive or inadequate notion of what art is, what poetry is. If the more we know about a thing, the uglier and more commonplace it becomes, then ignorance is indeed bliss, and every stage from helpless infancy up represents a decline in the potential beauty of the world. The fact is that most people find their enjoyment of any art form enhanced by a close study of its techniques. There are, of course, poems that collapse on close scrutiny, which only proves that they were insubstantial, inferior specimens to begin with. And it is probably a good idea to remind students of poetry, as one might remind medical students, that the purpose of their dissection is a better understanding of something which is alive and whole, rather than the creation of neatly mounted tissue cross sections. But poems are not destroyed by study and understanding of their interior workings. When one considers that some poems are over two-thousand years old and are still being read and enjoyed, it becomes fairly obvious that a well-made poem is a tough piece of craftsmanship.

We now turn to a consideration of that craftsmanship, and we begin with the basic feet and meters in English-American poetry. A foot is a group of syllables which constitute a metrical unit in poetry. All of the common feet in our poetry have one stressed syllable and one or two unstressed syllables. Stress (or accent or beat) refers to the relative force or loudness given to a syllable in its immediate context.

How English-American poetry came to develop a system like this is an interesting sidelight. Prior to 1066, the year of the Norman invasion, Old English poetry was based metrically on stress alone. In *Beowulf*, for example, each line has exactly four stressed syllables, but the number of unstressed syllables varies from three to as many as nine. Weak or unstressed syllables were not important metrically. After the Norman invasion, however, a new influence on English poetry developed. The French brought with them their culture, and their poetry was a good deal different metrically, since French is not a stressed language as is English. All syllables in a line of French poetry

9

receive about the same degree of stress or emphasis, so French poets counted syllables rather than stresses. As the English language and English poetry evolved, a new metrical form developed. By Chaucer's time, most poets counted both stresses and syllables, producing *accentual-syllabic meter*.

The basic accentual-syllabic feet in English are as follows.

*Iambic foot (iamb):* One unstressed syllable followed by one stressed syllable, as in alŏne, cŏllect, sĕcure.

*Trochaic foot (trochee):* One stressed syllable followed by one unstressed syllable, as in nĕver, wŏman, hŏly.

*Anapestic foot (anapest):* Two unstressed syllables followed by a stressed syllable, as in intercĕpt, ŏvercŏme, intervĕne.

*Dactylic foot (dactyl):* One stressed syllable followed by two unstressed syllables, as in thŭndering, pŏetry, ănimal.

*Spondaic foot (spondee):* Two stressed syllables. There are few natural spondees in English. Compound words, such as stŏp wătch and dĕsk tŏp, are usually considered spondaic, although most spondees occur through syntactic context.

*Pyrrhic foot (pyrrhus):* Two unaccented syllables. There are no naturally pyrrhic words in English because in any word of two or more syllables, one syllable always receives more stress. Context within the syntactic structure creates pyrrhic feet.

Meter is created when the various feet listed above recur in lines of poetry. Meter is designated in the following terms.

One iambic foot—iambic monometer
Two iambic feet—iambic dimeter
Three iambic feet—iambic trimeter
Four iambic feet—iambic tetrameter
Five iambic feet—iambic pentameter
Six iambic feet—iambic hexameter
Seven iambic feet—iambic heptameter
Eight iambic feet—iambic octometer

Similar designations are used for trochaic, anapestic, and dactylic meter. Trimeter, tetrameter, and pentameter are the most common meters.

Remember that these metrical designations are not laws engraved on stone and handed down from above. Our brief excursion into English history was taken primarily to demonstrate how language changes and grows, and how poetry changes in response to language change. Meter designations are only handy ways of talking about an art form which is being continually modified in the same way as music, dress, and other forms of human expression. The techniques of poetry "grow" in response to the poet's desire to communicate effectively.

We have suggested that rhythmic patterns affect human

10

behavior. Different rhythms produce different responses. Whether the poet has his say in a line which runs

di DUM di DUM di DUM di DUM

or in a line which runs

DUM di di DUM di di DUM di di

is going to affect what he says. In fact, the poet says something—not all he has to say, but something—by his choice of meter.

Each meter, as we will see, has its own "feel." A meter inappropriate to the mood and the subject matter of a poem can undercut the poet's attempt at emotional and intellectual contact with the reader. A meter which "works," however, is without doubt one of the most effective tools of the poet's trade.

## SCANSION

The process of determining which syllables in a line of poetry are stressed and which are unstressed is called *scansion*. In accentual-syllabic poetry, scansion will reveal the poetic foot and the number of feet in a line, as in this example.

My mistress' eyes are nothing like the sun.

The syllables receiving the most *stress*, or relatively more loudness and force, are MIS, EYES, NOTH, LIKE, SUN. The syllables "my," "tress'," "are," "ing," "the" are unstressed. The movement of the line, then, is

di DUM di DUM di DUM di DUM di DUM.

The "di DUM" pattern indicates the iambic foot. There are five such feet in the line; therefore the line is iambic pentameter. The diagonal slash separates the feet in scansion, like this.

My mis/tress' eyes/are noth/ing like/the sun.

Note the use of the single slash line over "like" and the "x" over the other stressed syllables. In this text we will be indicating two degrees of stress: "x" for primary and "/" for secondary. In the line quoted above, "like" is stressed relative to "ing" and "the." Yet it is not as heavily stressed as "noth" or "sun." Learning to hear and respond to such differences is vital to both understanding and appreciating poetry. And finally, while variations in the scansion of a given poem between

11

two scanners can be expected, nevertheless the difference in scansion
between two people sensitive to the flow of the English language
should be slight.

## The Iamb

Probably nine-tenths of English verse from Chaucer's time to our own
is iambic. The usual stress patterns of English more nearly approximate
iambic meter than any other meter, and therefore iambs are easier
to use in long passages without a sense of strain. Another reason for
iambic meter's prevalence is its flexibility. Iambic meter can be used
for passages of elevated and formal beauty, as in these lines from
Edward Fitzgerald's translation of the *Rubaiyyat* of Omar Khayyam.

> I sometimes think that never blows so red
> The Rose as where some buried Caesar bled.

On the other hand, iambic meter can be used very effectively for an
informal, conversational tone.

> I'm not afraid of them, though, if they're not
> Afraid of me. There's two can play at that.
>
> from *A Servant to Servants*, ROBERT FROST

Still another use of iambic meter is for gentle, flowing, lyrical effects.

> Whenas in silks my Julia goes,
> Then, then, methinks, how sweetly flows
> The liquefaction of her clothes.
>
> from *Upon Julia's Clothes*, ROBERT HERRICK

Or it can be used for sharp, witty, satiric effects.

> The hungry judges soon the sentence sign,
> And wretches hang that jury-men may dine.
>
> from *The Rape of the Lock*, ALEXANDER POPE

## The Trochee

By contrast with the flexible and adaptable iamb, the trochee is more
limited in its possibilities. Rising meters like the iamb, in which the
line normally ends on a stressed syllable, more closely approximate
the stress patterns of everyday English than do falling meters like the
trochee, in which the line ends on an unstressed syllable. A regular

trochaic line always begins with a stressed syllable, but not many
sentences in a random conversation or prose passage begin in this
way. It is easier to sound conversational in iambic than in trochaic
meter.

But the trochee has its uses. The very oddness of the stress
pattern in a trochaic line makes it arresting to the ear. Children's
nursery rhymes, which often approximate exercises in pure sound, are
full of trochaic meter.

> Peter, Peter, pumpkin eater,
> Had a wife and couldn't keep her. . . .
>
> Jack, be nimble, Jack be quick;
> Jack, jump [over the] candlestick.

The foot we have bracketed is a *substitution*—a foot different from
the dominant meter of the line. Substitutions are common in all meters,
but, while it is comparatively easy to find iambic passages which are
without substitutions, it is more difficult to find them in other meters,
like the trochee. Notice, also, that in "Jack, be nimble," the final
unstressed syllables at the end of the lines of a normal trochaic pattern
are missing. This is common in dactylic as well as trochaic meters.

The nursery rhymes we have quoted are jigging and playful.
They could be used (as many nursery rhymes are) to accompany games.
Shakespeare, by contrast, used the unusual stress contour of the
trochaic line for the witches' incantations in *Macbeth*.

> Round about the cauldron go;
> In the poisoned entrails throw . . .
> Double, double, toil and trouble;
> Fire burn and cauldron bubble.

The meter jigs, just as it did in "Peter, Peter, pumpkin eater," but
"poisoned entrails" and the setting tell us this is a witches' dance. The
use of nursery-rhyme meter, along with nursery-rhyme repetitions,
suggest correctly that the witches are playing a sinister game with
Macbeth.

John Masefield used the trochee to help evoke the foreign and
exotic in these lines.

> Stately Spanish galleon coming from the Isthmus,
> Dipping through the Tropics by the palm-green shores.

from *Cargoes*

13

And Henry Wadsworth Longfellow, in "A Psalm of Life,"
used the trochee's drumbeat to send his readers marching off into the
"living Present."

> Let us, then, be up and doing,
>> With a heart for any fate;
> Still achieving, still pursuing,
>> Learn to labor and to wait.

## THE ANAPEST

The anapest is lighter and quicker than either the iamb or the trochee.
Drop a syllable out of an anapest, and you are back with the familiar
iamb. Iambic substitution is common in anapestic meter, and vice versa.
The following selection illustrates what anapestic meter, intelligently
used, can achieve.

> Ere you open your eyes in the city, the blessed
>> church-bells begin:
> No sooner the bells leave off than the diligence rattles in;
> You get the pick of the news, and it costs you never a pin. . . .
> Noon strikes,—here sweeps the procession: our Lady borne
>> smiling and smart
> With a pink gauze gown all spangles, and seven swords
>> stuck in her heart
> Bang-whang-whang goes the drum, tootle-te-tootle the fife;
> No keeping one's haunches still: it's the greatest pleasure
>> in life.

> from *Up at a Villa—Down in the City*, ROBERT BROWNING

The last few lines illustrate the uses of this meter for lighthearted or
comic effect. The "Italian Person of Quality" who is the speaker of
Browning's poem is a feather-brained busybody to whom a statue of
the Virgin Mary, nominally an object of deep religious adoration, is
merely an interesting part of the procession, like a modern-day parade
float. While word choice has a good deal to do with the effectiveness of
these lines (notice "smiling and smart," as if the Mother of Christ were
a chic matron turned out in her best for afternoon tea, and the juxta-
position of "seven swords stuck in her heart" with "Bang-whang-
whang goes the drum"), the rollicking anapests are exactly right for
Browning's gossipy viewer.

The rapid lightness of the anapest is used for quite a different effect in Byron's "The Destruction of Sennacherib."

> The Assyrian came down like the wolf on the fold,
> And his cohorts were gleaming in purple and gold;
> And the sheen of their spears was like stars on the sea,
> When the blue wave rolls nightly on deep Galilee.

Here the effect is, appropriately enough, like the clatter of horses' hooves. While the subject matter of the poem is serious, it is handled with an emphasis on the picturesque rather than the tragic.

## THE DACTYL

The dactyl is the least common of English feet. Dactylic meter is nearly always used for a mournful or elegiac effect, as in this poem.

> Take her up tenderly
> Lift her with care;
> Fashioned so slenderly,
> Young and so fair!

from *The Bridge of Sighs*, THOMAS HOOD

In such a brief passage as this, dactylic meter, dimeter in this poem, is effective, but when Hood attempts to carry the meter through 106 lines of lament, the language becomes artificial and affected. Notice that even in this brief quotation, Hood deviates from strict dactylic meter through the use of *catalexis*—the omission of expected syllables at the end of a line. Lines two and four are catalectic. The omission of expected syllables from the beginning of a line or within a line is called *truncation*.

Probably the two best-known poems in dactylic meter are Longfellow's "Evangeline" and Tennyson's "The Charge of the Light Brigade." In Byron's "The Destruction of Sennacherib," used as an illustration of the anapest, the rapid, rising effect of that foot suggests the galloping of horses. So does the rapid, falling dactyl of the excerpt below, but the effects are much different.

> Forward, the Light Brigade:
> Was there a man dismayed?
> Not though the soldier knew
> Someone had blundered.

15

Theirs nŏt tō make rĕplý
Theirs nŏt tō rĕasŏn whȳ,
Theirs bŭt tō dŏ ănd dīe.
Ĭnto thē Vălley ŏf Dĕath
    Rŏde thē six hŭndrēd.

from *The Charge of the Light Brigade*, ALFRED TENNYSON

Byron's anapests give us this rhythm.

Ānd thē shĕen ōf thĕir spĕars wās līke stărs oñ thē sĕa . . .

di    di DUM di   di    DUM   di   di DUM di di DUM

The poem lifts and bounds with the galloping horses. By contrast, Tennyson's dactyls force a heavy, pounding emphasis at the
beginning of each line, an emphasis which is especially noticeable
because the lines are so short. Notice the ways in which meter underlines meaning. The heavy beginning stress in "Sŏmeone hăd blun-
dered" emphasizes the impersonal nature of the military machine
which sent these men out. With the three heavily stressed repetitions
of "Theirs," the meter underscores the hopeless situation of the
enlisted men who must die for officers' mistakes. Both meter and
meaning push Tennyson's Light Brigade forward into their valley, in a
way Byron's Assyrians are not pushed. Tennyson probably chose the
dactyl for this poem because he felt it would help him say what he
wanted to say with more emotional wallop.

In our next chapter, we will further discuss the ways in which
poets manipulate meter. In the meantime, the exercises which follow
will help you to "feel" your way into the basic meters available to
poets writing accentual-syllabic verse. You are asked to discover the
metrical patterns used in the poems, and to select the word or phrase
which you think was the poet's choice. Whenever possible, read the
poems out loud, in a singsong voice if necessary. Tap with your fingers
and toes. Poets from all ages have been swingers, in a fairly literal
sense, and unless you can swing with them, your understanding and
appreciation of their work will be short-changed.

*Exercise 1*

## THE GOLF LINKS

The golf links lie so near the mill,                          1
That nearly ————— day,                                         2

16

The laboring children can ——————,          3
And see the —————— at play.                 4


1. The missing word(s) in line 2 is/are (a) each, (b) every, (c) all, (d) most of the
2. The missing word(s) in line 3 is/are (a) spy, (b) notice, (c) watch, (d) look out.
3. The missing word in line 4 is (a) golfers, (b) masters, (c) men, (d) players.


ANSWERS

1. Have you felt the basic rhythm of the poem? This understated, ironic little poem moves quietly about its business: di DUM di DUM di DUM, etc. Line 2 therefore needs a DUM di in the blank. Of the choices, only (b) fits this iambic pattern.
2. In Line 3 "children" must be DUM di, so "can" is most likely stressed. Say (a) and (c) aloud as unstressed words, Do they sound right? They shouldn't, nor should (b), which also disturbs the quiet rhythm by the placement of two stresses—DUM DUM—in a row. Choice (d) keeps the established pattern and blends in smoothly.
3. Does the natural movement of this line seem to require a one or two syllable word? Do you feel the line start to gallop when (a), (b), or (d) is inserted? Is there any good reason that it should? If not, then choice (c) is the only reasonable possibility.


*Exercise 2*


from *THE RAVEN*

But the Raven still beguiling my sad fancy into smiling,    1
Straight I wheeled a —————— seat in front of bird
   and bust and door                                      2
Then, upon the velvet sinking, —————— myself
   to linking                                              3
   —————— unto fancy, thinking what this ominous
   bird of yore—                                           4
What this grim, ungainly, ghastly, gaunt, and
   ominous bird of yore                                    5
      Meant in croaking "——————."             6


17

1. The missing word in line 2 is (a) comfortable, (b) love, (c) soft, (d) cushioned.

2. The missing words in line 3 are (a) I betook, (b) I started, (c) I forced, (d) Forced I.

3. The missing word in line 4 is (a) Thought, (b) Fancy, (c) Clue, (d) Reply.

4. The missing word(s) in line 6 is/are (a) never, (b) It is you I adore, (c) Nevermore, (d) Cuspidor.

ANSWERS

1. The basic foot of this poem is the trochee, a DUM di pattern. Line 2, then, is "Straight I wheeled a . . . ," so the pattern requires a DUM di as the choice. Choice (a) is DUM di di di. Choices (b) and (c) are single syllable words and so cannot fit the pattern. Choice (d), however, is DUM di, and it was the poet's choice. If you did not choose the correct answer, you should check your other answers before going on.

2. "Sinking" must be pronounced DUM di; "myself" is di DUM. We need a stressed syllable after "sinking" and another stressed syllable before "myself." The words chosen will have to be DUM di DUM. Only choice (a)—"I betook"—fits the trochaic pattern that Poe developed.

3. As you have discovered, each line begins with a stressed syllable. Choices (a), (b), and (c) are possibilities, therefore. Choice (d) is not, since we do not say RE ply. However, "unto" is scanned DUM di. We need two syllables which will provide an initial stress followed by an unstressed syllable. Choice (b), "FAN cy," is the only possibility.

4. The need for a rhyming word rules out choice (a). As you have seen, the lines are trochaic octometer (and one of the few examples in our poetry of the eight-foot line). The sixth line, though, is shorter, having only four stresses. Choice (b) is thus ruled out. Both (c) and (d) can be read DUM di DUM, but (c) was Poe's choice. Give yourself one ego point for (d), because you did recognize the metrical pattern.

*Exercise 3*

# WHEN A MAN HATH NO FREEDOM TO FIGHT FOR AT HOME

| | |
|---|---|
| When a man hath no freedom to fight for at home, | 1 |
| Let him combat for that of his neighbors; | 2 |
| Let him think ————— of Greece and of Rome, | 3 |

And get knocked on his head for his labours.                    4
To do good ————— is the chivalrous plan,                        5
And is always as nobly requited;                                6
Then battle for freedom —————;                                  7
And, —————, you'll get knighted.                                8


1. The missing word(s) in line (3) is/are (a) somewhat, (b) of the glories, (c) earnestly, (d) of stories.

2. The missing words in line 5 are (a) to mankind, (b) to his fellow man, (c) to others, (d) for other men.

3. The missing words in line 7 are (a) where it began, (b) like a man, (c) where you can, (d) wherever you can.

4. The missing words in line 8 are (a) lucky, (b) with luck, (c) if not first hanged, (d) if not shot or hanged.


ANSWERS

1. The correct choices in this poem are particularly hard to find unless you first determine the way the poem swings. Read the first two lines over and over again until you feel your foot begin to tap. You should be going di di DUM, di di DUM, etc. The basic foot employed here is the anapest. Line three reads, "Let him THINK di di DUM di of GREECE and of ROME." Of the choices given, only "of the GLOR ies" fits the pattern.

2. If you count the feet per line, you'll discover that the lines are alternately tetrameter and trimeter, that is, lines 1, 3, 5, and 7 have four anapestic feet, while 2, 4, 6, and 8 have three. Line 5, therefore, needs a complete anapestic foot—di di DUM—to fit the established pattern. Only (a) can be read as an anapest.

3. Line 7, also, needs two more stresses to complete the pattern. Only choice (d) provides two stresses—"wher EV er you CAN"—and is anapestic too.

4. Here again we need two stressed syllables. Choices (a) and (b) can only have one each, while choice (c) cannot be read "if NOT first hang ED" without doing violence to the language. Choice (d) was Byron's choice.


*Exercise 4*


## SONG OF THE OPEN ROAD       *a parody*

I think that I shall never see                                  1
A billboard ————— as a tree.                                   2


19

Perhaps, unless the billboards —————,                3

I'll never ————— a tree at all.                      4

1. The missing word(s) in line 2 is/are (a) magnificent, (b) lovely,
   (c) developed, (d) with leaves.
2. The missing word(s) in line 3 is/are (a) perish, (b) fall down,
   (c) fall, (d) get broken.
3. The missing word(s) in line 4 is/are (a) observe, (b) look at,
   (c) chance upon, (d) see.

*Exercise 5*

## COUNTING-OUT RHYME

Silver bark of beech, and sallow                     1
Bark of yellow birch and yellow                      2
  Twig of willow.                                    3

Stripe of ————— moosewood maple,                     4
Color seen in leaf of —————,                         5
  Bark of popple.                                    6

————— popple pale as moonbeam,                       7
Wood of oak for yoke and barn-beam                   8
—————.                                               9

Silver bark of beech, and hollow                     10
————— of elder, tall and yellow                      11
  Twig of willow.                                    12

1. The missing words in line 4 are (a) green in, (b) chartreuse in,
   (c) a verdant, (d) the green in.
2. The missing word in line 5 is (a) elm, (b) redwood, (c) apple,
   (d) cottonwood.
3. The missing words in line 7 are (a) Wood of, (b) The wood of,
   (c) Lumber made from, (d) The log of.
4. The missing words in line 9 are (a) Hornbeam's wood, (b) A stick
   of hornbeam, (c) The wood hornbeam, (d) Wood of hornbeam.
5. The missing word in line 11 is (a) Wood, (b) Tree, (c) Stem, (d)
   Log.

*Exercise 6*

from *THE LOST LEADER*    Dactyl

Just for a handful of silver he left us,                                    1
  Just for a riband to ————— coat—                              2
Found  the one gift of which fortune bereft us,                            3
————— others she lets us devote:                                        4
They, with the gold to give, —————,                                    5
  So much was theirs who so little allowed: *Change in meter*   6
How all ————— had gone for his service!                               7
  Rags—were they purple, his heart had been —————!          8

1. The missing words in line 2 are (a) affix to the, (b) stick in his, (c) decorate his, (d) make gorgeous his.

2. The missing word(s) in line 4 is/are (a) Disposed of, (b) Lost, (c) Lost all the, (d) And he lost.

3. The missing words in line 5 are (a) doled him out silver, (b) gave him money, (c) bribed him with filthy lucre, (d) bought him with cash.

4. The missing words in line 7 are (a) our copper, (b) taxes we paid, (c) taxes collected, (d) our tax money.

5. The missing word(s) in line 8 is/are (a) made glad, (b) proud, (c) open to all, (d) heavy.

21

# 1

---

## Poems

*Out of Sight, Out of Mind*
BARNABE GOOGE (1540–1594)

*The Burning Babe*
ROBERT SOUTHWELL (1561–1595)

*Song: To Celia*
BEN JONSON (1572–1637)

*A Short Song of Congratulation*
SAMUEL JOHNSON (1709–1784)

*John Anderson, My Jo*
ROBERT BURNS (1759–1796)

*Sweet Afton*
ROBERT BURNS (1759–1796)

*The Destruction of Sennacherib*
GEORGE GORDON, LORD BYRON (1788–1824)

*Now Sleeps the Crimson Petal*
ALFRED, LORD TENNYSON (1809–1892)

*In Prison*
WILLIAM MORRIS (1834–1896)

*Directive*
ROBERT FROST (1874–1963)

*Cross*
LANGSTON HUGHES (1902–1967)

*All Quiet on the Metrical Front*
IRVING KREUTZ (b. 1917)

*In a Prominent Bar in Secaucus
One Day*
X. J. KENNEDY (b. 1929)

## OUT OF SIGHT, OUT OF MIND

*very formal*
*iambic tetrameter*
*(4 stresses)*

The oftener seen, the more I lust,
The more I lust, the more I smart,
The more I smart, the more I trust,
The more I trust, the heavier heart,
The heavy heart breeds mine unrest,
Thy absence, therefore, like I best.                          5

The rarer seen, the less in mind,
The less in mind, the lesser pain,
The lesser pain, less grief I find,
The lesser grief, the greater gain,                           10
The greater gain, the merrier I,
Therefore I wish thy sight to fly. *Trochae*

The further off, the more I joy,
The more I joy, the happier life,
The happier life, less hurts annoy,                           15
The lesser hurts, pleasure most rife, *Trochae*
Such pleasures rife shall I obtain
When distance doth depart us twain.

BARNABE GOOGE

## THE BURNING BABE

As I in hoary winter's night stood shivering in the snow,
Surpris'd I was with sudden heat which made my
    heart to glow;
And lifting up a fearful eye to view what fire was near,
A pretty Babe all burning bright did in the air appear;
Who, scorchéd with excessive heat, such floods of
    tears did shed,                                           5
As though his floods should quench his flames
    which with his tears were fed.
'Alas!' quoth he, 'but newly born in fiery heats I fry,
Yet none approach to warm their hearts or feel my
    fire but I.

My faultless breast the furnace is, the fuel wounding
    thorns;
Love is the fire, and sighs the smoke, the ashes shame
    and scorns;            10
The fuel Justice layeth on, the Mercy blows the coals;
The metal in this furnace wrought are men's defiléd souls;
For which, as now on fire I am to work them to their good,
So will I melt into a bath to wash them in my blood.'
With this he vanish'd out of sight and swiftly shrunk
    away,            15
And straight I calléd unto mind that it was
    Christmas Day.

ROBERT SOUTHWELL


## *SONG: TO CELIA*

Come, my Celia, let us prove,            Trochee
While we may, the sports of love;
Time will not be ours for ever:
He at length our good will sever.
Spend not then his gifts in vain:            5
Suns that set, may rise again;
But if once we lose this light,
'Tis with us perpetual night.
Why should we defer our joys?
Fame and rumour are but toys.            10
Cannot we delude the eyes
Of a few poor household spies?
Or his easier ears beguile,
Thus removèd by our wile?
'Tis no sin love's fruits to steal,            15
But the sweet theft to reveal:
To be taken, to be seen,
These have crimes accounted been.

BEN JONSON

24

# A SHORT SONG OF CONGRATULATION

Long-expected one and twenty
    Lingering year at last is flown,
Pomp and pleasure, pride and plenty,
    Great Sir John, are all your own.

Loosened from the minor's tether;          5
    Free to mortgage or to sell,
Wild as wind, and light as feather
    Bid the slaves of thrift farewell.

Call the Bettys, Kates, and Jennys
    Every name that laughs at care,        10
Lavish of your grandsire's guineas,
    Show the spirit of an heir.

All that prey on vice and folly
    Joy to see their quarry fly,
Here the gamester light and jolly         15
    There the lender grave and sly.

Wealth, Sir John, was made to wander,
    Let it wander as it will;
See the jockey, see the pander,
    Bid them come, and take their fill.        20

When the bonny blade carouses,
    Pockets full, and spirits high,
What are acres? What are houses?
    Only dirt, or wet or dry.

If the guardian or the mother         25
    Tell the woes of willful waste,
Scorn their counsel and their pother,
    You can hang or drown at last.

SAMUEL JOHNSON


# JOHN ANDERSON, MY JO

John Anderson, my jo, John,
    When we were first acquent;

Your locks were like the raven,
   Your bonie brow was brent;

But now your brow is beld, John,                  5
   Your locks are like the snow;
But blessings on your frosty pow,
   John Anderson, my jo.

John Anderson, my jo, John,
   We clamb the hill thegither;              10
And mony a cantie day, John,
   We've had wi' ane anither:

Now we maun totter down, John,
   And hand in hand we'll go,
And sleep thegither at the foot,           15
   John Anderson, my jo.

ROBERT BURNS

## SWEET AFTON

Flow gently, sweet Afton! among thy green braes,
Flow gently, I'll sing thee a song in thy praise;
My Mary's asleep by thy murmuring stream,
Flow gently, sweet Afton, disturb not her dream.

Thou stock-dove whose echo resounds thro' the glen,    5
Ye wild whistling blackbirds in yon thorny den,
Thou green crested lapwing, thy screaming forbear,
I charge you, disturb not my slumbering Fair.

How lofty, sweet Afton, thy neighbouring hills,
Far mark'd with the courses of clear, winding rills;    10
There daily I wander as noon rises high,
My flocks and My Mary's sweet cot in my eye.

How pleasant thy banks and green valleys below,
Where, wild in the woodlands, the primroses blow;
There oft, as mild ev'ning weeps over the lea,    15
The sweet-scented birk shades my Mary and me.

The crystal stream, Afton, how lovely it glides,
And winds by the cot where my Mary resides;

How wanton thy waters her snowy feet lave,
As, gathering sweet flowerets, she stems thy clear wave.          20

Flow gently, sweet Afton, among thy green braes,
Flow gently, sweet river, the theme of my lays;
My Mary's asleep by thy murmuring stream,
Flow gently, sweet Afton, disturb not her dream.

ROBERT BURNS


## *THE DESTRUCTION OF SENNACHERIB*

The Assyrian came down like the wolf on the fold,
And his cohorts were gleaming in purple and gold;
And the sheen of their spears was like stars on the sea,
When the blue wave rolls nightly on deep Galilee.

Like the leaves of the forest when Summer is green,          5
That host with their banners at sunset were seen:
Like the leaves of the forest when Autumn hath blown,
That host on the morrow lay withered and strown.

For the Angel of Death spread his wings on the blast,
And breathed in the face of the foe as he passed;          10
And the eyes of the sleepers waxed deadly and chill,
And their hearts but once heaved, and forever grew still!

And there lay the steed with his nostril all wide,
But through it there rolled not the breath of his pride;
And the foam of his gasping lay white on the turf,          15
And cold as the spray of the rock-beating surf.

And there lay the rider distorted and pale,
With the dew on his brow, and the rust on his mail:
And the tents were all silent—the banners alone—
The lances unlifted—the trumpet unblown.          20

And the widows of Ashur are loud in their wail,
And the idols are broke in the temple of Baal;
And the might of the Gentile, unsmote by the sword,
Hath melted like snow in the glance of the Lord!

GEORGE GORDON, LORD BYRON

## NOW SLEEPS THE CRIMSON PETAL

Now sleeps the crimson petal, now the white;
Nor waves the cypress in the palace walk;
Nor winks the gold fin in the porphyry font:
The fire-fly wakens: waken thou with me.

Now droops the milkwhite peacock like a ghost,          5
And like a ghost she glimmers on to me.

Now lies the Earth all Danaë to the stars,
And all thy heart lies open unto me.

Now slides the silent meteor on, and leaves
A shining furrow, as thy thoughts in me.          10

Now folds the lily all her sweetness up,
And slips into the bosom of the lake:
So fold thyself, my dearest, thou, and slip
Into my bosom and be lost in me.

ALFRED, LORD TENNYSON


## IN PRISON

Wearily, drearily,
Half the day long,
Flap the great banners
High over the stone;
Strangely and eerily          5
Sounds the wind's song,
Bending the banner-poles.

While, all alone,
Watching the loophole's spark,
Lie I, with life all dark,          10
Feet tether'd, hands fetter'd
Fast to the stone,
The grim walls, square letter'd
With prison'd men's groan.

Still strain the banner-poles          15
Through the wind's song,

28

Westward the banner rolls
Over my wrong.

WILLIAM MORRIS

## *DIRECTIVE*

Back out of all this now too much for us,
Back in a time made simple by the loss
Of detail, burned, dissolved, and broken off
Like graveyard marble sculpture in the weather,
There is a house that is no more a house          5
Upon a farm that is no more a farm
And in a town that is no more a town.
The road there, if you'll let a guide direct you
Who only has at heart your getting lost,
May seem as if it should have been a quarry—      10
Great monolithic knees the former town
Long since gave up pretense of keeping covered.
And there's a story in a book about it:
Besides the wear of iron wagon wheels
The ledges show lines ruled southeast-northwest,  15
The chisel work of an enormous Glacier
That braced his feet against the Arctic Pole.
You must not mind a certain coolness from him
Still said to haunt this side of Panther Mountain.
Nor need you mind the serial ordeal               20
Of being watched from forty cellar holes
As if by eye pairs out of forty firkins.
As for the woods' excitement over you
That sends light rustle rushes to their leaves,
Charge that to upstart inexperience.              25
Where were they all not twenty years ago?
They think too much of having shaded out
A few old pecker-fretted apple trees.
Make yourself up a cheering song of how
Someone's road home from work this once was,      30
Who may be just ahead of you on foot

29

Or creaking with a buggy load of grain.
The height of the adventure is the height
Of country where two village cultures faded
Into each other. Both of them are lost.                                    35
And if you're lost enough to find yourself
By now, pull in your ladder road behind you
And put a sign up CLOSED to all but me.
Then make yourself at home. The only field
Now left's no bigger than a harness gall.                                  40
First there's the children's house of make-believe,
Some shattered dishes underneath a pine,
The playthings in the playhouse of the children.
Weep for what little things could make them glad.
Then for the house that is no more a house,                                45
But only a belilaced cellar hole,
Now slowly closing like a dent in dough.
This was no playhouse but a house in earnest.
Your destination and your destiny's
A brook that was the water of the house,                                   50
Cold as a spring as yet so near its source,
Too lofty and original to rage.
(We know the valley streams that when aroused
Will leave their tatters hung on barb and thorn.)
I have kept hidden in the instep arch                                      55
Of an old cedar at the waterside
A broken drinking goblet like the Grail
Under a spell so the wrong ones can't find it,
So can't get saved, as Saint Mark says they mustn't.
(I stole the goblet from the children's playhouse.)                        60
Here are your waters and your watering place.
Drink and be whole again beyond confusion.

ROBERT FROST


# CROSS

My old man's a white old man
And my old mother's black.

If ever I cursed my white old man
I take my curses back.

If ever I cursed my black old mother                      5
And wished she were in hell,
I'm sorry for that evil wish
And now I wish her well.

My old man died in a fine big house.
My ma died in a shack.                                    10
I wonder where I'm gonna die,
Being neither white nor black?

LANGSTON HUGHES


## ALL QUIET ON THE METRICAL FRONT

Dactyls were corpulent, corseted, gussetted,
heady with hubris and fat as a cat who eats
nothing but cream with a touch of canary. If
courage is reckoned in pounds, then be merry, oh
Dactyls! You've nothing to fear. For the Anapests        5
(people will tell you too quickly) are fantasies
out of a book by a man with an ulcer, an
ill man who dines on the wing of a gull, Sir. No
need for concern. So just tighten your corsets and
let out your gussets. Remember, though horses may       10
stagger and pitch, though your armor may buckle, that
battles (they say) can be won on your stomachs.
                    (A chuckle is
history's answer to that!)
                    For the An-                          15
apests came: with a flutter of flutes down they danced
through the woods to the plain and their shadows were white
and their eyes were like stars and their hands made a light
like the scent of sweet night.
                    Charge! yelled the Dactyls and   20
puffed down the hill.
                    Now the Anapests lacked
any instinct to kill. Turning sideways they smiled.

31

Disappeared quite from sight.
                                Driven distract by the                    25
absence of presence the Dactyls fell pell over mell. They were
Dactyls united—together they fell!
                                With a delicate sniff
and the faintest of sneers
all the Anapests joined                                                   30
in a whis-
per of cheers.

IRVING KREUTZ


# IN A PROMINENT BAR
# IN SECAUCUS ONE DAY

In a prominent bar in Secaucus one day
Rose a lady in skunk with a topheavy sway,
Raised a knobby red finger—all turned from their beer—
While with eyes bright as snowcrust she sang high and clear:

'Now who of you'd think from an eyeload of me                            5
That I once was a lady as proud as could be?
Oh I'd never sit down by a tumbledown drunk
If it wasn't, my dears, for the high cost of junk.

'All the gents used to swear that the white of my calf
Beat the down of the swan by a length and a half.                        10
In the kerchief of linen I caught to my nose
Ah, there never fell snot, but a little gold rose.

'I had seven gold teeth and a toothpick of gold,
My Virginia cheroot was a leaf of it rolled
And I'd light it each time with a thousand in cash—                      15
Why the bums used to fight if I flicked them an ash.

'Once the toast of the Biltmore, the belle of the Taft,
I would drink bottle beer at the Drake, never draft,
And dine at the Astor on Salisbury steak
With a clean tablecloth for each bite I did take.                        20

'In a car like the Roxy I'd roll to the track,
A steel-guitar trio, a bar in the back,

32

And the wheels made no noise, they turned over so fast,
Still it took you ten minutes to see me go past.

'When the horses bowed down to me that I might choose,    25
I bet on them all, for I hated to lose.
Now I'm saddled each night for my butter and eggs
And the broken threads race down the backs of my legs.

'Let you hold in mind, girls, that your beauty must pass
Like a lovely white clover that rusts with its grass.    30
Keep your bottoms off barstools and marry you young
Or be left—an old barrel with many a bung.

'For when time takes you out for a spin in his car
You'll be hard-pressed to stop him from going too far
And be left by the roadside, for all your good deeds,    35
Two toadstools for tits and a face full of weeds.'

All the house raised a cheer, but the man at the bar
Made a phonecall and up pulled a red patrol car
And she blew us a kiss as they copped her away
From that prominent bar in Secaucus, N.J.    40

X. J. KENNEDY

33

# 2

## Rhythmic Variation

In Chapter 1 we first considered the appeal of rhythm, then the metrical tools used by poets writing in English. Put most simply, the use of meter in poetry in some ways parallels the use of "beat" in music. Now one frequently hears it said that one or another performing group has a "good beat." But if by "beat" we mean simply a regularly repeated sound or sound pattern, then pile drivers, factory machinery, and dripping taps have a beat also. Why is the performance of a good drummer exciting and the performance of a leaky water faucet maddening? The difference is basic and vitally important to those who would understand poetry: a drummer with a good beat does not merely keep time, as does a monotonously dripping faucet. The drummer establishes a basic rhythmic pulse which he then goes on to vary in interesting ways. Half the fun of the performance is having one's body mechanism, from the toes on up, anticipating the beat to come; the other half is in the little rhythmic surprises which a subtle drummer can introduce, without losing the force of his original rhythmic pattern.

In our discussion of meter, we have proceeded as if the poet were at all times laying down a perfectly unvarying beat—iambic, trochaic, anapestic, or dactylic. But in practice, the poet uses his meter as the drummer uses his percussion instruments: he sets up a rhythmic expectancy within the reader, and then he varies it in interesting ways. In fact, a lengthy passage in any meter which is perfectly regular and unvaried is rare, and in any foot but the iamb the structure of the language makes it very nearly impossible. For the pur-

34

poses of this text, the theoretical meter implied by metrical definitions —such as iambic pentameter, five iambic feet to the line—will be referred to as *normative meter*, the "norm" to which the actual rhythmic structure of the poem is referred. The actual rhythmic structure of the poem—the normative meter as the poet varies it—will be called *performance meter*. One should not expect complete agreement as to what constitutes the performance meter of a given line of poetry, since that will vary somewhat according to the insights and interpretations of individual readers or performers. The range of possible readings, however, is narrower than many readers might suspect.

Let us now compare normative and performance meter in a quatrain from the *Rubaiyyat* by Edward Fitzgerald. Since the first two lines are regular iambic pentameter in which normative meter and performance meter are the same, they were used earlier as an illustration of some of the uses of the iamb. Here is the entire quatrain.

> I sometimes think that never blows so red
> The rose as where some buried Caesar bled;
> That every Hyacinth the garden wears
> Dropt in her lap from some once lovely Head.

Why does Fitzgerald, after those first two regular lines, choose to vary his metrical pattern? The word "hyacinth" in line 3 can be read with identical stresses on HY and CINTH only by a distortion of normal pronunciation, and it takes an even grosser distortion to emphasize the preposition IN rather than the verb DROPT in line 4. If Fitzgerald were an incompetent amateur, one might assume that he violated normative meter because he was incapable of keeping his iambic pentameter marching straight. But in the performance of a recognized poetic craftsman, "he did it because he didn't know any better" is almost never a valid reason. For instance, Fitzgerald could have written these lines.

> That every virgin bloom the garden wears
> Was once the curl of some fair maiden's head.

However, he chose not to. Why?

The answers, we think, are not hard to find. In addition to problems of diction and imagery, our substitute lines are wooden and artificial; they thump rather than swing. After two lines of unvarying iambic pentameter, Fitzgerald may have wanted variation, and he utilized that variation to help him say what he wanted to say. For instance, in the third line, substitution of a pyrrhic foot (two unstressed syllables)

35

That every Hyacinth/the garden wears

enables Fitzgerald both to achieve variety and provide quickness
and lightness for his personification of a garden. In the fourth line, the
variations are even more pronounced. By inverting the expected
iambic foot at the beginning of the line, Fitzgerald jars us out of the
quietness induced by the preceding line. Not only do the semantic
implications of "drop" impress us, but the unexpected stressed syllable
at the beginning of the line "drops" on us as well. To further emphasize the serious turn which the quatrain takes in the fourth line,
Fitzgerald substituted a spondee (two heavy stresses) for an iamb in
the fourth foot. The effect of this substitution is to slow us down
and make us ponder over the temporality of human existence. Fitzgerald
has varied but three of twenty feet in his quatrain. Yet those three
are so effectively placed that the tone of the poem is significantly
altered by them. Furthermore, these variations allow him a more natural word choice than would strict adherence to normative iambic
meter. But most importantly, these variations work to intensify and
underline his meaning. Sound and sense converge.

While Fitzgerald's substitutions, feet different than the
normative feet of the poem, are made in an iambic poem, it is also
possible to substitute in trochiac, anapestic, and dactylic meters.
As we have already indicated, a good deal of substitution in these
less common meters is necessary if the language of the poem is to
sound unstrained. Any of the four basic feet may be substituted in
a poem written in another meter, as may the spondee and the pyrrhus.

In a general way, all purposeful metrical substitution serves
to catch and retain the reader's attention through the shifts, both
obvious and subtle, in the poem's rhythmic movement. While a poem's
rhythm is influenced by many factors, some of which will be discussed in succeeding chapters, this chapter will concentrate on metrical
variation and several prosodic techniques related to tempo.

Metrical substitution may be so slight as to be almost unno-
ticeable, or it may be abrupt in effect. Fine poetry has been written
in which there is little variation. The poetry written in England during
the eighteenth century, when "regularity" was accounted a chief virtue of the poet, was often of this type; conversely, fine poetry has
been written using a great deal of substitution. The amount of metrical
substitution a poet uses is determined, often, by the subject matter
of his poem, the character of his metaphors and imagery, and by the
taste of the poet and the taste of his age.

Even though the amount and kind of metrical variation change
from age to age and poet to poet, there are several generalizations
that can be made.

> By creating a line which contains extra unstressed syllables,
> the poet can reinforce effects of rapidity, lightness, ease,
> or conversational naturalness.

Consider the effect of anapestic substitution in Robert Browning's "Fra Lippo Lippi," a poem in normative iambic pentameter. A monk of unmonastic appetites is describing girls passing on the street at night.

> . . . Scarce had they turned the corner when a titter
> Like the skipping of rabbits by moonlight—three slim shapes,
> And a face that looked up—zooks, sir, flesh and blood,
> That's all I'm made of.

Working against the pattern of normative iambs, the three initial anapests in line 2 skip and titter like the girls Fra Lippo Lippi is describing. Not only that, but Browning has added an extra syllable at the end of the first line, an unstressed one, thus creating a *feminine ending*. Lines which end in unstressed syllables are termed feminine, while lines which end in accented syllables are *masculine*. The feminine ending "titter" falls away to an unstressed final syllable, so that lines 1 and 2 flow into each other. By contrast, "shapes" and "blood," both masculine endings, are strongly stressed words. (Though feminine endings are often used when effects of playfulness, uncertainty, or softness are desired, the term is not derived from theoretical assumptions that women are weak and men strong. It is called feminine because in French such endings are most often formed from the feminine form of the adjective.) After the light, skipping anapests in line 2, Browning concludes his line with an iamb (light—three) followed by a spondee (slim shapes). The line is not only interesting rhythmically, but it also parallels the mood of the speaker, on whom the light, tripping feet have had a forceful, even sensual, effect.

Notice also the conversational naturalness of these lines. Extra light syllables, introduced through the substitution of anapests, dactyls, or pyrrhics, can often give a feeling of naturalness and casualness. Here are some lines from a more recent poem called "Thorstein Breedlove in the Eloise Butler Wild Flower Garden."

> I promise not to smoke your flowers, Eloise,
> Or stomp them demonstrating. I think I dig you,
> Dead lady, in your grey newspaper picture,
> With your owl glasses and your spinster bun.

Here the various substitutions, such as a final pyrrhus in line 1, the spondee beginning line 3, and the three substitutions in line 4,

37

are used primarily to achieve an off-the-cuff, conversational tone. And yet the basic foot here is the iamb in the familiar pentameter line, loosely used in this poem.

A second generalization about the potential effects of metrical substitution is suggested by the metrics of these two examples.

> *By creating a line which contains stressed syllables without the normally intervening unstressed syllables, the poet can reinforce effects of slowness, weight, difficulty, tension, or intensity.*

Alexander Pope, in his "Essay on Criticism," versifies his examples of what he considers good poetic form. Here he is illustrating the coupling of form and content, by writing a couplet which parallels and underscores the physical effort of its subject by metrical means.

When Ajax strives some rock's vast weight to throw,
The line too labours, and the words move slow.

In the first line we have an iamb followed by a spondee—three heavy stresses (rock's vast weight). In the second line this same device is used twice. The spondee alone is frequently used for heavy stress, but it can be reinforced, as in Pope's poem, by following an iamb, or by preceding a trochee, as in this line from a poem by Gerard Manley Hopkins.

As a dare-gale skylark scanted in a dull cage.

The heavy stress combinations in this one line give an effect of constriction, entirely appropriate to the image of the caged bird.

In another of his poems, Hopkins uses accumulated heavy stresses in a different way. The first nine lines of "Pied Beauty" sing the praises of nature's variety—"dappled things," the freckled markings of trout, the varieties of landscape, and the quirks and eccentricities of the world. The contrasts and differences and seeming conflicts of the world, says Hopkins, are merely illustrations of the infinite capacity of an unchanging God.

He fathers-forth whose beauty is past change:
                    Praise Him.

The four successive final stresses, like the repeated "Hallelujas" of Handel's chorus, underscore a release of joyous worship. (Incidentally, any student who may still be unsure of the distinctions between prose and poetry is encouraged to reread this summary of "Pied Beauty" and then read the poem in its entirety.)

38

To this point in our discussion of metrical substitution, we have used only iambic examples. The popularity of the iambic foot is in part a result of its close proximity to the stress patterns of normal spoken English. The other less common feet use substitution also, but a good deal of that substitution is employed to avoid abnormally stilted word order. Since the natural iambic tendency of the language keeps breaking in upon the more artificial meters, the poet who wishes his poem to have any vitality will frequently compromise his trochaic, dactylic, or anapestic patterns for the sake of naturalness alone. But it is possible to use substitution effectively in the less common meters, and the consequences of its use will be quite similar to those we have already sketched. A light extra syllable would be hardly noticeable in the triple feet, but it would have much the same effects in trochaic patterns as it does in iambic. In any meter, heavy stress combinations will slow and intensify the line.

There is one final generalization which can be made about metrical substitution.

*A pronounced reversal in the rhythm of the line usually signals an important moment in the development of the poem.* By reversing the rhythm, a poet may be expressing a sense of discovery or illumination. He may be moving from general to specific, or from specific to general. A crucial shift of tone may be involved, such as a movement from doubt to faith. Or the poet may be rising to a new level of poetic intensification. But what is meant by a *reversal* of rhythm? Assume we have a normative iambic line. This is its pattern: di DUM di DUM di DUM di DUM di DUM. Of course a perfectly regular line of anything is quite rare, but nonetheless the moderately experienced reader of poetry expects this pattern to occur. In fact, the experienced reader of poetry who sees a familiar stanza conformation on the page will unconsciously expect iambic feet before he reads a word. Once an iambic pattern is established, let us assume that the poet introduces a regular trochaic line: DUM di DUM di DUM di DUM di DUM di. An experienced reader will still "hear" the normative iambic pulse beating in his nerve endings. But the performance meter of this line reverses what has gone before. The tension between normative and performance meter gives an extra dimension of excitement to the language of the poem.

A reversal, or counter-rhythm, such as the above, would be an absolute reversal. Absolute anythings occur but rarely in poetry. But less absolute reversals are common. We have already discussed one such reversal—that which occurred in the fourth line of the quatrain by Fitzgerald. Here are the critical two lines again.

That every Hyacinth the garden wears
Dropt in her lap from some once lovely Head.

The initial trochaic stress in line 2 both sharpens and intensifies the poem's language and underscores the falling of the rose; the prevailing gentleness of the first three lines is offset by the bittersweet fourth line.

Fitzgerald's quatrain is a conservative example of metrical reversal. One of the most famous and dramatic reversals in the language occurs in Shakespeare's *King Lear*. The dialogue, like most elevated dialogue in Shakespeare's works, is in a freely varied blank verse. King Lear, humiliated, impoverished, ultimately driven mad by the maltreatment of his daughters, Goneril and Regan, is finally reunited with his loyal daughter, Cordelia. But the reunion is brief. Cordelia is hanged. Lear tries to convince himself that his loyal daughter ("my poor fool") still lives, but, failing to do so, cries out above her corpse:

> And my poor fool is hang'd: No, no, no life!
> Why should a dog, a horse, a rat, have life,
> And thou no breath at all? Thou'lt come no more,
> Never, never, never, never, never!

Here we have all the resources of metrical variation marshalled to intensify one of the peak moments of drama. In the first line, the performance meter breaks the iambic pattern with two clusters of three heavy stresses (my poor fool—hang'd: No, no). The second line emphasizes the futility of the question by beginning with a trochee, but the balance of the line is without significant variation. Line 3 is iambic with the exception of the final foot, in which a spondee is substituted. The fourth line, however, totally reverses the iambic pattern. The marching iambs stumble and fall away, like a man falling into an abyss of grief. The metrical reversal is absolute, as is the fact of Cordelia's death and Lear's recognition of his error and his loss. Although metrical substitution is the most frequently used prosodic device for altering a poem's rhythm, several other techniques can be employed to produce rhythmic variation.

## ONE-SYLLABLE WORDS

The tempo of a line is slowed if the line contains a high proportion of one-syllable words. The reason for this is that we make an almost imperceptible pause after discrete words so that the word is registered as an entity in itself. Consider, for example, the differences in tempo between the following pairs: futile-few/till; intensity-in/ten/see/tea; butter-but/her. Obviously, a poet may use many one-syllable words when he wishes to convey a feeling of slowness or deliberateness.

## Diaresis

Diaresis is the correspondence between the beginning and ending of words, and the beginning and ending of metrical feet. As with lines dominated by one-syllable words, diaresis is often effectively used to convey a feeling of slowness, or, as in this passage from Pope's "Essay on Criticism," of restraint and order. (The feet enclosed in parentheses mark the occurrence of diaresis.)

*[handwritten note: end of foot unit; does not come w/ the end of a word.]*

> (Hear how) (learn'd Greece) her useful rules (indites)
> (When to) (repress) (and when) (indulge) (our flights:)
> (High on) Parnassus' top (her sons) (she show'd,)
> And pointed out those ard'ous paths (they trod;)
> (Held from) (afar,) (aloft,) th' immortal prize,
> (And urged) (the rest) by equal steps (to rise.)

Pope's meter, though generally regular, has several substitutions. Four out of six iambic lines begin with trochees, for instance, and these variations from the norm prevent monotony.

But continued diaresis without metrical substitution tends toward choppy or singsong effects. Consider these lines from Longfellow's "Song of Hiawatha."

> From his lodge went Hiawatha,
> Dressed for travel, armed for hunting;
> Dressed in deer-skin shirt and leggings,
> Richly wrought with quills and wampum;
> On his head his eagle feathers,
> Round his waist his belt of wampum,
> In his hand his bow of ash-wood,
> Strung with sinews of the reindeer;
> In his quiver oaken arrows,
> Tipped with jasper, winged with feathers. . . .

Hiawatha may have been able to leave the wigwam under all that regalia, but the mere listing of it in Longfellow's diaretic leaden verse becomes exhausting to read.

## Caesura

A caesura is a pause or a break *within* a line of poetry. In most instances caesuras occur through natural syntactic pauses. The following passage from John Donne's "Holy Sonnet 14" illustrates several instances in which syntax creates a caesura.

Batter my heart, ‖ three person'd God; ‖ for you      1
As yet but knock, ‖ breathe, ‖ shine, ‖ and seek to mend;      2
That I may rise, ‖ and stand, ‖ o'erthrow me, ‖ and bend      3
Your force, to break, ‖ blow, ‖ burn and make me new.      4
I, ‖ like an usurp'd town, ‖ to another due,      5
Labor to admit you, ‖ but O, ‖ to no end!      6

The caesura after "heart" in the first line (indicated by a double vertical line) is needed because "three person'd God" is a term of direct address. The caesura after "God" in the first line occurs because the independent clause ends at that point. In the second line, light caesuras are needed after "knock," "breathe," and "shine" to indicate that they are items in a series—not elements of an invented compound verb. In line 3, the caesura after "rise" indicates that the two actions—rising and standing—are independent; the speaker may rise, but he will not necessarily then be standing. The caesura after "stand" is required so that the phrase "and stand" is clearly a part of the noun clause beginning with "that." After "me," in the third line, the caesura indicates the end of the first independent clause in a compound sentence. In the fourth line, no caesura is needed after "force," even though a comma is used, but caesuras are needed after "break," and "blow," for the same reason they are needed in line 2 after "knock." The caesuras in line 5 after "I" and "town" occur for quite a different reason. The phrase, "like an usurp'd town," is a syntactic interrupter. Without the pause after "I," the reader or hearer would understand that the speaker in the poem likes "usurp'd towns." The caesura is essential to prevent a gross misreading. Finally, in line 6, the ejaculatory phrase "but O" is set off by caesuras to unmistakably indicate that it is an interrupting element.

    In the exercises which follow, you will be asked to deal with metrical substitutions and with some of the other prosodic techniques affecting a poem's rhythm. While logical thought processes will be of some assistance to you in making your choices, an attentive ear and live nerve endings will be even more helpful.

*Exercise 1*

## IAMBIC FEET CONSIDERED AS HONORABLE SCARS

You see these little scars? That's where my wife      1
—The principle of order everywhere—      2

_____ _c_ , shooting at the sloppy bear     3

That _____ _a_ _____ the urinals of life.     4

He is the principle of god knows what;     5

He wants things to be shapeless and all hair.     6

_____ _b_ _____ would want to fight him fair,     7

Only a woman would think he could be shot.     8

1. The missing words in line 3 are (a) Hits me, (b) Assaults me, (c) Grazes me, (d) Has wounded me.

2. The missing words in line 4 are (a) lurches from, (b) steps out of, (c) walks out from, (d) plugs up.

3. The missing words in line 7 are (a) A fool; (b) Only a fool, (c) A hunter brave, (d) Another bear.

ANSWERS

1. As you have discovered, the basic foot of this poem is the iamb. How many feet are in each line? You'll need to know that in order to make choices in questions 2 and 3. In any case, the action implied is somewhat violent—consider "scars," "shooting," and "fight." Would regular iambic feet at the beginning of line 3 reinforce that implied violence? Of the four choices, only (b) and (c) have three syllables—the number required to make the line iambic pentameter. Choice (c) was the poet's choice.

2. If you have discovered the number of feet per line, then choice (d) is not a possibility. (a), (b), and (c), however, are potential choices, and all three of them can be read as normative iambic meter. Consider the implications, though, of "sloppy" in line 3. How would a "sloppy" bear walk? The poet had him walk like this: di DUM di di di DUM di di di DUM. Choice (a) was the poet's preference, and doesn't the line seem to "lurch" with that bear?

3. The text stated that a metrical reversal at the beginning of a line can arrest our attention and signal a reversal of emphasis. Lines 1 and 2 focused on "my wife." Lines 3 through 6 on the bear. Line 7 switches from the bear to choice (b)—"Only a fool..." The substitution of the trochee for the iamb identifies that change of emphasis; none of the others do.

_Exercise 2_

## A SLUMBER DID MY SPIRIT SEAL

A slumber did my spirit seal;     1

I had no human fears:     2

43

She seemed a thing that could not feel       3
    The touch of earthly years.       4

No motion has she ____*d*____ :       5
    She neither hears nor sees;       6
____*a*____ in earth's diurnal course,       7
    With rocks, ____*b*____, and trees.       8

1. The missing words in line 5 are (a) to enforce, (b) through the gorse, (c) now or force, (d) now, no force.
2. The missing words in line 7 is/are (a) Rolled around, (b) Revolved, (c) Interred, (d) Turning.
3. The missing word(s) in line 8 is/are (a) grass, (b) and stones, (c) brambles, (d) and bones.

ANSWERS

1. The regular iambic meter of this poem should be easy to detect. Since the first stanza of the poem suggests a resigned, gentle attitude, one should not expect a great deal of variation, and indeed the variations are few. In line 5, choice (b) does fit the metrical expectation, but seems irrelevant. Choices (a) and (c) are both metrically and semantically acceptable. However, it is in this line that we see the irony of the speaker's early heedless slumber; his loved one was mortal and is now dead. In order to emphasize this irony, the poet has incorporated metrical variations in choice (d). The caesura after "now" interrupts the smooth motion of the line, thereby calling our attention to the cessation of her life. The words "no force" both can be and should be read as a spondee, a substitution which further emphasizes the fact of death.

2. Here again all four choices are metrically possible. Choices (b) and (c) maintain the normative iambic meter; choice (d) is a trochee which reverses or inverts the meter initially; choice (a) can be read as an iamb, but it is more natural to read it as a spondee— "Rolled round." Choice (a) was the poet's choice, emphasizing as it does the fact that the dead beloved one has lost all power to move of her own volition; she now moves only with the natural movements of the earth.

3. The diurnal movement of the earth is, of course, highly regular and predictable. Choices (a) and (c) would disrupt this regular rhythmic expectation. Both (b) and (d), however, are metrically acceptable; furthermore, either seems to make sense. Perhaps (b) is repetitive, since rocks and stones are essentially the same. Choice (d) would appear to add an element to rocks (inorganic) and trees (organic), since bones are from the animal world which neither of the others is. Choice (b), though, was the poet's choice. Give yourself a pat on the back for (d).

*Exercise 3*

## ENGLAND IN 1819

| | |
|---|---|
| An old, ————, despised, and dying king; | 1 |
| Princes, the dregs of their dull race, who flow | 2 |
| Through public scorn—mud from a muddy spring; | 3 |
| Rulers who neither see, nor feel, nor know, | 4 |
| But leech-like to their fainting country cling | 5 |
| Till they drop, ————, without a blow; | 6 |
| A people starved and stabbed in the untilled field; | 7 |
| An army, which liberticide and prey | 8 |
| Makes as a two-edged sword to all who wield; | 9 |
| Golden and sanguine laws which tempt and slay; | 10 |
| Religion Christless, Godless—a book sealed; | 11 |
| A Senate—Times worst statute unrepealed,— | 12 |
| Are graves, from which a glorious ———— | 13 |
| ————, to illumine our tempestuous day. | 14 |

1. The missing word(s) in line 7 is/are (a) and dumb, (b) ugly, (c) mad, blind, (d) insane.
2. The missing word(s) in line 6 is/are (a) blind in blood, (b) fainting, (c) cowards in common, (d) soundlessly.
3. The missing words in line 13 are (a) Corpse will, (b) Phantom may, (c) Apparition will, (d) Light may.
4. The missing word in line 14 is (a) Appear, (b) Burst, (c) Materialize, (d) Evolve.

*Exercise 4*

A    O, west wind please blow now soon for me,
      And let the sky make rain.
      And then my love and I may be
      Together in bed again.

B    O wind from the west will you blow
      And let again come rain?
      And my love then can be in my arms
      And I? I in my bed again.

45

C      Western wind, when wilt thou blow,
          The small rain down can rain?
          Christ, if my love were in my arms,
          And I in my bed again!

1. The "genuine" poem of these three is (1)A, (2) B, (3) C.
2. Give three reasons for preferring the one you do prefer.

# 2

---

## Poems

47

## THEY FLEE FROM ME

They flee from me that sometime did me seek,
  With naked foot stalking in my chamber.
I have seen them gentle, tame, and meek,
  That now are wild and do not remember
  That sometime they put themselves in danger      5
    To take bread at my hand; and now they range
    Busily seeking with a continual change.

Thankt be fortune, it hath been otherwise
  Twenty times better; but once, in special,
In thin array, after a pleasant guise,      10
  When her loose gown from her shoulders did fall,
  And she me caught in her arms long and small,
    Therewith all sweetly did me kiss,
    And softly said: "Dear heart, how like you this?"

It was no dream; I lay broad waking:      15
  But all is turned thorough my gentleness
Into a strange fashion of forsaking;
  And I have leave to go of her goodness;
  And she also to use new-fangleness.
    But since that I so kindely am served,      20
    I fain would know what she hath deserved.

SIR THOMAS WYATT

## SLOW, SLOW, FRESH FOUNT

Slow, slow, fresh fount, keep time with my salt tears:
  Yet slower, yet: oh, faintly, gentle springs,
List to the heavy part the music bears,
  Woe weeps out her division when she sings.
    Droop herbs and flowers;      5
    Fall grief in showers,
    Our beauties are not ours;
    Oh, I could still,
Like melting snow upon some craggy hill,
    Drop, drop, drop, drop,      10
Since nature's pride is now a withered daffodil.

BEN JONSON

48

## DELIGHT IN DISORDER

A sweet disorder in the dress
Kindles in clothes a wantonnesss
A lawn about the shoulders thrown
Into a fine distraction,
An erring lace, which here and there          5
Enthrals the crimson stomacher,
A cuff neglectful, and thereby
Ribbands to flow confusedly,
A winning wave, deserving note,
In the tempestuous petticoat,               10
A careless shoe-string, in whose tie
I see a wild civility,
Do more bewitch me, than when art
Is too precise in every part.

ROBERT HERRICK


## TO ALTHEA FROM PRISON

When Love with unconfinéd wings
   Hovers within my gates,
And my divine Althea brings
   To whisper at the grates;
When I lie tangled in her hair             5
   And fetter'd to her eye,
The birds that wanton in the air
   Know no such liberty.

When flowing cups run swiftly round
   With no allaying Thames,               10
Our careless heads with roses crown'd,
   Our hearts with loyal flames;
When thirsty grief in wine we steep,
   When healths and draughts go free,
Fishes that tipple in the deep            15
   Know no such liberty.

When, linnet-like confinéd, I
   With shriller throat shall sing

49

The sweetness, mercy, majesty
   And glories of my King;            20
When I shall voice aloud how good
   He is, how great should be,
Enlarged winds, that curl the flood,
   Know no such liberty.

Stone walls do not a prison make,          25
   Nor iron bars a cage;
Minds innocent and quiet take
   That for an hermitage:
If I have freedom in my love
   And in my soul am free,           30
Angels alone, that soar above,
   Enjoy such liberty.

RICHARD LOVELACE

## LA BELLE DAME SANS MERCI

generally iambic tentameter

"Ah, what can ail thee, knight-at-arms,
   Alone and palely loitering?
The sedge is withered from the lake,
   And no birds sing.

"Ah, what can ail thee, knight-at-arms!      5
   So haggard and so woe-begone?
The squirrel's granary is full,
   And the harvest's done.

"I see a lily on thy brow,
   With anguish moist and fever dew;     10
And on thy cheek a fading rose
   Fast withereth too."

"I met a lady in the meads
   Full beautiful, a faery's child;
Her hair was long, her foot was light,     15
   And her eyes were wild.

"I made a garland for her head,
   And bracelets too, and fragrant zone;

50

She looked at me as she did love,
  And made sweet moan.                              20

"I set her on my pacing steed,
  And nothing else saw all day long;
For sideways would she lean, and sing
  A faery's song.

"She found me roots of relish sweet,               25
  And honey wild, and manna dew;
And sure in language strange she said,
  I love thee true.

"She took me to her elfin grot,
  And there she wept and sighed full sore,         30
And there I shut her wild, wild eyes—
  With kisses four.

"And there she lullèd me asleep,
  And there I dreamed, ah woe betide,
The latest dream I ever dreamed                    35
  On the cold hill's side.

"I saw pale kings, and princes too,
  Pale warriors, death-pale were they all;
They cried—'La belle dame sans merci
  Hath thee in thrall!'                            40

"I saw their starved lips in the gloom
  With horrid warning gapèd wide,
And I awoke, and found me here
  On the cold hill's side.

"And this is why I sojourn here                    45
  Alone and palely loitering,
Though the sedge is withered from the lake,
  And no birds sing."

JOHN KEATS

## DAYS

Daughters of Time, the hypocritic Days,
Muffled and dumb like barefoot dervishes,

And marching single in an endless file,
Bring diadems and fagots in their hands.
To each they offer gifts after his will,                    5
Bread, kingdoms, stars, and sky that holds them all,
I, in my pleached garden, watched the pomp,
Forgot my morning wishes, hastily
Took a few herbs and apples, and the Day
Turned and departed silent. I, too late,                   10
Under her solemn fillet saw the scorn.

RALPH WALDO EMERSON


## BREAK, BREAK, BREAK

Break, break, break,
   On thy cold gray stones, O Sea!
And I would that my tongue could utter
   The thoughts that arise in me.

O well for the fisherman's boy,                             5
   That he shouts with his sister at play!
O well for the sailor lad,
   That he sings in his boat on the bay!

And the stately ships go on
   To their haven under the hill;                           10
But O for the touch of a vanished hand,
   And the sound of a voice that is still!

Break, break, break,
   At the foot of thy crags, O Sea!
But the tender grace of a day that is dead                  15
   Will never come back to me.

ALFRED, LORD TENNYSON


## PROSPICE

Fear death?—to feel the fog in my throat,
   The mists in my face,

When the snows begin, and the blasts denote
    I am nearing the place,
The power of the night, the press of the storm,         5
    The post of the foe;
Where he stands, the Arch  Fear in a visible form,
    Yet the strong man must go:
For the journey is done and the summit attained,
    And the barriers fall,         10
Though a battle's to fight ere the guerdon be gained,
    The reward of it all.
I was ever a fighter, so—one fight more,
    The best and the last!
I would hate that death bandaged my eyes, and forebore,   15
    And bade me creep past.
No! let me taste the whole of it, fare like my peers
    The heroes of old,
Bear the brunt, in a minute pay glad life's arrears
    Of pain, darkness, and cold.         20
For sudden the worst turns the best to the brave,
    The black minute's at end.
And the element's rage, the fiend-voices that rave,
    Shall dwindle, shall blend,
Shall change, shall become first a peace out of pain,     25
    Then a light, then thy breast,
O thou soul of my soul! I shall clasp thee again,
    And with God be the rest!

ROBERT BROWNING


## THE BREEZE IS SHARP

The breeze is sharp, the sky is hard and blue,—
Blue with white tails of cloud. On such a day,
Upon a neck of sand o'erblown with spray,
We stood in silence the great sea to view;
And marked the bathers at their shuddering play
Run in and out with the succeeding wave,
While from our footsteps broke the trembling turf:

53

*(margin note: Secondary slash (/) - between X & —.)*

Again I hear the drenching of the wave;
The rocks rise dark, with wall and weedy cave;
Her voice is in mine ears, her answer yet:                    10
Again I see, above the froth and fret,
The blue loft standing like eternity!
And white feet flying from the surging surf   *(margin note: anapestic)*
And simmering suds of the sea!

FREDERIC TUCKERMAN


## SPRING AND FALL: TO A YOUNG CHILD

Márgarét, are you grieving
Over Goldengrove unleaving?
Leáves, like the things of man, you
With your fresh thoughts care for, can you?
Áh! ás the heart grows older                                  5
It will come to such sights colder
By and by, nor spare a sigh
Though worlds of wanwood leafmeal lie;
And yet you wíll weep and know why.
Now no matter, child, the name:                              10
Sórrow's spríngs áre the same.
Nor mouth had, no nor mind, expressed
What heart heard of, ghost guessed:
It ís the blight man was born for,
It is Margaret you mourn for.                                15

GERARD MANLEY HOPKINS


## DUST IN THE EYES

If, as they say, some dust thrown in my eyes
Will keep my talk from getting overwise,
I'm not the one for putting off the proof.
Let it be overwhelming, off a roof
And round a corner, blizzard snow for dust.                  5
And blind me to a standstill if it must.

ROBERT FROST


54

## *JUGGLER*

A ball will bounce, but less and less. It's not
A light-hearted thing, resents its own resilience.
Falling is what it loves, and the earth falls
So in our hearts from brilliance,
Settles and is forgot.                                    5
It takes a sky-blue juggler with five red balls

To shake our gravity up. Whee, in the air
The balls roll round, wheel on his wheeling hands,
Learning the ways of lightness, alter to spheres
Grazing his finger ends,                                   10
Cling to their courses there,
Swinging a small heaven about his ears,

But a heaven is easier made of nothing at all
Than the earth regained, and still and sole within
The spin of worlds, with a gesture sure and noble          15
He reels that heaven in,
Landing it ball by ball,
And trades it all for a broom, a plate, a table.

Oh, on his toe the table is turning, the broom's
Balancing up on his nose, and the plate whirls             20
On the tip of the broom! Damn, what a show, we cry:
The boys stamp, and the girls
Shriek, and the drum booms
And all comes down, and he bows and says good-bye.

If the juggler is tired now, if the broom stands           25
In the dust again, if the table starts to drop
Through the daily dark again, and though the plate
Lies flat on the table top,
For him we batter our hands
Who has won for once over the world's weight.              30

RICHARD WILBUR

# 3

## Rhyme

Since the essence of poetry is rhythm, we began with a consideration of rhythm as it is traditionally expressed in English and American verse, that is, in accentual-syllabic meter. However, if one asked a random hundred people on a street to define poetry, the chances are excellent that more of them would mention rhyme than any other feature of poetry. The reason for this is that rhyme, especially full rhyme, has been the most conspicuous and pervasive feature of English and American poetry for the lay audience.

There have, of course, been exceptions. Blank verse—unrhymed iambic pentameter—is the language of Shakespeare's drama, Milton's epic poems *Paradise Lost* and *Paradise Regained*, many of Wordsworth's major poems, and Browning's dramatic monologues. In addition, the popularity of free verse in the twentieth century has meant a rejection of both rhyme and meter. But rhyme is far from dead. In contemporary poetry, for example, many poets feel free to choose between traditional and self-devised forms, and also to combine the two, moving from metered to unmetered lines and from unrhymed to rhymed lines. In this chapter, in addition to discussing the principle forms of rhyme in English, we will be looking at some of the strengths the use of rhyme can bring to poetry. In the process, perhaps we will discover some of the reasons why rhymed verse has not gone the way of the buggy whip and the 78 RPM record.

Rhyme, broadly defined, is any correspondence in sound between words. However, since alliteration, assonance, consonance, and sound coloration deserve a chapter of their own, this chapter will deal only with rhyme in its narrow definition.

The most common form of rhyme is *full rhyme.* A rhyme is "full" if (1) the rhyming words have different initial sounds, but identical following sounds (doom-room, near-cheer), or (2) the rhyming words are polysyllabic and correspond at every point but one (tenderly-slenderly, relent-repent). Technically, homonym or *repeat rhyme,* in which the same word is repeated, or words with identical sounds, such as "heir-air," are rhymed, is also a form of full rhyme. So is *sight rhyme,* in which two words rhyme to the eye but not to the ear, as in "come-home" or "food-blood." But in serious poetry such rhymes are rarely used. Some apparent sight rhymes are the result of pronunciation differences (rain-again). Others reflect changes in the language over a period of time: "good/food/blood" were all full rhymes at one time.

The origin of full rhyme is obscure. It is not common in the poetry of most cultures. It appears first in the literature of Western Europe in religious chants and hymns. It may have originated in Ireland, in the fourth or fifth century A.D., and traveling Irish monks may have spread rhyme throughout Europe. In any case, though there is some full rhyme in *Beowulf,* the use of full rhyme as a basic part of poem structure did not become established in English poetry till the fourteenth century.

Rhyming words can be classified as *masculine* or *feminine.* Masculine rhymes include all rhyming words of one syllable, as well as all polysyllabic words in which the final syllable is stressed (posséss-caréss). Feminine rhymes, softer and more graceful in effect, are words of two or more syllables in which the final syllable is not stressed (mérrily-áirily).

*End rhyme,* in which the rhyming words occur as the final words in lines, is the most common form of rhyme in English and American poetry. *Internal rhyme* is rhyme occurring within lines, as in Poe's famous poem, "The Raven."

Ah, distinctly I *remember,* it was in the bleak *December.*

Categorizing the types of rhyme is useful to a limited degree, but even more essential to the student of poetry is understanding the varied functions of rhyme.

One of the oldest and simplest uses of rhyme is for *mnemonic effect*—to help the hearer or reader remember what he has heard. Numerous traditional sayings or proverbs incorporate rhyme, such as, "Thirty days hath September, April, June, and November"; or "Red sky in the morning, sailor, take warning." The rhyme helps the proverb stick in our minds.

A second use of rhyme is for what might be broadly described as *musical effect*. Recurring sounds, as long as they are sufficiently varied, are pleasant to the ear. Small children not only enjoy having Mother Goose and A. A. Milne read to them, they joyously use—and sometimes invent—all kinds of rhyming games: "Ink-a-dink, a bottle of ink, the cork fell out and you stink!" "Red Rover, Red Rover, tell Joey to come over." And even apoetic adults frequently cherish a well-worn limerick or two, largely because the cleverness or incongruity of the rhyme gives the joke more kick.

When employed by a consummate poetic lyricist, though, rhyme is more than merely clever. Notice how much the music of rhyme adds to the following poem.

> Under the greenwood tree
> Who loves to lie with me,
> And turn his merry note
> Unto the sweet bird's throat,
> Come hither, come hither, come hither;
> Here shall he see
> No enemy
> But winter and rough weather.

"Song" from *As You Like It*, WILLIAM SHAKESPEARE

Many readers, as we suggested in our introduction, approach poems as if they were grocery lists, road maps, or sermons—as if the devices of poetry (meter, rhyme, sound patterns, imagery) were so much wrapping paper. No doubt the paper is pretty, they believe, and it may even be artfully applied, but it is not really important. What counts is the present inside, the little hard nugget of fact or moral admonition under the pretty paper. In order to penetrate to the "hidden meaning" you must ignore the wrapping paper, and once you have the present out of the paper, you can safely throw the paper away.

How much of "Song" can we throw away? Can we throw away the rhyme?

> Under the greenwood bough
> Who loves to lie with me,
> And turn his merry song
> Unto the sweet bird's warble,
> Come here, come here, come here;
> Here shall he find
> No enemy
> But winter and rough weather.

A great deal of the "poemness" of the poem is discarded along with the rhyme. There is still music in the lines, for to destroy wholly the music of Shakespeare's poem we would have to find substitutes for nearly all of his words. We would discover, if we did so, that changing the words had altered the meaning to some extent. ("Lie with me" in Shakespeare's time could be taken as an invitation to sexual pleasure. Try substituting any word or phrase with the same meaning. Is the overall effect of the poem the same?)

The poet's meaning and the poet's devices are in fact inseparable. You can't throw out the wrapping paper, including rhyme and its musical potential, without throwing out the present.

Not all poetry is musical in the way that "Song" is. There is more than one kind of music, and rhyme can be used musically even if it is not "pretty" in an obvious way. It can be dignified or spritely, serious or witty. Rhyme can be the keystone of a cathedral arch. It can also be the punchline of a joke.

A third use of rhyme, very closely related to rhyme as music, is *structural*. English poetry has many traditional stanza forms which make use of set rhyme patterns, usually in combination with the conventional accentual-syllabic feet and established meters. In its structural (sometimes called architectonic) function, the various rhyming combinations both create and emphasize the outline or divisions within the poem. See how rhyme functions structurally in this brief poem by Emily Dickinson, "Faith Is a Fine Invention."

| | |
|---|---|
| Faith is a fine invention | *x* |
| When gentlemen can see, | *a* |
| But microscopes are prudent | *x* |
| In an emergency. | *a* |

Though only a single rhyme is involved in this poem, it is certainly more than a decoration. The unrhymed lines are parallel not only in their rhymelessness, but also in their subject matter. Both are concerned with different ways of gaining information about the world. The use of the word "invention" to describe faith suggests that faith, like the microscope, is a kind of information-gathering instrument. The rhymed lines are also parallel, each describing a state of affairs or human condition—"when gentlemen can see" parallels "in an emergency," with the rhyme emphasizing the parallel.

Despite its brevity, this is definitely a poem in two equal parts. Lines 1 and 2 describe the conditions under which faith is an adequate means of dealing with life; lines 3 and 4 describe the conditions under which "microscopes" represent a "prudent" approach to life. Taken together, the two halves of the poem make a single unified statement. The *xaxa* rhyme scheme emphasizes both the two-part division and the overall unity. The *x*, incidentally, is used to indicate nonrhyming lines in otherwise rhymed poems.

We will discuss the structural function of rhyme in more depth in the chapters dealing with traditional stanzaic forms.

A fourth use of rhyme, one which to some extent incorporates the three we have been discussing, is *intensification*. One of the reasons why rhyme helps us to remember, is pleasing to the ear, and is structurally useful to the poet is because rhyme, like rhythm, both creates and satisfies a psychic expectation. Once a rhyme pattern is established (and establishing a rhyme pattern is easier than establishing a rhythm pattern, since it takes only two rhyming words at the ends of lines), we anticipate further rhyme. The poet can then play with our expectation of rhyme, much as he plays with our expectation of rhythm when he manipulates meter.

Rhyming words are nearly always prominent words in poems. They are usually at the ends of lines, the position of greatest prominence, and our unconscious expectation of them makes us dwell on them more than we do on nonrhymed words. Therefore, the poet often chooses rhyme words that create an area of meaning which is greater than the potential of each word taken individually. For example, in Shakespeare's "Song," the full rhymes "note" and "throat" are used. Without being particularly aware of it, we quickly sense an appropriateness or logic to this combination, since "notes" are produced by "throats." Suppose Shakespeare had written a different line that resulted in "boat" or "moat" or "tote" rhyming with "note." In that instance, all we would have had were two words which met the basic rhyming requirements, but whose rhyming would make no special contribution toward the entire sense of the poem.

The potential of rhyme to intensify a poem is especially evident in the following lines excerpted from a poem which describes soldiers in retreat.

> Bent double, like old beggars under sacks,
> Knock-kneed, coughing like hags, we cursed through sludge,
> Till on the haunting flares we turned our backs,
> And towards our distant rest began to trudge.

from *Dulce et Decorum Est,* WILFRED OWEN

The rightness of the combination "sacks" and "backs" is readily apparent; sacks are frequently carried on backs, so the rhyme reinforces the comparison in line 1. Even more striking, though, is the intensification engendered by the rhyme combination of "sludge" and "trudge." These are not "pretty" rhyme words, but deliberately

60

ugly ones, chosen to match the ugliness, both physical and moral, of the scene described. These four lines are part of an introductory stanza which leads into a description of a man strangled by poison gas. Both "sludge" and "trudge are heavy, clumsy-sounding words, as strained and awkward as the movements of the exhausted soldiers. And how does a person walk in sludge? Does he stride, march, or skip? No, he trudges. The rhyming words, then, intensify both the physical details of the poem and the emotional attitude which the poet is projecting.

Rhyme intensification is in some ways more obvious in humorous poetry. Here Lord Byron, describing the education of Don Juan at the hands of his prudish but ambitious mother, lets a deft rhyme make his point for him.

> In case our lord the king should go to war again,
> He learn'd the arts of riding, fencing, gunnery,
> And how to scale a fortress—or a nunnery.

from *Don Juan*, Canto I

Robert Burns deflates some romantic clichés in "The Jolly Beggars" with intensifying rhyme. A contest for the charms of a woman between a Caird, or tinker, and an itinerant fiddler is won by the tinker. (Scots words are glossed in the right margin.)

> The Caird prevailed: th' unblushing fair
> In his embraces sunk,
> Partly wi' love o'ercome sae sair ....                 *sae sair,*
>                                                          so sore, so deeply

So far we have a touching embrace except for "unblushing fair"—ladies are supposed to blush at moments like that—and the curious word "sunk," a most unromantic word for an embrace. But "sunk" is there for a reason, as we find when Burns finishes the rhyme sequence.

> The Caird prevailed: th' unblushing fair
> In his embraces sunk,
> Partly wi' love o'ercome sae sair,
> And partly she was drunk.

Burns extends and complicates his use of intensive rhyme in "Holy Willie's Prayer." The speaker has already described himself to

61

God as "a pillar in Thy temple,/Strong as a rock,/A guide, a buckler, an example/To a' thy flock." Further on in the poem, however, he does some confessing.

> O Lord! yestreen, Thou kens, wi' Meg—     *yestreen*, last night
> Thy pardon I sincerely beg,                              *kens*, knows
> O! may it ne'er be a living plague
>             To my <u>dishonor</u>!
> An' I'll ne'er lift a lawless leg
>             Again <u>upon her</u>.

If we look only at the rhyme words, "Meg" and "beg" immediately suggest a female involvement. "Plague" suggests bad consequences. "Dishonor," which breaks the rhyme scheme, is a high-flown, moralistic word. (Notice that Holy Willie is only concerned about his honor, not Meg's.) Then the bawdy word "leg" takes us back to the original rhyme scheme ("Meg," "beg," "plague") while letting us know what previously unspecified dishonorable action Holy Willie has committed. The precise physical description of the last two lines (An' I'll ne'er lift a lawless leg/Again upon her.") undercuts Willie's high-toned concern for his honor. The final clinching reinforcement which helps us to see Holy Willie as a lecherous old hypocrite is the rhyme of "dishonor" with "upon her."

Our discussion so far has centered on full rhyme, which, until the twentieth century, was the dominant form in English and American poetry. Unlike full rhymes, which are comparatively rare in English, the looser, approximate *slant rhyme* (also called near, oblique, half, off, or imperfect rhyme) is easy to achieve and to vary. For instance, here is a pair of full rhymes: "mellow-yellow." After differing initial consonants, the words have identical sounds. Here are some slant-rhyme variations of "mellow" with italics to indicate those common letter-sounds which identify them as slant rhymes: "*mel*on, wil*low*, *m*i*ll*er, *lem*on, be*ll*, be*low*." Notice that the number of sounds in common between two slant rhymes is variable, as is the order in which they occur. (The "mel" sound in "mellow" is reversed in the "lem" sound of "lemon.") Sometimes it is hard to decide the exact point at which slant rhyme ends and no-rhyme begins. Perhaps the safest way to make the distinction is to say that when the ear hears a correspondence approximating rhyme, and the words in question occur at points in the poem where rhyme would normally be anticipated, then slant rhyme exists.

Admittedly this definition is somewhat looser and more cumbersome than the definition of full rhyme. Full rhyme in English has been used, experimented with, and gradually standardized over a period of roughly seven hundred years. By contrast, slant rhyme has only been used as a serious alternative for full rhyme for about a century, and it has been widely accepted and practiced only for the last forty or fifty years. It is, comparatively, a new and experimental form. This makes it more difficult to define briefly and absolutely.

The major reason for the use of slant rhyme and for its proliferation, once it was recognized as a legitimate form of rhyme, is the rhyme-poor nature of English. As John Ciardi points out, an Italian poet ending a line with "vita" (life) has literally hundreds of possible rhyme words available. On the other hand, when a poet writing in English ends a line with "life" he can choose from "strife, wife, knife, fife, rife"; he has no other possibilities. Since the end of a line, like the end of a sentence, is a position of great emphasis in English, the poet wants his key words at the ends of lines. Also, if possible, he wants correspondence in more than just sound between those key words. He wants intensification—word correspondences that work on more than one level. As a result, some words involving concepts very central to poetry have been used, reused, and then used again to the point that they have become rhyme clichés. Consider the following combinations, for example: life-strife, death-breath, earth-birth, trees-breeze, moon-June. The use of slant rhyme allows poets to avoid clichéd rhymes such as these as well as to use many words which have few or no rhymes in English. Perhaps the two most obvious examples of the limitations which full rhyme has created for poets writing in English are "orange" and "silver." Hundreds of poems have been written with words specifying color in rhyming positions—all colors, that is, except orange, silver, and perhaps purple. However, once the possibilities of slant rhyme are admitted, the potential rhyming combinations are many.

Slant rhyme has never quite the musical effect of full rhyme. Slant rhymes are always a bit dissonant. But sometimes a little dissonance is exactly what the poet wants.

Emily Dickinson, one of slant rhyme's pioneers, was especially gifted in making the dissonances of slant rhyme work for her, as is evident in "I Heard a Fly Buzz."

> I heard a Fly buzz—when I died—
> The Stillness in the Room
> Was like the Stillness in the Air
> Between the Heaves of Storm—
>
> The Eyes around—had wrung them dry—
> And Breaths were gathering firm

63

For that last Onset—when the King
Be witnessed—in the Room—

I willed away my Keepsakes—Signed away
What portion of me be
Assignable—and then it was
There interposed a Fly—

With Blue—uncertain stumbling Buzz—
Between the light—and me—
And then the Windows failed—and then
I could not see to see—

Notice how effectively here the dissonance of slant rhyme
carries out and helps create the uneasy, uncertain, and foreboding
feeling of the poem. Then, too, the slant rhyme used in the first three
stanzas sets up and underlines the full rhyme used in the chillingly
final stanza.

Slant rhyme can also be utilized in a more neutral way, as an
alternate or supplement to full rhyme. Here is the first stanza of
William Butler Yeats's "Among School Children."

I walk through the long schoolroom questioning;
A kind old nun in a white hood replies;
The children learn to cipher and to sing,
To study reading-books and history,
To cut and sew, be neat, in everything
In the best modern way—the children's eyes
In momentary wonder stare upon
A sixty-year-old smiling public man.

Here the rhymes weave together in a quietly unassertive pattern,
giving structural strength to the poem. Yeats has freely intermixed
full rhyme (sing-everything; replies-eyes) with slant rhyme (replies-
history; history-eyes; upon-man). The last stanza of this eight-stanza
poem well illustrates the musical and intensifying qualities latent in
poems employing both full and slant rhyme.

Labour is blossoming or dancing where
The body is not bruised to pleasure soul,
Nor beauty born out of its own despair
Nor blear-eyed wisdom out of midnight oil.

O chestnut-tree, great-rooted blossomer,
Are you the leaf, the blossom or the bole?
O body swayed to music, O brightening glance,
How can we know the dancer from the dance?

The stanzaic rhyme scheme in this poem is *abababcc*. Yeats ingeniously combines both full and slant rhymes in the triple rhymes (where-despair-blossomer; soul-oil-bole), before resolving both this stanza as well as the question implicit in the poem with the resounding full rhyme "glance-dance."

Poetic techniques, like styles of women's clothes, go in and out of fashion. Rhyme has been alternately praised and denounced by English and American poets for many, many years. Of the making of bad rhymes there is no end. But good rhymes—memorable rhymes, rhymes which intensify while they decorate—are always powerful, even when out of fashion.

*Exercise 1*

## OUT UPON IT

| | |
|---|---|
| Out upon it! I have loved | 1 |
| Three whole days together. | 2 |
| And am like to love three more, | 3 |
| If it prove _____. | 4 |
| Time shall molt away his wings | 5 |
| Ere he shall _____ | 6 |
| In the whole wide world again | 7 |
| Such a constant lover. | 8 |
| But the spite on't is, no _____ | 9 |
| Is due at all to me: | 10 |
| Love with me had made no stays, | 11 |
| Had it any been but she. | 12 |
| Had it any been but she, | 13 |
| And that very _____, | 14 |
| There had been at least ere this | 15 |
| A dozen dozen in her place. | 16 |

65

1. The missing words in line 4 are (a) fair weather, (b) fair lore, (c) a happy chore, (d) a kind tether.
2. The missing word in line 6 is (a) revere, (b) discover, (c) uncover, (d) deliver.
3. The missing word in line 9 is (a) admiration, (b) sigh, (c) scorn, (d) praise.
4. The missing word in line 14 is (a) face, (b) form, (c) shape, (d) case.

ANSWERS

1. Does this poem have a consistent rhyme scheme?
Except for stanza three, the pattern is *xaxa*. Therefore, the possible choices are (a) and (d). Of these two, which one is metrically right? Choice (a).
2. Would you expect to find slant rhyme in this poem? If not, then only choices (b) and (c) will do, and both of these are metrically acceptable. However, is one more likely to discover or uncover a lover? Choice (b).
3. You're right; a one-syllable word is needed. Only choices (c) and (d) would seem to make sense. Sir John breaks his pattern here and uses rhyme. Choice (d).
4. Only choices (a) and (d) provide the full rhyme needed. To refer to this lovely young lady, though, as a "case" wouldn't be flattering. Choice (a).

*Exercise 2*

## ARMS AND THE BOY

| | |
|---|---|
| Let the boy try along this bayonet-blade | 1 |
| How cold steel is, and keen with hunger of blood; | 2 |
| Blue with all malice, like a madman's flash; | 3 |
| And thinly drawn with famishing for _____. | 4 |
| Lend him to stroke these blind, blunt bullet-heads | 5 |
| Which long to nuzzle in the hearts of _____, | 6 |
| Or give him cartridges of fine zinc teeth, | 7 |
| Sharp with the sharpness of grief and death. | 8 |
| For his teeth seem for laughing round _____. | 9 |
| There lurk no claws behind his fingers _____; | 10 |
| And God will grow no talons at his heels, | 11 |
| Nor antlers through the thickness of his curls. | 12 |

66

1. The missing word in line 4 is (a) food, (b) flesh, (c) cash, (d) meat.
2. The missing word in line 6 is (a) lads, (b) soldiers, (c) men, (d) humans.
3. The missing words in line 9 are (a) an orange, (b) a peach, (c) a pear, (d) an apple.
4. The missing word in line 10 is (a) flippers, (b) neat, (c) fair, (d) supple.

ANSWERS

1. Lines 1 and 2, 7 and 8, and 11 and 12 reveal that the rhyming principle of this poem is slant rhyme. Since choice (c) is a full rhyme and choice (d) is neither full nor slant, they can not be considered. Choice (a) does have the "f" in common with "flash," but choice (b), "flesh," more fully satisfies the requirements of slant rhyme, in that most poets attempt to get at least two sounds in common.
2. In this line, only choices (a) and (d) have more than one sound in common with "heads." (Don't be deceived by the "d" in "soldiers.") Since the syllable count is somewhat irregular, choice (d) is possible, but choice (a) has the "ds" in common with "heads," and it also blends in well with the term "boy" which is used in line 1.
3/4. Since lines 9 and 10 will be completed by a slant rhyme pair, read them over to yourself with the various pairs of possibilities, if you have not done so already. The only word that can meaningfully modify "fingers" in line 10 is choice (d), "supple." Therefore, the choice in line 9 must also be (d).

*Exercise 3*

## WHEN FIRST MY WAY TO FAIR I TOOK

When first my way to fair I took          1
Few pence in purse had I.          2
And long I used to stand and look          3
At things I could not ____.          4

Now times are altered: if I care          5
To buy a thing, I can;          6
The pence are here and here's the ____,          7
But where's the lost young man?          8

To think that two and two are ____          9
And neither five nor three          10

67

The heart of man has long been sore          11
And long 'tis ___*b*___.                      12


1. The missing word in line 4 is (a) brook, (b) buy, (c) tie, (d) share.
2. The missing word in line 7 is (a) affair, (b) chair, (c) fair, (d) fare.
3. The missing word in line 9 is (a) four, (b) more, (c) plenty, (d) same.
4. The missing word(s) in line 12 is/are (a) likely, (b) likely to be, (c) like to be, (d) going to be.


## Exercise 4

1. Write five full rhymes for *June*.
2. Write five full rhymes for *emotion*.
3. Write five slant rhymes for *orange*.
4. Write five slant rhymes for *death*.
5. Write three full rhymes which could work to intensify each other (see pp. 60-62). Be prepared to explain your choices.
6. Write three slant rhymes which could work to intensify each other. Be prepared to explain your choices.

# 3

## Poems

## WHY SO PALE AND WAN

Why so pale and wan, fond lover?
　　Prithee, why so pale?
Will, when looking well can't move her,
　　Looking ill prevail?
　　Prithee, why so pale?　　　　　　　　　　　　　　　5

Why so dull and mute, young sinner?
　　Prithee, why so mute?
Will, when speaking well can't win her,
　　Saying nothing do 't?
　　Prithee, why so mute?　　　　　　　　　　　　　10

Quit, quit for shame! This will not move;
　　This cannot take her.
If of herself she will not love,
　　Nothing can make her:
　　The devil take her!　　　　　　　　　　　　　　15

SIR JOHN SUCKLING

## SHE WALKS IN BEAUTY

She walks in beauty, like the night
　　Of cloudless climes and starry skies;
And all that's best of dark and bright
　　Meet in her aspect and her eyes:
Thus mellowed to that tender light　　　　　　　　5
　　Which heaven to gaudy day denies.

One shade the more, one ray the less,
　　Had half impaired the nameless grace
Which waves in every raven tress
　　Or softly lightens o'er her face;　　　　　　　10
Where thoughts serenely sweet express
　　How pure, how dear their dwelling-place.

And on that cheek, and o'er that brow
　　So soft, so calm, yet eloquent,
The smiles that win, the tints that glow,　　　　15
　　But tell of days in goodness spent,

70

A mind at peace with all below,
    A heart whose love is innocent!

GEORGE GORDON, LORD BYRON

## ODE ON MELANCHOLY

No, no, go not to Lethe, neither twist
    Wolf's-bane, tight-rooted, for its poisonous wine;
Nor suffer thy pale forehead to be kissed
    By nightshade, ruby grape of Proserpine;
Make not your rosary of yew-berries,            5
    Nor let the beetle, nor the death-moth be
        Your mournful Psyche, nor the downy owl
A partner in your sorrow's mysteries;
    For shade to shade will come too drowsily,
        And drown the wakeful anguish of the soul.     10

But when the melancholy fit shall fall
    Sudden from heaven like a weeping cloud,
That fosters the droop-headed flowers all,
    And hides the green hill in an April shroud;
Then glut thy sorrow on a morning rose,          15
    Or on the rainbow of the salt sand-wave,
        Or on the wealth of globed peonies;
Or if thy mistress some rich anger shows,
    Emprison her soft hand, and let her rave,
        And feed deep, deep upon her peerless eyes.     20

She dwells with Beauty—Beauty that must die;
    And Joy, whose hand is ever at his lips
Bidding adieu; and aching Pleasure nigh,
    Turning to poison while the bee-mouth sips:
Ay, in the very temple of Delight            25
    Veiled Melancholy has her sovran shrine,
        Though seen of none save him whose strenuous tongue
Can burst Joy's grape against his palate fine:
His soul shall taste the sadness of her might,
    And be among her cloudy trophies hung.     30

JOHN KEATS

## AMONG SCHOOL CHILDREN

I WALK through the long schoolroom questioning;
A kind old nun in a white hood replies;
The children learn to cipher and to sing,
To study reading-books and history,
To cut and sew, be neat in everything                5
In the best modern way—the children's eyes
In momentary wonder stare upon
A sixty-year-old smiling public man.

I dream of a Ledaean body, bent
Above a sinking fire, a tale that she              10
Told of a harsh reproof, or trivial event
That changed some childish day to tragedy—
Told, and it seemed that our two natures blent
Into a sphere from youthful sympathy,
Or else, to alter Plato's parable,                 15
Into the yolk and white of the one shell.

And thinking of that fit of grief or rage
I look upon one child or t'other there
And wonder if she stood so at that age—
For even daughters of the swan can share           20
Something of every paddler's heritage—
And had that colour upon cheek or hair,
And thereupon my heart is driven wild:
She stands before me as a living child.

Her present image floats into the mind—            25
Did Quattrocento finger fashion it
Hollow of cheek as though it drank the wind
And took a mess of shadows for its meat?
And I though never of Ledaean kind
Had pretty plumage once—enough of that,            30
Better to smile on all that smile, and show
There is a comfortable kind of old scarecrow.

What youthful mother, a shape upon her lap
Honey of generation had betrayed,
And that must sleep, shriek, struggle to escape    35
As recollection or the drug decide,

Would think her son, did she but see that shape
With sixty or more winters on its head,
A compensation for the pang of his birth,
Or the uncertainty of his setting forth?                    40

Plato thought nature but a spume that plays
Upon a ghostly paradigm of things;
Solider Aristotle played the taws
Upon the bottom of a king of kings;
World-famous golden-thighed Pythagoras                      45
Fingered upon a fiddle-stick or strings
What a star sang and careless Muses heard:
Old clothes upon old sticks to scare a bird.

Both nuns and mothers worship images,
But those the candles light are not as those                50
That animate a mother's reveries,
But keep a marble or a bronze repose.
And yet they too break hearts—O Presences
That passion, piety or affection knows,
And that all heavenly glory symbolise—                      55
O self-born mockers of man's enterprise;

Labour is blossoming or dancing where
The body is not bruised to pleasure soul,
Nor beauty born out of its own despair,
Nor blear-eyed wisdom out of midnight oil.                  60
O chestnut-tree, great-rooted blossomer,
Are you the leaf, the blossom or the bole?
O body swayed to music, O brightening glance,
How can we know the dancer from the dance?

WILLIAM BUTLER YEATS

THE BRACELET OF GRASS
The opal heart of afternoon
Was clouding on to throbs of storm,
Ashen within the ardent west
The lips of thunder muttered harm,

73

And as a bubble like to break          *a*          5
Hung heaven's trembling amethyst, *b*
When with the sedge-grass by the lake *a*
I braceleted her wrist. *b*

And when the ribbon grass was tied, *slant*
Sad with the happiness we planned, *b*          10
Palm linked in palm we stood awhile
And watched the raindrops dot the sand; *b*
Until the anger of the breeze
Chid all the lake's bright breathing down,
And ravished all the radiancies          15
From her deep eyes of brown.

We gazed from shelter on the storm,
And through our hearts swept ghostly pain
To see the shards of day sweep past,
Broken, and none might mend again.          20
Broken, that none shall ever mend;
Loosened, that none shall ever tie.
O the wind and the wind, will it never end?
O the sweeping past of the ruined sky!

WILLIAM VAUGHN MOODY


## DULCE ET DECORUM EST

Bent double, like old beggars under sacks,
Knock-kneed, coughing like hags, we cursed through sludge,
Till on the haunting flares we turned our backs
And towards our distant rest began to trudge.
Men marched asleep. Many had lost their boots          5
But limped on, blood-shod. All went lame; all blind;
Drunk with fatigue; deaf even to the hoots
Of tired, outstripped Five-Nines that dropped behind.

Gas! Gas! Quick, boys!—An ecstacy of fumbling,
Fitting the clumsy helmets just in time;          10
But someone still was yelling out and stumbling
And flound'ring like a man in fire or lime . . .

Dim, through the misty panes and thick green light,
As under a green sea, I saw him drowning.

In all my dreams, before my helpless sight,          15
He plunges at me, guttering, choking, drowning.

If in some smothering dreams you too could pace
Behind the wagon that we flung him in,
And watch the white eyes writhing in his face,
His hanging face, like a devil's sick of sin;          20
If you could hear, at every jolt, the blood
Come gargling from the froth-corrupted lungs,
Obscene as cancer, bitter as the cud
Of vile, incurable sores on innocent tongues,—
My friend, you would not tell with such high zest       25
To children ardent for some desperate glory,
The old Lie: Dulce et decorum est
Pro patria mori.

WILFRED OWEN

## THE PRIVATE DINING ROOM *internal*

Miss Rafferty wore taffeta,
Miss Cavendish wore lavender.
We ate pickerel and mackerel
And other lavish provender.
Miss Cavendish was Lalage,          5
Miss Rafferty was Barbara.
We gobbled pickled mackerel
And broke the candelabara,
Miss Cavendish in lavender,
In taffeta, Miss Rafferty,          10
The girls in taffeta lavender,
And we, of course, in mufti.

Miss Rafferty wore taffeta,
The taffeta was lavender,
Was lavend, lavender, lavenderest,        15
As the wine improved the provender.
Miss Cavendish wore lavender,

The lavender was taffeta.
We boggled mackled pickerel,
And bumpers did we quaffeta.                     20
And Lalage wore lavender,
And lavender wore Barbara,
Rafferta taffeta Cavender lavender
Barbara abracadabra.

Miss Rafferty in taffeta                          25
Grew definitely raffisher.
Miss Cavendish in lavender
Grew less and less stand-offisher.
With Lalage and Barbara
We grew a little pickereled.                       30
We ordered Mumm and Roederer
Because the bubbles tickereled.
But lavender and taffeta
Were gone when we were soberer.
I haven't thought for thirty years                35
Of Lalage and Barbara.

OGDEN NASH


## THE DEAD IN EUROPE

After the planes unloaded, we fell down
Buried together, unmarried men and women;
Not crown of thorns, not iron, not Lombard crown,
Not grilled and spindle spires pointing to heaven
Could save us. Raise us, Mother, we fell down      5
Here hugger-mugger in the jellied fire:
Our sacred earth in our day was our curse.

Our Mother, shall we rise on Mary's day
In Maryland, wherever corpses married
Under the rubble, bundled together? Pray          10
For us whom the blockbusters marred and buried;
When Satan scatters us on Rising-day,
O Mother, snatch our bodies from the fire:
Our sacred earth in our day was our curse.

76

Mother, my bones are trembling and I hear                    15
The earth's reverberations and the trumpet
Bleating into my shambles. Shall I bear,
(O Mary!) unmarried man and powder-puppet,
Witness to the Devil? Mary, hear,
O Mary, marry earth, sea, air and fire;                      20
Our sacred earth in our day is our curse.

ROBERT LOWELL


## AMERICAN PRIMITIVE

Look at him there in his stovepipe hat,
His high-top shoes, and his handsome collar;
Only my Daddy could look like that,
And I love my Daddy like he loves his Dollar.

The screen door bangs, and it sounds so funny—          5
There he is in a shower of gold;
His pockets are stuffed with folding money,
His lips are blue, and his hands feel cold.

He hangs in the hall by his black cravat,
The ladies faint, and the children holler:              10
Only my Daddy could look like that,
And I love my Daddy like he loves his Dollar.

WILLIAM JAY SMITH


## TOADS

Why should I let the toad *work*
    Squat on my life?
Can't I use my wit as a pitchfork
    And drive the brute off?

Six days of the week it soils                           5
    With its sickening poison—
Just for paying a few bills!
    That's out of proportion.

77

Lots of folk live on their wits:
    Lecturers, lispers,                                10
Losels, loblolly-men, louts—
    They don't end as paupers;

Lots of folk live up lanes
    With fires in a bucket,
Eat windfalls and tinned sardines—                  15
    They seem to like it.

Their nippers have got bare feet,
    Their unspeakable wives
Are skinny as whippets—and yet
    No one actually *starves*.                         20

Ah, were I courageous enough
    To shout *Stuff your pension*!
But I know, all too well, that's the stuff
    That dreams are made on:

For something sufficiently toad-like             25
    Squats in me, too;
Its hunkers are heavy as hard luck,
    And cold as snow,

And will never allow me to blarney
    My way to getting                             30
The fame and the girl and the money
    All at one sitting.

I don't say, one bodies the other
    One's spiritual truth;
But I do say it's hard to lose either,          35
    When you have both.

PHILIP LARKIN


# MY SON, MY EXECUTIONER

My son, my executioner,
    I take you in my arms,
Quiet and small and just astir,
    And whom my body warms.

78

Sweet death, small son, our <u>instrument</u>                    5
  Of <u>immortality</u>,
Your cries and hungers <u>document</u>
  Our bodily <u>decay</u> slant

We twenty-five and twenty-<u>two</u>,
  Who seemed to live <u>forever</u>,                              10
Observe enduring life in <u>you</u>
  And start to die <u>together</u>.

I take into my arms the <u>death</u>
  Maturity <u>exacts</u>,
And name with my imperfect <u>breath</u>                          15
  The mortal paradox. slant

DONALD HALL


## THE THOUGHT-FOX

  I imagine this <u>midnight moment</u>'s <u>forest</u>:
  Something else is alive
  Beside the clock's <u>loneliness</u> slant
  And this blank page where my fingers move.

  Through the window I see no <u>star</u>:                        5
  Something more near
  Though deeper within <u>darkness</u> Slant
  Is entering the loneliness:

  Cold, delicately as the dark <u>snow</u>,
  A fox's nose touches twig, leaf;                               10
  Two eyes serve a movement, that <u>now</u> font
  And again now, and now, and <u>now</u> Same

  Sets neat prints into the <u>snow</u>
  Between trees, and warily a lame
  Shadow lags by stump and in <u>hollow</u> Slant               15
  Of a body that is bold to come

  Across clearings, an eye,
  A widening deepening <u>greenness</u>,
  Brilliantly, concentratedly,
  Coming about its own <u>business</u> slant                     20

Till, with a sudden sharp hot stink of fox
It enters the dark hole of the <u>head.</u>
The window is starless still; the clock ticks,
The page is <u>printed.</u> Silent

TED HUGHES

# 4

## Sound and Meaning

The sound is the gold in the ore. Then we will have
the sound out alone and dispense with the inessential.

ROBERT FROST

All sounds . . . call down among us certain
disembodied powers, whose footsteps over our hearts
we call emotions.

WILLIAM BUTLER YEATS

In poetry the function of sound purely as sound has for
centuries been a source of both confusion and contention.
Some critics maintain that speech sounds divorced from the
semantics of the words in which they occur are meaningless.
Others assert that while the semantics of a word is the
most important consideration, still certain sounds or types
of sounds are somehow appropriate in some contexts. And
others, while recognizing the primacy of denotative and
connotative word values, nonetheless insist that individual
speech sounds and combinations of sounds within poems are
exceedingly important in their message-bearing potential.
It is our position that sound is an important aspect of
poetry, first because it is meaningful itself, and secondly
because individual speech sounds are often built into
structures of sound for important reasons.
      Before going further, it would perhaps be a good idea
to get a clearer notion of what a speech sound is. As every
first-grader knows, our alphabet has twenty-six letters,

and as all first-graders quickly realize, the correspondence between the letters of the alphabet and the sounds they represent is far from perfect. Linguists, those who make formal studies of languages and their structures, have identified twenty-four consonants and about fifteen vowels and vowel combinations in English. The reason we say "about" is that the number of vowels in a person's idiolect or a group's dialect varies considerably. Some people speaking English may have as many as twenty different vowels and vowel combinations while others may have but ten. Theoretically, there are thirty-six vowels and combinations in English.

In describing these "sounds," the technical term phoneme is useful. A phoneme is defined by linguists as that minimal unit of speech which distinguishes one meaningful utterance from another. Thus, the fact that the words "pit" and "bit" are two distinct names for two distinct things is signalled by the difference we hear between "p" and "b" sounds. The same is true of vowels. We know that "pit" and "pet" have two different meanings because each uses a different vowel sound. Moreover, it is helpful to have a system which has a greater correspondence between sound and symbol than does our alphabet. For example, although "cat," "ocean," and "celery" all have the letter "c," this letter is pronounced differently in each word: as a "k," an "sh," and an "s" sound, respectively.

The following chart lists the consonants of English and their pronunciations in initial, medial, and final positions. The chart also includes the approximate occurrence* per 100 phonemes of each of the phonemes, information which is sometimes used to determine whether or not given phonemes are occurring in greater than random chance in a given line of poetry. The information on the class and voicing of the phonemes is provided for those who may wish to pursue more sophisticated analysis.

The vowels of English and key words indicating their pronunciation are also listed in the vowel chart. The position in the oral cavity where each is formed is indicated, along with their approximate occurrence per 100 phonemes in the standard language.

Information such as that presented in these charts is at least mildly interesting, but unless we have some way of utilizing it in the analysis of poetry, it is of little value. We now turn to an examination of the way sounds can have meaning and how poets use sound to achieve certain effects and communicate certain feelings.

---

* The percentage of approximate occurrence represents a composite or average derived from phoneme counts on several different kinds of discourse. Research has not yet given us the specific percentages for poetry written in English.

CONSONANT CHART

| Symbol | Class | Voicing | %* | Initial | Medial | Final |
|--------|-------|---------|-----|---------|--------|-------|
| /b/ | stop | voiced | 2½ | bag | neighbor | grab |
| /p/ | stop | voiceless | 3 | peg | dropper | drop |
| /d/ | stop | voiced | 4 | dog | rider | rid |
| /t/ | stop | voiceless | 7 | tag | flatter | gnat |
| /g/ | stop | voiced | 1 | goat | tiger | rag |
| /k/ (c) | stop | voiceless | 3½ | coat | broken | back |
| /v/ | fricative | voiced | 2 | vat | river | live |
| /f/ | fricative | voiceless | 3 | fat | effort | laugh |
| /z/ | fricative | voiced | 2½ | zeal | raisin | noise |
| /s/ | fricative | voiceless | 5 | sin | recent | moss |
| /ð/ | fricative | voiced | 2 | then | either | bathe |
| /θ/ | fricative | voiceless | ½ | thin | ether | bath |
| /ž/ | fricative | voiced | 0+ | Zsa Zsa | azure | beige |
| /š/ | fricative | voiceless | 1 | shoe | assure | fish |
| /ǰ/ | affricate | voiced | 1 | gin | frigid | edge |
| /č/ | affricate | voiceless | 1 | chin | teacher | wretch |
| /l/ | liquid | voiced | 5 | lick | pillar | pill |
| /r/ | liquid | voiced | 6½ | rap | quarry | deer |
| /m/ | resonant | voiced | 3 | map | amber | dam |
| /n/ | resonant | voiced | 6½ | knee | annual | dean |
| /ŋ/ | resonant | voiced | 1 | ——— | singer | ring |
| /h/ | semi-vowel | voiceless | 1½ | hat | ahead | hah |
| /w/ | semi-vowel | voiced | 2 | were | about | now |
| /y/ | semi-vowel | voiced | ½ | yes | shale | lay |

*The % (percentage) indicates the approximate occurrence per 100 phonemes.

VOWEL CHART

| Symbol | Formation | % Occurrence | Key Words |
|--------|-----------|--------------|-----------|
| /i/ | high front | 5½ | bit, knit |
| /iy/ | high front | 3 | beat, feet |
| /e/ | mid-front | 3 | bet, fret |
| /ey/ | mid-front | 2 | bait, mate |
| /ae/ | low front | 3 | bat, mass |
| /ɨ/ | high central | 0+ | rebel (v.), Not usual in most Am. dialects |
| /ə/ | mid-central | 6 | but, sofa |
| /a/ | low central | 3 | hall, father |
| /aw/ | low central | 1 | bough, chow |
| /ay/ | low central | 2½ | bite, light |
| /u/ | high back | 1 | bush, good, put |
| /uw/ | high back | 1½ | blew, shoot |
| /ow/ | mid-back | 2 | boat, tow, moan |
| /ɔ/ | low back | 1 | taught, bought |
| /ɔy/ | low back | ½ | oyster, joint |

## ONOMATOPOEIA

Onomatopoeia is one of the time-honored devices of sound encountered in poetry. Briefly defined, onomatopoeia is the use of sounds to imitate natural sounds in the environment, so that the sound of a word strongly suggests its meaning. Some words commonly regarded as onomatopoetic are "buzz," "swish," and "clang." While there are many words like these which seem to reproduce phonemically the actions or objects they describe, onomatopoetic effects in poetry are rare, and easily recognizable. Of far greater importance and interest to poets is the overall capacity of the language's phonemic resources to create more subtle effects. These effects are sometimes referred to as "sound color," or "sound painting." We can talk about "sound color" more precisely if we use the concept of phonetic symbolism.

## PHONETIC SYMBOLISM

The capacity of speech sounds to suggest nonacoustic meanings, such as feelings of size, or brightness and darkness, solemnity or delight, beauty or ugliness, is attested by the statements of poets as well as hundreds of research studies done over the years in phonetic symbolism. Frost and Yeats, quoted at the beginning of this chapter, show an awareness of the subtle uses of sound to engender feelings in us. Dylan Thomas is even more specific. In a letter to a friend he said that the self-created word "drome" gave him a vision of heaven. The "m" sound, he said, was the source of the celestial association, and the long "o" sound conveyed the movement of God.

Phonetic symbolism is also validated by research. While the results are not completely definitive, they do lead toward one rather strong conclusion: within a language community there is a surprising amount of agreement among speakers as to what a given phoneme "means." For example, suppose you were asked to choose a definition for the following nonsense syllables: "keek" and "mool." Suppose you were told that one is a small, sharp stone, and the other is a large, soft, warm pillow. The chances are good that nine out of ten people would say that a "keek" is a small, sharp stone, and that a "mool" is a large, soft, and warm pillow. The reasons for such choices, though complex, are worth understanding. The testimony of practicing poets should convince us that sounds are capable of creating definite moods, and of qualifying the meaning of words in various ways. Furthermore, recent etymological studies, the analysis of phonemes in semantic differential studies, as well as the research in phonetic symbolism alluded to above, all point toward the same conclusion: that phonemes, singly and in combination, seem capable of producing effects which cannot be accounted for by conventional semantic analysis alone.

84

Researchers employing the semantic differential scales of the psychologist C. E. Osgood have identified three force-fields within which the "felt" meanings of words coalesce. In other words, just as we tend to think abstractly and intellectually in certain categories, so too we tend to feel concretely and emotionally in at least three broad categories. The accumulated evidence now also seems to indicate that individual phonemes, as well as words, can be considered from the same perspectives: as evoking feelings which are of three broad types. These three classes of emotional response are called the evaluative, potency, and activity factors. The list below indicates some of the possible positive and negative meanings which given phonemes can carry. All of the adjectives in each category share a certain degree of connotative meaning. The evaluative category generally deals with a sound's overall good or bad connotations. The potency factor describes the strength or weakness of a phoneme, and the activity factor indicates its ability to evoke feelings of movement or stasis, dynamism or inertness. While each of the lists could be made much more extensive, the polarized adjectives listed for each of the factors should be enough to suggest the possible ways in which phonemic "meaning" might be discovered or defined.

| EVALUATIVE FACTOR | | POTENCY FACTOR | | ACTIVITY FACTOR | |
|---|---|---|---|---|---|
| *Positive* | *Negative* | *Positive* | *Negative* | *Positive* | *Negative* |
| (+) | (−) | (+) | (−) | (+) | (−) |
| good | bad | large | small | fast | slow |
| beautiful | ugly | strong | weak | active | passive |
| pleasant | unpleasant | thick | thin | sharp | dull |
| sweet | sour | hard | soft | moving | static |
| optimistic | pessimistic | rugged | delicate | angular | round |
| bright | dark | serious | humorous | solid | liquid |

In order to proceed with further analysis, though, we need to indicate the evaluative, potency, and activity content of each vowel and consonant phoneme. The following chart indicates in a general way how each of the phonemes carries an evaluative, potency, and activity meaning. Bear in mind, however, that a positive or negative rating does not automatically mean that all possible meanings that could be applied under the factor heading necessarily do apply. What the chart does indicate are the *tendencies* of a given phoneme to elicit more positive than negative responses, or vice versa.

85

EPA FACTOR CHART

| Phoneme | Eval. | Pot. | Act. | Phoneme | Eval. | Pot. | Act. |
|---|---|---|---|---|---|---|---|
| b | + | + | − | i | + | − | + |
| p | + | − | + | iy | + | − | + |
| d | − | + | − | e | + | − | + |
| t | + | − | + | ey | + | − | + |
| g | − | + | + | ae | + | − | + |
| k | + | * | + | ɨ | + | − | + |
| v | + | + | * | ə | * | * | * |
| f | + | − | * | a | − | + | − |
| z | − | − | − | aw | − | + | − |
| s | + | − | − | ay | − | + | − |
| ð | − | * | * | u | − | + | − |
| θ | + | * | * | uw | − | + | − |
| ž | − | − | − | ow | − | + | − |
| š | * | − | + | ɔ | − | + | − |
| j | − | + | + | ɔy | − | + | − |
| č | − | + | − | | | | |
| l | + | − | − | Key to symbols: | | | |
| r | + | + | + | + Positive | | | |
| m | * | + | − | − Negative | | | |
| n | − | − | − | * Insufficient data or not | | | |
| ŋ | * | * | − | generalizable | | | |
| h | * | − | * | | | | |
| w | * | − | * | | | | |
| y | * | − | * | | | | |

Let us look at a few examples. The vowels are all fairly regular in their emotional meanings. The high front vowels, such as /iy/*, are universally *negative* in potency and *positive* in evaluation. That is, they are felt by people to be small, weak, thin, delicate, and so on, and at the same time they seem good, beautiful, pleasant, and bright. The back vowels, such as /a/, have opposite meanings: large, strong, thick, rugged, bad, ugly, unpleasant, dark. The consonants are, however, more irregular, probably because there are more different types of them, and more articulatory cues in their make-up. One research study indicates that the /k/ sound evokes feelings of thinness, shallowness, and smallness, but it is also quite 'strong." In other words, /k/ is negative in potency in all respects save one: strength. Likewise, the /m/ sound is mixed in its evaluative content. It is sad and dark, but also beautiful and sweet. Perhaps some day we will have a definitive description of the responses which every phoneme in English evokes, but until then we will have to be content with approximations or rely on our own intuitions.

---

*Linguists often put slash marks around phonemes to distinguish them from letters of the alphabet.

At first encounter, much of the material presented so far in this chapter might seem too technical to help us understand and appreciate poetry. Indeed, some might feel that the magic of poetry is destroyed by such analytic procedures. After all, no one in reading or hearing a poem is going to pull out charts and do an "instant replay" of what he has just experienced.

And yet, the comparison to "instant replay" technique, so popular on televised sports events, is not entirely inappropriate. Surely all of us enjoy the fluid double play, the long touchdown run, or the tie-breaking goal in hockey all the more when we see, through instant replays, the skill and finesse which made it possible—and which we were perhaps unaware of in the blur and excitement of the developing play. So too in poetry. Even without technical insight, our scalps may tingle and our breath grow tight as the poem moves toward its culmination. But with the right information and analytic skills at our disposal, our appreciation of the poet's "moves" will be greater and our understanding of the poem more profound. We will still have the immediate thrill, but we will also have the satisfactions which come from recognizing the deeper structures of the poet's craft.

Even so, it is undeniable that minute analysis, such as is suggested by the foregoing charts, is difficult. Furthermore, since the individual phonemes always appear in combinations in poetry, it is not likely that a poem will reveal itself through phonemic analysis alone. For instance, a poem in which vowels with a high positive potency content predominate might employ consonants which are largely negative in potency. In such a case one must consider other analytic alternatives. Perhaps potency, as a meaning factor, is unimportant in the poem. Perhaps potency, positive or negative, is achieved through diction which is highly charged emotionally.

There are two other possibilities. Perhaps the sounds in a poem are being used metaphorically, or ironically. Consider the first stanza of Brother Antoninus' poem "The Stranger." (pp. 95–96). In this stanza, the high front vowels predominate, especially /i/. From the EPA Chart, we know that this phoneme is positive in evaluation and negative in potency, that it contributes feelings of smallness, weakness, and delicacy to what the poet is otherwise saying. These feelings of smallness are perhaps meant to reflect the girl's immaturity or innocence, and to contrast with the harshness and brazenness of her "bed-lore brag." In this way, sounds can metaphorically qualify what a poet says: a "small" idea is a trivial one; a "small" man is a petty man.

"The Stranger" also illustrates how sounds can be used ironically. The sixth line is a good example.

She prattles the lip-learned, light-love list.

87

There are six /l/ phonemes in this line—far more than one would expect to hear in normal, everyday speech. Moreover, the /l/ is commonly felt to be one of the most beautiful sounds in the language, but here it seems ironic: its repetition emphasizes instead the banality and triteness of the young girl's behavior.

Some shortcuts in determining the role of phonemic patterns in poetry are available, and these are offered as additions or alternatives to the analytical procedures we have suggested. These are what might be called "common sense" uses of consonant and vowel phonetic patterns. A listing of some of them and their potential effects follows.

## PLOSIVENESS

The consonant stops /b, p, t, d, g/ and /k/ are produced by stopping the breath stream before producing the sound. Once these consonants have been articulated, they cannot be continued. Thus, they lend themselves to abrupt, percussive, or popping effects. The voiced members of this class also have high positive potency content. Coleridge's use of stops in this excerpt from "Kubla Khan" is well-suited to the explosive, crackling, forceful scene he is describing.

> A mighty fountain momently was forced:
> Amid whose swift half-intermitted burst
> Huge fragments vaulted like rebounding hail . . .
>
> (18 stops)

As we shall see, the use of the many /m/ sounds and back vowels also contributes to the feeling of power in these lines.

## STRIDENCY

The fricatives are /f, v, θ, ð, s, z, š, ž/. These phonemes, unlike the plosives, can be continued as long as the breath lasts. However, the air stream is released through narrowed openings which produce a more turbulent air stream and a different quality of sound color. These sounds can suggest frying, hissing, chirping, or breezy effects, among others. Keats uses these fricatives beautifully in "To Autumn."

> Season of mists and mellow fruitfulness,
>     Close bosom-friend of the maturing sun;
> Conspiring with him how to load and bless
>     With fruit the vines that round the thatch eaves run.
>
> (28 fricatives)

88

One can almost hear the crickets and locusts as they buzz and move on a warm fall day. The numerous resonants also contribute significantly to the total effect of lazy warmth and mellowness.

Two other closely related sounds are /ǰ/ and /č/. These differ from the other strident sounds because they have abrupt beginnings rather than gradual ones. They are similar to the plosives in their ability to suggest strength. Notice the unique effect of firm power in these lines from W. S. Merwin's poem "Leviathan" (pp. 110–111), due to the plosives and /ǰ/, /č/, and /š/ sounds.

> The hulk of him is like hills heaving,
> Dark, yet as crags of drift-ice, crowns cracking in thunder,
> Like land's self by night black-looming, surf-*ch*urning
>     and trailing
> Along his *sh*ores' ru*sh*ing, *sh*oal-water boding
> About the dark of his *j*aws; and who *sh*ould moor at his e*dg*e
> And fare on afoot would find gates of no gardens.

## Resonance

The phonemes /m/, /n/, and /ŋ/ are called resonants, sounds which can be formed and then continued for as long as one has breath. When making these sounds, the air vibrates through the nasal cavity. Because they have this additional resonance, and because they can be held, they have a dark, dense quality and lend themselves to the humming, lingering, continuing effects which characterize the following lines.

> Five *m*iles *m*eandering with a *m*azy *m*otio*n*
> Through wood a*n*d dale the sacred river ra*n*,
> The*n* reached the caver*n*s measureless to *m*a*n* . . .
>
>                                          (14 resonants)

These lines, though from the same stanza of "Kubla Khan" that was quoted above for its plosives, have quite a different effect. The fourteen resonants enable Coleridge to let his sound patterns flow with the river. By way of contrast, this second quotation has but nine stops, only half as many as the first excerpt.

## Liquids and Semivowels

The liquids /l/ and /r/ are so called because unlike most of the other consonants the breath stream is interrupted only slightly when they

are articulated. Like the resonants, they can be held as long as the
breath lasts, and they are both voiced. Many feel that the /r/ sound
has a dark tone color. Although it lacks the harshness of the plosives
and fricatives, it has a quiet power and is positive in evaluation.

The /l/ sound, on the other hand, feels shallow, weak, and
small. And though it is usually felt to be one of the most beautiful
phonemes, it also evokes feelings of darkness and sadness. Like the
resonants, both /l/ and /r/ are well suited for expressing langorous,
effortless beauty, as in these lines from Coleridge's "Christabel."

> Beneath the *lamp* the *lady* bowed,
> And *slowly rolled* her eyes around;
> Then *drawing* in her breath a*loud,*
> *Like* one that shudder*ed* she unbound
> The cincture from beneath her breast . . .

(17 liquids)

Notice also the twelve liquids in the second passage from "Kubla
Khan" quoted above, and how well they blend in with the resonants.

The /w/ and /y/ phonemes are called semivowels because
they have even fewer characteristics of consonants than the liquids do:
that is, there is almost no interruption of the air stream when they
are produced. The /y/ sound of "yes" is produced at the front of the
mouth, and is very much like the high front vowels. The /w/ sound,
on the other hand, is like the back vowels because the lips are rounded
and the tongue is at the back of the mouth when it is articulated.
In fact, as the Vowel Chart shows, several of the vowels are symbolized by adding /y/ and /w/ to another vowel. Perhaps the best way
to understand the emotional meanings of these two sounds is to look
at the vowels themselves.

## FRONT AND BACK VOWELS

As we mentioned a while ago, the vowels are the most regular of the
phonemes in their meanings, and are probably the most intense in
their ability to convey the types of meaning we have been discussing.
As indicated on the EPA Chart, the vowels /i, iy, e, ey, ae/ and /i/
are generally perceived as weak, small, bright, and pleasant. That is,
they are negative in potency and positive in evaluation. On the other
hand, the back vowels /a, aw, ay, u, uw, ow, ɔ/, and /ɔy/ which are
produced toward the back of the mouth, are felt to be strong, large,
dark, bad, and unpleasant. Or, in other words, they are positive in
potency and negative in evaluation. How they work in a poetic context
can be seen in the following excerpts. The first is from John Milton's
"L'Allegro"; the second is from Milton's "Il Penseroso."

90

> Sport that wrinkled care derides,
> And Laughter holding both his sides,
> Come, and trip it as ye go,
> On the light fantastic toe . . .

Of the twenty-nine vowels in these four lines, twenty are on the high
or front end of the scale. The effect of these lines is one of lightness,
happiness, and delight, just as we would expect based on the EPA
factors of the vowels.

> Oft, on a plat of rising ground,
> I hear the far-off curfew sound
> Over some wide-watered shore,
> Swinging slow with sullen roar . . .

Of the thirty vowels here, fifteen of them are on the low or back end
of the scale. Of the fifteen remaining, about eight are the neutral
"Schwa" /ə/. Clearly, the more somber, dark, melancholy feeling
these lines achieve is very much a function of Milton's choice of words
containing the larger vowels.

We have spent a great deal of time talking about the meanings
of sounds and the capacity of the phonemic resources of the language
to evoke unique kinds of feelings in us. We should perhaps now turn
to the question of how and when sounds become important in a poem.
To return to our "instant replay" analogy, it is obvious that not every
play in a football game is a significant one, and not every hit in a ball
park is a home run. There are comparatively few plays that stand out
as being particularly surprising, and there are only a few that are
amazingly well executed. Yet these are the ones that evoke our cheers,
partly because they are in contrast to the events around them, and
partly because they are well done. Likewise with poetry. Not every
sound in a line or group of lines is significant or meaningful, and only
occasionally are the sounds so well patterned that they capture our
attention. In discussing these uses of sound in poetry, the concepts of
*foregrounding* and *phonemic patterning* may be useful.

You will recall that the Consonant and Vowel Charts also give
information concerning the relative frequencies of the various
phonemes in the language as a whole. In poetry, however, which is a
special use of language, these sounds are often overrepresented. That
is, they are used more frequently than they are in standard language.
When we run across a passage which is particularly dense with one
type of sound or another, that sound is *foregrounded*—it becomes

noticeable and meaningful. Consider again the line of "The Stranger" quoted earlier: "She prattles the lip-learned, light-love list." Of the thirty-one phonemes in this line, six or 20 percent of them, are /l/ sounds. The Consonant Chart tells us that /l/ makes up only 5 percent of the standard language. It is this greater than average representation of the phoneme in a poetic line that renders the /l/ sounds noticeable and foregrounds their emotive content.

In addition to foregrounding, however, there are several more conventional devices for approaching the functions of sound in poetry, devices which describe the way sounds are *patterned*. These are the traditional devices of alliteration, assonance, and consonance.

## ALLITERATION

Alliteration occurs when the initial consonants of words in close proximity are identical. A broader—and more useful—definition, however, includes the repetition of identical consonants in stressed syllables, just so long as they are reasonably close together. The second type is also called *consonance*. The following quotation illustrates both types.

> I know the grass beyond the door,
>     The sweet, keen smell,
> The sighing sound, the light around the shore.

## ASSONANCE

Assonance occurs when the vowel phonemes of words in close proximity are identical. In the preceding excerpt, the /iy/ vowel in "sweet" and "keen" are assonantal, as are /ay/ in "sighing" and "light." "Sound" and "around" are better defined as internal rhyme since the two words are actually full rhymes.

As an illustration of all the sound devices we have been discussing, let's look at a short but splendid poem by Carl Sandburg, called "Splinter."

> The voice of the last cricket
> across the first frost
> is one kind of good-bye.
> It is so thin a splinter of singing.

It is difficult to imagine another short poem which is as densely packed with sound and meaning patterns as this one. In the first, second, and fourth lines, the /s/ and /st/ sounds are represented twice as often as they normally are. These sounds are particularly appropriate to express the dryness, smallness, and slight harshness of the cricket's last, fading song. Of most importance, though, is the key last line. Sandburg's use of the front vowel /i/ is expressive of smallness, weakness, thinness, and delicacy. The /i/ sound accounts for 23 percent of the phonemes in this line, whereas it makes up only 5 percent of the phonemes in the standard language.

In addition to the denseness of expressive sound symbols, however, the phonemes occur in finely executed patterns of alliteration, consonance, and assonance which bind the poem together. Notice the consonance of the /s/ and /st/ sounds in lines 1 and 2. The /s/'s of "splinter" and "singing" in the last line are alliterative, as are the /f/ sounds of "first" and "frost" in the second line. Finally, there is a good deal of assonance in this short poem, especially the repetition of the significant /i/ in the last line.

Thus, the structural patterning of sounds and their meanings can function to draw attention to themselves and the contexts in which they occur. Well used, they can bind ideas, as well as sound structures, more closely together, adding also a dimension of meaning which the normal denotative and connotative resources of the language do not provide for. Poorly used, they can draw attention to concepts, attitudes, or emotions which deserve neither attention nor emphasis.

As is obvious to anyone who has pursued the discussion of the functions of sounds in poetry to this point, there is still a great deal that needs to be discovered and clarified about the subject. In the absence of the kind of certainty that we have in discussing meter or imagery, for example, both the devotee of poetry and those who are but mildly interested in it need to constantly remind themselves that open minds and keen ears are fundamental requirements for understanding and appreciation.

*Exercise 1*

DIRECTIONS

Without referring to the text or any of the charts, take the following "test" to see how your reactions to the phonetic symbolism of sounds compares to the reactions of others who have taken this same test. Since you have not yet mastered the phonemic symbols, the nonsense syllables are written in patterns which should make their pronunciations clear. Match the nonsense syllable to its definition.

1. Shawsh    A. a deep pool of water
   Sheesh    B. a shallow pool of water

2. Lowl      A. a small bottle of perfume
   Leel      B. a large bottle of shaving lotion
3. Zezh      A. a beautiful, sweet plum
   Rel      B. an ugly, smelly fish
4. Peesh—————A. a fast, rippling river
   Dowch————B. a huge, jagged rock

ANSWERS

| Shawsh—A | Lowl—B | Zezh—B | Peesh—A |
| Sheesh—B | Leel—A | Rel—A | Dowch—B |

On previous tests, students have reacted with over 90% agreement on these items. To see why their reactions (and hopefully yours, too) are predictable, check the EPA Factor Chart.

*Exercise 2*

# SKERRYVORE

| | |
|---|---|
| For love of lovely words, and for the sake | 1 |
| Of those, my kinsmen and my countrymen, | 2 |
| Who early and late in the windy ocean ———— | 3 |
| To plant a star for seamen, where was then | 4 |
| The surfy ———— of seals and ————: | 5 |
| I, on the lintel of this cot, inscribe | 6 |
| The name of a ————. | 7 |

1. The missing word in line 3 is (a) worked, (b) builded, (c) toiled, (d) delved.
2. The first missing word in line 5 is (a) haunt, (b) dwelling, (c) quarters, (d) residence.
3. The second missing word in line 5 is (a) terns, (b) gulls, (c) penguins, (d) cormorants.
4. The missing words in line 7 are (a) strong tower, (b) big spire, (c) massive mast, (d) large parapet.

ANSWERS

1. The feeling one should get from this poem is one of seriousness, tinged perhaps with melancholy. In this, as in the other choices, which word has the vowel coloration which best conveys such feelings? Only choice (c) has a low and back vowel.

94

2. In addition to the vowel color needed, the correct choice here should also fit the basically iambic pattern of this poem. Choice (a).

3. Again the name of only one of these four birds has a vowel pattern which suggests power and sadness. In fact choice (d), cormorants, has three such vowels. It also has the requisite number of syllables to fill out the pentameter line.

4. Choice (a) was the poet's choice, even though the line is less than ten syllables long. "Skerryvore" was the name of a lighthouse off the coast of England. It was built in 1844 by Stevenson's uncle, and built so well that it still stands. Later, Stevenson built a house (the "cot" referred to in line 6) and named it Skerryvore.

## Exercise 3

1. Drop a pen or pencil from a distance of 18 inches or so onto a wooden surface. Invent a sequence of sounds which reproduces what you hear.

2. Riffle the pages of a book close to your ear. Invent a sequence of sounds which reproduces what you hear.

3. Invent a two-syllable sequence of sounds which would express disgust or contempt.

4. Invent a three-syllable sequence of sounds that would describe your feelings at a time when you are utterly content, at peace with yourself and with the world.

## Exercise 4

# THE STRANGER

| | |
|---|---|
| Pity this girl. | 1 |
| At callow sixteen, | 2 |
| Glib in the press of rapt ——————— | 3 |
| She bruits her smatter, | 4 |
| Her bed-lore brag. | 5 |
| She prattles the lip-learned, light-love list. | 6 |
| In the new itch and squirm of sex, | 7 |
| How can she foresee? | 8 |
| How can she foresee the thick stranger, | 9 |
| ————————————————, | 10 |
| Who will ————— her across a hired bed, | 11 |
| Open the loins, | 12 |

Rive the breach                                                13
And set the foetus wailing within the womb,                    14
To hunch toward the knowledge of its disease,                  15
And shamble ——————————.                                        16


1. The missing word in line 3 is (a) listeners, (b) friends, (c) companions, (d) buddies.
2. The missing line 10 is (a) through the valley from Ypsilanti, (b) over the ridge from Albuquerque, (c) fresh from the big city, (d) over the hills from Omaha.
3. The missing word in line 11 is (a) break, (b) lay, (c) place, (d) put.
4. The missing words in line 16 are (a) without hope to eternity, (b) ramble, amble, forever, (c) to judgment, (d) down time to doomsday.

# 4

## Poems

## UPON JULIA'S CLOTHES

Whenas in silks my Julia goes,
Then, then, methinks how sweetly flows
That liquefaction of her clothes.

Next, when I cast mine eyes and see
That brave vibration each way free;                              5
O how that glittering taketh me!

ROBERT HERRICK

## THE THREE PIGEONS

Let schoolmasters puzzle their brain,
    With grammar, and nonsense, and learning;
Good liquor, I stoutly maintain,
    Gives genius a better discerning.
Let them brag of their heathenish gods,                          5
    Their Lethes, their Styxes, and Stygians,
Their Quis and their Quaes and their Quods,
    They're all but a parcel of pigeons.
        *Toroddle, toroddle, toroll.*

When Methodist preachers come down,                              10
    A-preaching that drinking is sinful,
I'll wager the rascals a crown,
    They always preach best with a skinful.
But when you come down with your pence,
    For a slice of their scurvy religion,                    15
I'll leave it to all men of sense,
    But you, my good friend, are the pigeon.
        *Toroddle, toroddle, toroll.*

Then come, put the jorum about,
    And let us be merry and clever,                          20
Our hearts and our liquors are stout,
    Here's the Three Jolly Pigeons for ever!
Let some cry up woodcock or hare,
    Your bustards, your ducks, and your widgeons;
But of all the gay birds in the air,                             25
    Here's a health to the Three Jolly Pigeons!
        *Toroddle, toroddle, toroll.*

OLIVER GOLDSMITH

## KUBLA KHAN

In Xanadu did Kubla Khan
A stately pleasure-dome decree:
Where Alph, the sacred river, ran
Through caverns measureless to man
  Down to a sunless sea.      5

So twice five miles of fertile ground
With walls and towers were girdled round:
And there were gardens bright with sinuous rills,
Where blossomed many an incense-bearing tree;
And here were forests ancient as the hills,   10
Enfolding sunny spots of greenery.

But oh! that deep romantic chasm which slanted
Down the green hill athwart a cedarn cover!
A savage place! as holy and enchanted
As e'er beneath a waning moon was haunted   15
By woman wailing for her demon-lover!
And from this chasm, with ceaseless turmoil seething,
As if this earth in fast thick pants were breathing,
A mighty fountain momently was forced:
Amid whose swift half-intermitted burst   20
Huge fragments vaulted like rebounding hail,
Or chaffy grain beneath the thresher's flail:
And 'mid these dancing rocks at once and ever
If flung up momently the sacred river.
Five miles meandering with a mazy motion   25
Through wood and dale the sacred river ran,
Then reached the caverns measureless to man,
And sank in tumult to a lifeless ocean:
And 'mid this tumult Kubla heard from far
Ancestral voices prophesying war!     30
  The shadow of the dome of pleasure
  Floated midway on the waves;
  Where was heard the mingled measure
  From the fountain and the caves.
It was a miracle of rare device,     35
A sunny pleasure-dome with caves of ice!

99

A damsel with a dulcimer
In a vision once I saw:
It was an Abyssinian maid,
And on her dulcimer she played,　　　　　40
Singing of Mount Abora.
Could I revive within me
Her symphony and song,
To such a deep delight 'twould win me,
That with music loud and long,　　　　　45
I would build that dome in air,
That sunny dome! those caves of ice!
And all who heard should see them there,
And all should cry, Beware! Beware!
His flashing eyes, his floating hair!　　　　　50
Weave a circle round him thrice,
And close your eyes with holy dread,
For he on honey-dew hath fed,
And drunk the milk of Paradise.

SAMUEL TAYLOR COLERIDGE

## TO AUTUMN

*apostrophe – device used to speaking to Autumn.*

Season of mists and mellow fruitfulness,
　Close bosom-friend of the maturing sun: *" is personified – thought of as a living force.*
Conspiring with him how to load and bless
　With fruit the vines that round the thatch-eves run;
To bend with apples the mossed cottage-trees,　　　　　5
　And fill all fruit with ripeness to the core;
　　To swell the gourd, and plump the hazel shells
With a sweet kernel; to set budding more,
　And still more, later flowers for the bees,
　　Until they think warm days will never cease,　　　　　10
　　For summer has o'er-brimmed their clammy cells.

Who hath not seen thee oft amid thy store?
　Sometimes whoever seeks abroad may find
Thee sitting careless on a granary floor,
　Thy hair soft-lifted by the winnowing wind;　　　　　15

100

Or on a half-reaped furrow sound asleep,
　　Drowsed with the fume of poppies, while thy hook
　　　Spares the next swath and all its twinèd flowers:
And sometimes like a gleaner thou dost keep
　　Steady thy laden head across a brook;　　　　　　　20
　　Or by a cider-press, with patient look,
　　　Thou watchest the last oozings hours by hours.

Where are the songs of Spring? Ay, where are they?
　　Think not of them, thou hast thy music too,—
While barrèd clouds bloom the soft-dying day,　　　　25
And touch the stubble-plains with rosy hue;
Then in a wailful choir the small gnats mourn
　　Among the river sallows, borne aloft
　　　Or sinking as the light wind lives or dies;
And full-grown lambs loud bleat from hilly bourn;　　30
　　Hedge-crickets sing; and now with treble soft
　　The red-breast whistles from a garden-croft;
　　And gathering swallows twitter in the skies.

JOHN KEATS


## SONG OF THE CHATTAHOOCHEE

　　　Out of the hills of Habersham,
　　　Down the valleys of Hall,
　　I hurry amain to reach the plain,
　　Run the rapid and leap the fall,
　　Split at the rock and together again,　　　　　　　5
　　Accept my bed, or narrow or wide,
　　And flee from folly on every side
　　With a lover's pain to attain the plain
　　Far from the hills of Habersham,
　　Far from the valleys of Hall.　　　　　　　　　　10

　　　All down the hills of Habersham,
　　　All through the valleys of Hall,
　　The rushes cried *Abide, abide,*
　　The willful waterweeds held me thrall,
　　The laving laurel turned my tide,　　　　　　　　15

101

The ferns and the fondling grass said *Stay,*
The dewberry dipped for to work delay,
And the little reeds sighed *Abide, abide,*
    *Here in the hills of Habersham,*
    *Here in the valleys of Hall.*                        20

    High o'er the hills of Habersham,
    Veiling the valleys of Hall,
The hickory told me manifold
Fair tales of shade, the poplar tall
Wrought me her shadowy self to hold,                       25
The chestnut, the oak, the walnut, the pine,
Overleaning, with flickering meaning and sign,
Said, *Pass not, so cold, these manifold*
    *Deep shades of the hills of Habersham,*
    *These glades in the valleys of Hall.*                 30

    And oft in the hills of Habersham,
    And oft in the valleys of Hall,
The white quartz shone, and the smooth brook-stone
Did bar me of passage with friendly brawl,
And many a luminous jewel lone                             35
—Crystals clear or a-cloud with mist,
Ruby, garnet and amethyst—
Made lures with the lights of streaming stone
    In the clefts of the hills of Habersham,
    In the beds of the valleys of Hall.                    40

    But oh, not the hills of Habersham,
    And oh, not the valleys of Hall
Avail: I am fain for to water the plain.
Downward the voices of Duty call—
Downward, to toil and be mixed with the main,              45
The dry fields burn, and the mills are to turn,
And a myriad flowers mortally yearn,
And the lordly main from beyond the plain
    Calls o'er the hills of Habersham,
    Calls through the valleys of Hall.                     50

SIDNEY LANIER

102

## GOD'S GRANDEUR

The world is charged with the grandeur of God.
  It will flame out, like shining from shook foil;
  It gathers to a greatness, like the ooze of oil
Crushed. Why do men then now not reck his rod?
Generations have trod, have trod, have trod;                    5
  And all is seared with trade; bleared, smeared with toil;
  And wears man's smudge and shares man's smell: the soil
Is bare now, nor can foot feel, being shod.

And for all this, nature is never spent;
  There lives the dearest freshness deep down things;          10
And though the last lights off the black West went
  Oh, morning, at the brown brink eastward, springs—
Because the Holy Ghost over the bent
  World broods with warm breast and with ah! bright wings.

GERARD MANLEY HOPKINS *called it Sprung Rhythm — diff. use of stresses. (un-even)*

## THE LAKE ISLE OF INNISFREE

I will arise and go now, and go to Innisfree,
*Planned things to do* And a small cabin build there, of clay and wattles made;
Nine bean rows will I have there, a hive for the honey bee,
And live alone in the bee-loud glade.

And I shall have some peace there, for peace comes
    dropping slow,                                              5
Dropping from the veils of the morning to where the
    cricket sings;
There midnight's all a glimmer, and noon a purple glow,
And evening full of the linnet's wings.

I will arise and go now, for always night and day
I hear lake water lapping with low sounds by the shore;        10
While I stand on the roadway, or on the pavements gray,
I hear it in the deep heart's core.

WILLIAM BUTLER YEATS

103

## PATTERNS

I walk down the garden paths,
And all the daffodils
Are blowing, and the bright blue squills.
I walk down the patterned garden-paths
In my stiff, brocaded gown.                                    5
With my powdered hair and jewelled fan,
I too am a rare
Pattern. As I wander down
The garden paths.

My dress is richly figured,                                    10
And the train
Makes a pink and silver stain
On the gravel, and the thrift
Of the borders.
Just a plate of current fashion                                15
Tripping by in high-heeled, ribboned shoes.
Not a softness anywhere about me,
Only whalebone and brocade.
And I sink on a seat in the shade                              20
Of a lime tree. For my passion
Wars against the stiff brocade.
The daffodils and squills
Flutter in the breeze
As they please.                                                25
And I weep;
For the lime-tree is in blossom
And one small flower has dropped upon my bosom.

And the plashing of waterdrops                                 30
In the marble fountain
Comes down the garden-paths.
The dripping never stops.
Underneath my stiffened gown
Is the softness of a woman bathing in a marble basin,          35
A basin in the midst of hedges grown
So thick, she cannot see her lover hiding,
But she guesses he is near,

And the sliding of the water                          40
Seems the stroking of a dear
Hand upon her.
What is Summer in a fine brocaded gown!
I should like to see it lying in a heap upon the ground.    45
All the pink and silver crumpled up on the ground.

I would be the pink and silver as I ran along the paths,
And he would stumble after,                          50
Bewildered by my laughter.
I should see the sun flashing from his sword-hilt
     and buckles on his shoes.
I would choose
To lead him in a maze along the patterned paths,     55
A bright and laughing maze for my heavy-booted lover.
Till he caught me in the shade,
And the buttons of his waistcoat bruised my body
     as he clasped me,                               60
Aching, melting, unafraid.
With the shadows of the leaves and the sundrops,
And the plopping of the waterdrops,
All about us in the open afternoon—                  65
I am very like to swoon
With the weight of this brocade,
For the sun sifts through the shade.

Underneath the fallen blossom
In my bosom,                                         70
Is a letter I have hid.
It was brought to me this morning by a rider from the Duke.
"Madam, we regret to inform you that Lord Hartwell    75
Died in action Thursday se'nnight."
As I read it in the white, morning sunlight,
The letters squirmed like snakes.
"Any answer, Madam," said my footman.                80
"No," I told him.
"See that the messenger takes some refreshment.
No, no answer."
And I walked into the garden,                         85
Up and down the patterned paths,

In my stiff, correct brocade.
The blue and yellow flowers stood up proudly in the sun,
Each one.                                                                  90
I stood upright too,
Held rigid to the pattern
By the stiffness of my gown.
Up and down I walked.
Up and down.                                                               95

In a month he would have been my husband.
In a month, here, underneath this lime,
We would have broken the pattern;
He for me, and I for him,                                                  100
He as Colonel, I as Lady,
On this shady seat.
He had a whim
'That sunlight carried blessing.
And I answered, "It shall be as you have said."                           105
Now he is dead.

In Summer and in Winter I shall walk
Up and down
The patterned garden-paths                                                110
In my stiff, brocaded gown.
The squills and daffodils
Will give place to pillared roses, and to asters, and to snow.
I shall go                                                                 115
Up and down,
In my gown.
Gorgeously arrayed,
Boned and stayed.
And the softness of my body will be                                       120
    guarded from embrace
By each button, hook, and lace.
For the man who should loose me is dead,
Fighting with the Duke in Flanders,                                       125
In a pattern called a war.
Christ! What are patterns for?

AMY LOWELL

## SUNDAY MORNING

### I

Complacencies of the peignoir, and late
Coffee and oranges in a sunny chair,
And the green freedom of a cockatoo
Upon a rug mingle to dissipate
The holy hush of ancient sacrifice.      5
She dreams a little, and she feels the dark
Encroachment of that old catastrophe,
As a calm darkens among water-lights.
The pungent oranges and bright, green wings
Seem things in some procession of the dead,      10
Winding across wide water, without sound.
The day is like wide water, without sound,
Stilled for the passing of her dreaming feet
Over the seas, to silent Palestine,
Dominion of the blood and sepulchre.      15

### II

Why should she give her bounty to the dead?
What is divinity if it can come
Only in silent shadows and in dreams?
Shall she not find in comforts of the sun,
In pungent fruit and bright, green wings, or else      20
In any balm or beauty of the earth,
Things to be cherished like the thoughts of heaven?
Divinity must live within herself:
Passions of rain, or moods in falling snow;
Grievings in loneliness, or unsubdued      25
Elations when the forest blooms; gusty
Emotions on wet roads on autumn nights;
All pleasures and all pains, remembering
The bough of summer and the winter branch.
These are the measures destined for her soul.      30

### III

Jove in the clouds had his inhuman birth.
No mother suckled him, no sweet land gave
Large-mannered motions to his mythy mind.

He moved among us, as a muttering king,
Magnificent, would move among his hinds, 35
Until our blood, commingling, virginal,
With heaven, brought such requital to desire
The very hinds discerned it, in a star.
Shall our blood fail? Or shall it come to be
The blood of paradise? And shall the earth 40
Seem all of paradise that we shall know?
The sky will be much friendlier then than now,
A part of labor and a part of pain,
And next in glory to enduring love,
Not this dividing and indifferent blue. 45

IV
She says, "I am content when wakened birds,
Before they fly, test the reality
Of misty fields, by their sweet questionings;
But when the birds are gone, and their warm fields
Return no more, where, then, is paradise?" 50
There is not any haunt of prophecy,
Nor any old chimera of the grave,
Neither the golden underground, nor isle
Melodious, where spirits gat them home,
Nor visionary south, nor cloudy palm 55
Remote on heaven's hill, that has endured
As April's green endures; or will endure
Like her remembrance of awakened birds,
Or her desire for June and evening, tipped
By the consummation of the swallow's wings. 60

V
She says, "But in contentment I still feel
The need of some imperishable bliss."
Death is the mother of beauty; hence from her,
Alone, shall come fulfilment to our dreams
And our desires. Although she strews the leaves 65
Of sure obliteration on our paths,
The path sick sorrow took, the many paths
Where triumph rang its brassy phrase, or love
Whispered a little out of tenderness,

She makes the willow shiver in the sun                    70
For maidens who were wont to sit and gaze
Upon the grass, relinquished to their feet.
She causes boys to pile new plums and pears
On disregarded plate. The maidens taste
And stray impassioned in the littering leaves.            75

VI

Is there no change of death in paradise?
Does ripe fruit never fall? Or do the boughs
Hang always heavy in that perfect sky,
Unchanging, yet so like our perishing earth,
With rivers like our own that seek for seas               80
They never find, the same receding shores
That never touch with inarticulate pang?
Why set the pear upon those river-banks
Or spice the shores with odors of the plum?
Alas, that they should wear our colors there,            85
The silken weavings of our afternoons,
And pick the strings of our insipid lutes!
Death is the mother of beauty, mystical,
Within whose burning bosom we devise
Our earthly mothers waiting, sleeplessly.                 90

VII

Supple and turbulent, a ring of men
Shall chant in orgy on a summer morn
Their boisterous devotion to the sun,
Not as a god, but as a god might be,
Naked among them, like a savage source.                  95
Their chant shall be a chant of paradise,
Out of their blood, returning to the sky;
And in their chant shall enter, voice by voice,
The windy lake wherein their lord delights,
The trees, like serafin, and echoing hills,             100
That choir among themselves long afterward.
They shall know well the heavenly fellowship
Of men that perish and of summer morn.
And whence they came and whither they shall go
The dew upon their feet shall manifest.                  105

109

## VIII

She hears, upon that water without sound,
A voice that cries, "The tomb in Palestine
Is not the porch of spirits lingering.
It is the grave of Jesus, where he lay."
We live in an old chaos of the sun,                          110
Or old dependency of day and night,
Or island solitude, unsponsored, free,
Of that wide water, inescapable.
Deer walk upon our mountains, and the quail
Whistle about us their spontaneous cries;                    115
Sweet berries ripen in the wilderness;
And, in the isolation of the sky,
At evening, casual flocks of pigeons make
Ambiguous undulations as they sink,
Downward to darkness, on extended wings.                     120

WALLACE STEVENS

## THE GENIUS

Waked by the pale pink
Intimation to the eastward,
Cock, the prey of every beast,
Takes breath upon the hen-house rafter,
Leans above the fiery brink                                  5
And shrieks in brazen obscene burst
On burst of uncontrollable derisive laughter:
Cock has seen the sun! He first! He first!

ARCHIBALD MACLEISH

## LEVIATHAN

This is the black sea-brute bulling through wave-wrack,
Ancient as ocean's shifting hills, who in sea-toils
Travelling, who furrowing the salt acres
Heavily, his wake hoary behind him,

110

Shoulders spouting, the fist of his forehead                                    5
Over wastes gray-green crashing, among horses unbroken
From bellowing fields, past bone-wreck of vessels,
Tide-ruin, wash of lost bodies bobbing
No longer sought for, and islands of ice gleaming,
Who ravening the rank flood, wave-marshalling,                        10
Overmastering the dark sea-marches, finds home
And harvest. Frightening to foolhardiest
Mariners, his size were difficult to describe:
The hulk of him is like hills heaving,
Dark, yet as crags of drift-ice, crowns cracking in thunder,   15
Like land's self by night black-looming, surf churning
     and trailing
Along his shores' rushing, shoal-water boding
About the dark of his jaws; and who should moor at his edge
And fare on afoot would find gates of no gardens,
But the hill of dark underfoot diving,                                       20
Closing overhead, the cold deep, and drowning.
He is called Leviathan, and named for rolling,
First created he was of all creatures,
He has held Jonah three days and nights,
He is that curling serpent that in ocean is,                                25
Sea-fright he is, and the shadow under the earth.
Days there are, nonetheless, when he lies
Like an angel, although a lost angel
On the waste's unease, no eye of man moving,
Bird hovering, fish flashing, creature whatever                        30
Who after him came to herit earth's emptiness.
Froth at flanks seething soothes to stillness,
Waits; with one eye he watches
Dark of night sinking last, with one eye dayrise
As at first over foaming pastures. He makes no cry       35
Though that light is a breath. The sea curling,
Star-climbed, wind-combed, cumbered with itself still
As at first it was, is the hand not yet contented
Of the Creator. And he waits for the world to begin.

W. S. MERWIN

111

## WINTER OCEAN

Many-maned scud-thumper, tub
of male whales, maker of worn wood, shrub-
ruster, sky-mocker, rave!
portly pusher of waves, wind-slave.

JOHN UPDIKE

# 5

---

## Diction

Poems, like all other literary forms, are made out of words. This statement sounds blatantly obvious. Still, it is not uncommon to read discussions of poems which proceed from the assumption that the poem is made out of ideas, or pictures, or the poet's subconscious emotional kinks, or his glandular secretions, or divine emanations transmitted through the muse. Of course, poems do contain and are directed by ideas and emotional states of the poet. And of course, there is something mysterious about the process of poetic composition, just as there is something mysterious about falling in love, about courage or cowardice, about any of the important choices human beings make. But whether he is writing to impress a girl, to make money (highly unlikely), to start a revolution or to express simple pleasure in being alive, and whether he is inspired by scripture, sex, Scotch, or sunrise, the poet at some point takes pen in hand and puts words on paper in a particular order. The words that the poet puts on paper in a specific slot in a poem constitute his *diction*—the individual word choices he makes from the options available to him.

As semanticists have emphasized, words are not neutral building blocks, so many bricks, all the same size, shape, and color, which the poet can order as he will. And they are not clay, which the poet can push into any shape he pleases. Words are sounds, and, purely as sounds, words can move us. Words have rhythmic potential, and rhythm can move us. And, of course, words have meaning. The primary meaning of any word is its *denotation*—

its meaning apart from emotional association or coloration. A cat
is, in the phraseology of the dictionary, a domesticated carnivorous
mammal of various colors, having retractile claws. This is the
original, primary, or denotative meaning of the word "cat." But
a cat is also a backbiting, gossipy woman. To be "catty" is to be
the sort of person who purringly demolishes the reputations of her
friends. "She has the morals of an alleycat" means "She has no morals
at all." "To cat around" is to philander. All these references draw on
negative *connotations* of the word "cat." The connotation of a
word is its extensional meaning, the positive or negative charge it
carries with it. The ordinary housecat, by reason of his footloose
ways and casual sex life, has acquired one set of largely negative
connotations.

But not all the connotations of the word "cat" are negative.
"Cat" as an equivalent for "man" or "person" ("Who's that cat?") is
fairly neutral, while "He moves like a big cat" is complimentary.

Words like "cat," "mousy," "coyote," "hawk," and "dove"
in their connotative extensions retain some trace of denotative
description. A political "hawk" does not have feathers and a beak,
but he does favor an aggressive foreign policy, and is more likely
to prefer swooping down on an enemy to cooing at him. But there are
some words in which the important thing communicated is not a
description of the person or object referred to, but the attitude of
the speaker. Compare "Candidate X favors increased spending
for social welfare" with "Candidate X is a spendthrift bleeding heart."
All of us are familiar with many abuse words, political, racial,
and cultural.

At any given time there are likely to be two or three blanket
terms of abuse in currency for describing things we do not like.
These expressions vary from group to group and, indeed, the joint
use of them is one way in which people who identify themselves
with any given group, whatever its makeup, assert their common
identity and mutual interests.

And as there are blanket terms of abuse, so there are blanket
terms of approval. "Nice," "fine," and "good" are examples of
words which, unless said in a sarcastic way, merely tell us whether
the speaker approves of the weather or the meal or the movie.

Virtually all words, except articles and prepositions, have a
connotative "feel" to them. Even scientific terminology is not neutral;
it smells of scholarship. Water is water, but $H_2O$ is water in a
laboratory. In our ordinary social intercourse, we learn to pick up
the appropriate "feel" of words at an early age. We do not describe
our best friend's mother as a "broad" or his pedigreed Afghan
hound as a "mutt."

While a feeling for the connotations of words is important

114

in any kind of verbal communication, careful attention to the nuances
of words is even more important in poetry. Consider with us, if
you will, what Emily Dickinson does with the nuances of words
in "The Snake."

A narrow Fellow in the Grass
Occasionally rides—
You may have met Him—did you not
His notice sudden is—

The Grass divides as with a Comb—
A spotted shaft is seen—
And then it closes at your feet
And opens further on—

He likes a Boggy Acre
A floor too cool for Corn—
Yet when a Boy, and Barefoot—
I more than once at Noon
Have passed, I thought, a Whip lash
Unbraiding in the Sun
When stooping to secure it,
It wrinkled, and was gone—

Several of Nature's People
I know, and they know me—
I feel for them a transport
Of cordiality—

But never met this Fellow
Attended or alone
Without a tighter breathing
And Zero at the Bone—

In the fourth stanza, "a transport/ of cordiality" sounds a
little overdone at first, if Miss Dickinson merely means that she
likes "Nature's People." Why not merely a "sentiment" or "feeling"
of cordiality? We discover the answer to that when we encounter
"tighter breathing" in the last stanza. To be transported is not simply
to be moved, but to be carried. Usually, the speaker says, "Nature's
People" take him out of himself and make him feel more at home with
the rest of his fellow creatures. But the snake produces the opposite
effect; in its constrictive impact, it produces "tighter Breathing/
And Zero at the bone." Why "zero" rather than coldness or chilling?

"Cold" and "chill" are relative words; "zero" is not. It is mathematical and scientific—and absolute. It is as cold as you can get. Throughout the poem, "Nature's People"—even the "narrow Fellow in the Grass" who is its subject—are treated in domestic terms. He "rides" and parts grass like a "comb." He is referred to as "Him" and "He," not the impersonal "it." He is never called a snake; he is a friend, a fellow creature, except for that "tighter breathing/ And Zero at the Bone." And it is this phrasing which describes the poet's reaction to the snake. "Zero" is not a domestic, household word, as the cold it describes is not an everyday kind of cold.

In addition of having sound, rhythmic potential, denotations and connotations, words have histories. The etymology of a word often gives an extra dimension to our understanding of its present-day meaning. Again, consider the phrase "transport/ Of cordiality." "Cordiality" means warmth, sincerity of feeling. But "cordial" from the Latin cor, cordis (heart) at one time in English meant "pertaining to the heart." We could paraphrase "transport of cordiality" as "feeling of friendliness." That is roughly what it means, but only roughly. Considered closely, "transport of cordiality"—being moved or carried by a warmth coming from the heart—is in exact opposition to "tighter breathing/ And Zero at the Bone." One is an image of warmth and expansion, the other an image of cold and constriction. If one remembers that "cordial," in addition to meaning "with heartfelt warmth," also means "a liquor or medical stimulant"—that is, something that revives the heart—and that the snake, which produces "tighter breathing/ And Zero at the Bone" belongs to a species, some of whom kill by constriction, and is cold- rather than warm-blooded, he will get some notion of the care with which good poets choose their words.

The connotations of words often grow out of their histories. English has an extremely rich vocabulary, in part because it has a long history of accommodating words from other languages. But some words have been in the language much longer than others. From the original Anglo-Saxon, for example, come many of the most common words in our daily vocabulary: bread, home, water, tree; and father, mother, brother, wife; and love, hate, happy, fear. After the Norman conquest (1066), French became the language of the court, of education, and of the judicial system. That influence is still evident today in that words of French derivation provide most of the terminology for government, theology, military affairs, law, medicine, the arts, society, and gastronomy. Many of the words which came in through French were, of course, originally from Latin or Greek.

In a general way, "native" English words—words of Teutonic origin—tend to be more homely (native English) and simpler in their connotations than later word imports. Compare "home" with

116

"domicile"; "brotherly" with "fraternal"; "loving" with "amorous."
In addition to having different connotations, the word which came
later into the language often has a somewhat narrower and more
specialized denotative meaning. Thus, while a "home" is a "domicile,"
most of us would prefer to go home rather than to our domiciles.
A domicile seems, somehow, too legal—and too cold. If we compare
"loving" with "amorous," we see a similar process of specialization
at work. One may feel loving toward his wife, his children, his
friends, his country, but he can only feel amorous towards an actual
or potential sexual partner. "Loving" is an old word, with serious
associations, a homespun, bread-and-butter word; "amorous" is
comparatively a new word, a word of the courts where fine ladies
and gentlemen had "paramours" and met at "rendezvous."

In addition to having sound, denotation, connotation, and
history, words have a sense appeal. They may have visual impact, as
does Miss Dickinson's description of the snake's progress.

> The Grass divides as with a Comb—
> A spotted shaft is seen—
> And then it closes at your feet
> and opens further on—

In this stanza we are urged to visualize the snake's progress: it
"divides" the grass, much as one parts his hair; the grass "closes"
behind the snake which is almost underfoot; the snake's movement
is deduced as the grass "opens further on." Without our ability and
willingness to see, the delight of this stanza would escape us.

Poems also appeal to our ears. We have already discussed a
good many of the aural devices which poets use: rhythm, rhyme,
assonance, alliteration, and onomatopoeia.

Of the remaining senses, the vocabulary of taste and
smell overlap considerably. "Salt," "sweet," "bitter," "acrid" can
equally well describe things smelled and things tasted. The sense
of touch is often appealed to with diction which can also yield a
visual image. "Velvet," "downy," "coarse," "gossamer" primarily
arouse the sense of touch, but also have visual suggestiveness.
The sense of touch is also related to the muscular or kinesthetic
sense, the ability to feel bodily tensions; and the thermal sense,
the ability to feel heat and cold. One gets them both in the line, "a
tighter breathing/ And Zero at the Bone."

Just as the reading of poetry helps us to an increased awareness
of the different sound possibilities, suggestive possibilities of words,
and histories of words, so it may help us to see the world with
new eyes or hear it with new ears. Far from being a man in an ivory

117

tower, thinking abstract thoughts, the poet is likely to be out in the garden, walking in the woods, or raiding the icebox: intellection grows out of sensation.

The task of the poet, then, is to find the words that will most honestly and accurately depict the concepts that grow out of his sensations. As Mark Twain once described it, ". . . the difference between the almost right word and the right word is really a large matter—'tis the difference between the lightning bug and the lightning." While lightning bugs have their own fascination, what the poet wants is to be a conductor for the world's voltage. To do this he must choose his words with care.

How meticulously the skilled poet approaches words became obvious as we discussed the qualities of words. The poet must be aware, as the ordinary user of the language is not, that there are no exact synonyms. "Awake" is not the same as "wake up"; one word is more formal and elevated than the other. "Fly," "soar," "flutter," "sweep," "swoop" are all possible descriptions of the flight of a bird; but when the exiled Macduff hears that his wife and children have been killed by Macbeth, he exclaims, "What, all my pretty ones at one fell swoop?" The other choices just would not convey the feeling of one powerful, silent movement. Any bird can fly, but it takes a killer-predator to "swoop."

In addition to making exact distinctions—not settling for lightning bugs in place of lightning—the poet must be conscious of the associative impact his words will have. Tennyson's "The splendor falls on castle walls" immediately awakens chivalric and medieval images in a way that "The sunlight falls on castle walls" does not. "Splendor," of course, is reinforced by "castle walls"; the effect of the line would be quite different if Tennyson had written, "The splendor falls on garbage dumps." But even with the castle walls, much of the impact of the line still comes from "splendor." Consider "The strobe light falls on castle walls"—an interesting image in its own way, but with entirely different semantic dimensions.

In a general way, poetry is active rather than passive, concrete rather than abstract. The psalmist, describing his confidence in his God, says: "He leadeth me beside the still waters." One can imagine a psychology textbook with the words: "Belief in the existence of an onmipotent, omniscient, personally involved diety frequently induces in believers a high degree of emotional security and tends to minimize anxiety symptoms." Of course, the psychologist is writing to convey scientific observations about general human behavior while the psalmist is writing to induce prayerful awe and reverence. The psychologist, though he could probably write a more elegant sentence than ours and though he might personally admire the Twenty-Third Psalm, might not be willing to accept "He leadeth

118

me beside the still waters" as a paraphrase for his sentence, because
it is too subjective, too emotionally loaded. The scientist chooses
the neutral third person: "Belief in the existence of . . ." The psalmist
chooses the immediate personal involvement of "He leadeth me."
The scientist describes, and, for those who are familiar with
psychoanalytic jargon, the description is quite precise. But the psalmist
dramatizes. The scientist is abstract. There is nothing in his sentences
likely to trigger a physical reaction. The psalmist is concrete and
sensuous. Instead of "a high degree of emotional security," we have
"still waters." Instead of "minimize anxiety symptoms" we have
"Yea, though I walk through the valley of the shadow of death I will
fear no evil, for Thou art with me." Just as the psalmist's nouns
and adjectives are more vivid and concrete, his verbs are more directly
concerned with movement. Instead of "induces" and "tends" we
have (modernizing the verb forms) "makes," "leads," "restores,"
"anoints" and so on. Notice the active verb forms. Suppose we wrote,
"I am made to lie down in green pastures. I am led beside still waters.
My soul is restored." Some of the vitality goes out of the language
with the active verbs.

The diction a poet employs is also instrumental in establishing
the poem's *tone*—that feeling a reader senses which tells him how
the poet feels about his audience, his subject, and himself in relation
to his poem. Consider the tone implicit in these opening lines of
well-known poems.

1. That time of year thou may'st in me behold
   When yellow leaves, or none, or few, do hang;

2. A bunch of the boys were whooping it up in the Malemute
   saloon;

3. I am enamoured of growing outdoors,
   Of men that live among cattle or taste of the ocean
   or woods,
   Of the builders and steerers of ships, of the wielders
   of axes and mauls, of the drivers of horses,
   I can eat and sleep with them week in and week out.

4. I wandered lonely as a cloud/That floats on high o'er vales
   and hills.

5. For God's sake hold your tongue and let me love;

The difference in tone among these five selections could be made
even greater, for no humorous poems have been included and all but

one of the poems is in a conventional foot and meter. Quotation 1, Shakespeare's "Sonnet 73," is nowhere near the same wavelength as 2, Robert W. Service's "Shooting of Dan McGrew." Quotation 3, from Walt Whitman's *Leaves of Grass*, begins "I am enamoured of growing outdoors," but Whitman's "outdoorsiness" is of a different order than that implied in quotation 4, William Wordsworth's "I Wandered Lonely as a Cloud." Quotation 5, John Donne's "The Canonization," is a love poem, as is Shakespeare's sonnet, but each is distinctive; the fact that they are love poems does not create a common tone.

Looking more closely at the diction of these brief excerpts, we can see how word choice helps create the tone. The melancholy we sense in Quotation 1 would be subtly altered if we substituted "golden" for "yellow." "Golden" has almost wholly positive connotations: wealth, richness. "Golden" as a description of autumn leaves suggests richness, completion, even warmth. "Yellow," in this context, evokes loss, age, and aging.

In quotation 2, notice what happens to the tone when several key words are altered: "A few of the men were enjoying themselves in the Yukon Country Club." Service's words, "bunch," "boys," "whooping it up," and "saloon," not only work together, but they also prepare us for the rough-and-tumble, deadly action which follows.

Whitman's use of "enamoured" in quotation 3 at first glance is strange; yet the very strangeness of that term is part of its effectiveness in creating the tone of this passage. The other words in the passage and the images they convey are fairly common. Whitman wants us to know that he does not just like the outdoors and common people and tasks: he loves them passionately. More than any other single word in the passage, "enamoured" is the word that sets the overall tone.

In quotation 4, consider the terms "lonely," "floats," and "high." The impression immediately given is of someone isolated and adrift and remote. The tone is pensive and introspective, but it is not melancholy in the way that quotation 1 is.

We have said that quotation 5 begins a poem dealing with love. Obviously we are not faced with a bashful lover with a creampuff-and-perfume approach. The speaker is direct and unequivocal: love and loving are too serious and personal to be interrupted by idle chatter or even the affairs of state.

In many poems, we must first determine who the speaker of the poem is before we can determine what the tone is, and just as often we will need to determine to whom the speaker is addressing his words. Sometimes the title gives us both answers. "The Passionate Shepherd to His Love" tells us in what character the poet is writing. "To His Coy Mistress" leaves no doubt as to whom the audience is.

Frequently the first few lines tell us: "Since there's no help, come let us kiss and part," is certainly from lover to lover, although we still need to know what sort of "lovers" they are. A line beginning, "This is my letter to the world" speaks to a broader audience. Some forms of poetry, such as the dramatic monologue, have a designated speaker, usually one named in the title, and often a specific audience: others, such as the epistle or love sonnet, have a specified hearer. It is important to note that the poet does not always speak through his own voice, but may, for the purposes of the poem, speak through somebody else. Then, too, poets do not always speak directly to the audience. For the purposes of the poem, the general audience may "overhear" the poet.

Sometimes the word "poetic" is used to describe prose, usually nature writing or inspirational writing. And occasionally one encounters a list of the "Ten Most Beautiful Words" in the English language, as determined by a poll. Poetry, it is frequently assumed (usually by people who do not read it or like it, or by people who prefer bad poetry to good poetry), is beautiful thoughts in beautiful words. It should be clear by this point in our discussion that poets write about practically anything, not just "beautiful" things, and that the words they use are frequently not "beautiful" words. A poet may, indeed, wish to use an elevated tone, with diction to suit; but there are poems for which a casual tone, or a tough tone, may be appropriate. The level of diction a poet employs will vary from poem to poem, to meet the demands of the voices which the poet chooses.

So we end where we began. Poems are made out of words. Words can amuse or irritate or soothe us by the way they sound singly and together. Words as poets use them can enhance our appreciation of the words we speak ourselves. The words of poems can sharpen our sensory appreciation of the world around us. And words as the poet uses them can let us hear other voices and take us into the minds and hearts of other men.

*Exercise 1*

## ON THE LIFE OF MAN

| | |
|---|---|
| What is our life? a play of passion, | 1 |
| Our mirth the music of division; | 2 |
| Our mother's wombs the tiring houses be, | 3 |
| Where we are dressed for this short ___a___; | 4 |
| Heaven the judicious sharp ___d___ is, | 5 |

121

That sits and marks still who doth ___*b*___ amiss;  6
Our graves that hide us from the searching sun,  7
Are like ___*b*___ when the play is done.  8
Thus march we playing to our latest rest,  9
Only we die in earnest, that's no jest.  10

1. The missing word in line 4 is (a) time, (b) agony, (c) comedy, (d) tragedy.
2. The missing word in line 5 is (a) spectator, (b) judge, (c) observer, (d) director.
3. The missing word in line 6 is (a) look, (b) act, (c) move, (d) rehearse.
4. The missing word(s) in line 8 is/are (a) scenery, (b) drawn curtains, (c) empty stages, (d) sun's setting.

ANSWERS

1. While metrical considerations are of some aid to us in this poem, the primary clue is provided by the first line: life is a play. The diction of the poem, then, must carry out this metaphor. Both choices (c) and (d) are possibilities. Line 10, though, indicates that what has gone before has not been fully serious. Choice (c) was Sir Walter Raleigh's choice.
2. Metrical needs demand more than one syllable, so choice (b) is out. Of the remaining three choices, (a) and (d) are more clearly related to the theatre than (c). Either a "spectator" or a "director" might "sit and mark" the performance, but ultimately it is the audience of spectators who determine the success or failure of a play by choosing to attend or not attend. Choice (a).
3. Line 4 tells us that "we" are the actors in the play; the spectators sit and watch our acting and judge is quality. Choice (b).
4. Line 7 reminds us that the corpse in a grave is hidden from the sun; likewise, the actors in a play are hidden from the audience at the end of the play. Choice (b) is the only one that sustains the metaphor through the appropriate diction.

*Exercise 2*

## A DIRGE

Rough wind, that ___*b*___ loud  1
   Grief too sad for song;  2
Wild wind, when ___*b*___ cloud  3
   Knells all the night long;  4

Sad storm, whose tears are vain,                                    5

Bare woods, whose branches strain,                                 6

   Deep caves and ___*a*___ main—                       7

   ___*b*___, for the world's wrong!                     8

1. The missing word(s) in line 1 is/are (a) singest, (b) moanest, (c) purrs so, (d) croonest.
2. The missing word in line 3 is (a) puffy, (b) threatening, (c) sullen, (d) thunder.
3. The missing word in line 7 is (a) dreary, (b) surging, (c) surfy, (d) rolling.
4. The missing word in line 8 is (a) Cry, (b) Wail, (c) Revolt, (d) Laugh.

ANSWERS

1. A dirge is a song of sorrow, a funeral song. One should expect, therefore, that the diction of this poem be consistent with that fact. Choice (a) is a neutral term; Choices (c) and (d) are better suited for a children's lullaby. Choice (b) has the proper funereal tinge.
2. Choice (a) is too light and soft to be a serious possibility. Of the remaining choices, which one best maintains a foreboding tone? All of the vowels in "threatening" are front vowels, and "thunder" is implied by "Knells" in line 4. Shelley's word was "Sullen," choice (c).
3. The "main" of this line refers to the open sea. All choices, therefore, would fit. Choices (b), (c), and (d) are neutrally descriptive. Choice (a), though, conveys the speaker's emotional attitude and maintains the diction of the poem.
4. Read line 8 aloud to yourself with each of the four choices. All matters of diction aside, one of the choices should feel much more appropriate than the others. Considerations of diction should rule out choices (c) and (d), as they are out of place in a dirge. While "cry" and "wail" are roughly synonymous, a "cry" can be a cry of joy as well as sorrow. A "wail" is only expressive of deep sorrow, and in this line it alliterates with "world's wrong," thereby binding the line more tightly together. Choice (b).

*Exercise 3*

## SONNET 50

Thus piteously Love closed what he begat:                          1

The union of this ever-diverse pair!                               2

These two were rapid falcons in a snare,                                    3
——————— to do the flitting of the bat.                                      4
Lovers beneath the singing sky of May,                                      5
They wandered once; clear as the dew on flowers.                            6
But they fed not on the advancing hours;                                    7
Their hearts held cravings for the ———————.                                 8
Then each applied to each that fatal knife,                                 9
Deep questioning, which probes to endless dole.                            10
Ah! what a ——————— gets the soul                                           11
When hot for certainties in this our life!—                                12
In tragic hints here see what evermore                                     13
Moves ——————— as yonder midnight oceans' force,                            14
Thundering like ramping hosts of warrior horse,                            15
To throw that faint thin line upon the shore.                              16

1. The missing word in line 4 is (a) agreed, (b) likely, (c) condemned,
   (d) determined.
2. The missing words in line 8 are (a) buried day, (b) sunny day,
   (c) sunlit day, (d) cool, clear day.
3. The missing words in line 11 are (a) silly reply, (b) dusty answer,
   (c) stupid retort, (d) wretched sermon.
4. The missing word in line 14 is (a) fast, (b) murderous, (c) slow,
   (d) dark.

*Exercise 4*

## THERE CAME A WIND LIKE A BUGLE

There came a wind like a bugle.                                             1
It quivered through the grass,                                              2
And a green chill upon the heat                                            3
So ominous did pass.                                                       4
We ——————— the windows and the doors                                       5
As from an emerald ghost.                                                   6
The ——————— electric moccasin                                              7
That very instant passed.                                                  8
On a strange mob of ———————                                                 9
And fences fled away                                                       10
And rivers where the houses ran                                            11

| Those looked that lived, that day. | 12 |
| The bell within the ————— | 13 |
| The flying tidings told— | 14 |
| How much can come | 15 |
| And much can go, | 16 |
| And yet abide the world. | 17 |

1. The missing word in line 5 is (a) closed, (b) shut, (c) barred, (d) secured.
2. The missing word in line 7 is (a) doom's, (b) day's, (c) atmosphere's, (d) city's.
3. The missing words in line 9 are (a) waving flowers, (b) panting trees, (c) laughing lads, (d) little girls.
4. The missing words in line 13 are (a) steeple wild, (b) school belfrey, (c) firehouse loud, (d) lovely tower.

# 5

---

## Poems

126

# SHE DWELT AMONG THE UNTRODDEN WAYS

She dwelt among the untrodden ways
   Beside the springs of Dove,
A maid whom there were none to praise
   And very few to love:

A violet by a mossy stone          5
   Half hidden from the eye!
—Fair as a star, when only one
   Is shining in the sky.

She lived unknown, and few could know
   When Lucy ceased to be;         10
But she is in her grave, and, oh,
   The difference to me!

WILLIAM WORDSWORTH

# I AM A PARCEL OF VAIN STRIVINGS TIED

I am a parcel of vain strivings tied
   By a chance bond together,
  Dangling this way and that, their links
   Were made so loose and wide,
      Methinks,         5
   For milder weather.

A bunch of violets without their roots,
   And sorrel intermixed,
  Encircled by a wisp of straw
   Once coiled about their shoots,         10
      The law
   By which I'm fixed.

A nosegay which Time clutched from out
   Those fair Elysian fields,
With weeds and broken stems, in haste,         15
   Doth make the rabble rout
      That waste
   The day he yields.

And here I bloom for a short hour unseen,
    Drinking my juices up,               20
  With no root in the land
      To keep my branches green,
        But stand
      In a bare cup.

Some tender buds were left upon my stem        25
    In mimicry of life,
  But ah! the children will not know,
    Till time has withered them,
      The woe
    With which they're rife.             30

But now I see I was not plucked for naught,
    And after in life's vase
  Of glass set while I might survive,
    But by a kind hand brought
      Alive                35
    To a strange place.

That stock thus thinned will soon redeem its hours,
    And by another year,
  Such as God knows, with freer air,
    More fruits and fairer flowers       40
      Will bear,
    While I droop here.

HENRY DAVID THOREAU


# I AM OF OLD AND YOUNG

I am of old and young, of the foolish as much as the
    wise,
Regardless of others, ever regardful of others,
Maternal as well as paternal, a child as well as a man,
Stuffed with the stuff that is coarse, and stuffed with the    5
    stuff that is fine,
One of the great nation, the nation of many nations—the
    smallest the same and the largest the same,

A southerner soon as a northerner, a planter nonchalant
    and hospitable,                                                    10
A Yankee bound my own way....ready for trade....my
    joints the limberest joints on earth and the sternest
    joints on earth,
A Kentuckian walking the vale of the Elkhorn in my
    deerskin leggings,                                                 15
A boatman over the lakes or bays or along coasts....a
    Hoosier, a Badger, a Buckeye,
A Louisianian or Georgian, a poke-easy from sandhills and
    pines.
At home on Canadian snowshoes or up in the bush, or        20
    with fishermen off Newfoundland,
At home in the fleet of iceboats, sailing with the rest and
    tacking,
At home on the hills of Vermont or in the woods of
    Maine or the Texan ranch,                                          25
Comrade of Californians....comrade of free north-
    westerners, loving their big proportions,
Comrade of raftsmen and coalmen—comrade of all who
    shake hands and welcome to drink and meat;
A learner with the simplest, a teacher of the thoughtfulest, 30
A novice beginning experient of myriads of seasons,
Of every hue and trade and rank, of every caste and
    religion,
Not merely of the New World but of Africa Europe or
    Asia....a wandering savage,                                        35
A farmer, mechanic, or artist....a gentleman, sailor, lover
    or quaker,
A prisoner, fancy-man, rowdy, lawyer, physician or priest.

I resist anything better than my own diversity,
And breathe the air and leave plenty after me,             40
And am not stuck up, and am in my place.

The moth and the fisheggs are in their place,
The suns I see and the suns I cannot see are in their place,
The palpable is in its place and the impalpable is in its place.

WALT WHITMAN

129

## THE MALDIVE SHARK

About the Shark, phlegmatical one,
Pale sot of the Maldive sea,
The sleek little pilot-fish, azure and slim,
How alert in attendance be.
From his saw-pit of mouth, from his charnel of maw          5
They have nothing of harm to dread,
But liquidly glide on his ghastly flank
Or before his Gorgonian head;
Or lurk in the port of serrated teeth
In white triple tiers of glittering gates,                 10
And there find a haven when peril's abroad,
An asylum in jaws of the Fates!
They are friends; and friendly they guide him to prey,
Yet never partake of the treat—
Eyes and brains to the dotard lethargic and dull,          15
Pale ravener of horrible meat.

HERMAN MELVILLE

## DOVER BEACH     *Simple to more complex*

*Sea used as a metaphor*

The sea is calm to-night.
The tide is full, the moon lies fair
Upon the straits;—on the French coast the light
Gleams and is gone; the cliffs of England stand,
Glimmering and vast, out in the tranquil bay.              5
Come to the window, sweet is the night-air!
Only, from the long line of spray
Where the sea meets the moon-blanch'd land,
Listen! you hear the grating roar
Of pebbles which the waves draw back, and fling,           10
At their return, up the high strand,
Begin, and cease, and then again begin,
With tremulous cadence slow, and bring
*Bridging the element of Time* { The eternal note of sadness in.
Sophocles long ago                                         15
Heard it on the Ægaean, and it brought

130

Into his mind the turbid ebb and flow ~~Ocean~~
Of human misery; we
Find also in the sound a thought,
Hearing it by this distant northern sea.                    20

The Sea of Faith     *a ? of Faith. Is there anything a Man can believe in?*
Was once, too, at the full, and round earth's shore
Lay like the folds of a bright girdle furl'd.
But now I only hear
Its melancholy, long, withdrawing roar,                     25
Retreating, to the breath
Of the night-wind, down the vast edges drear
And naked shingles of the world.

Ah, love, let us be true     *wistful - a plea almost*
To one another! for the world, which seems    *world is a fantasy*    30
To lie before us like a land of dreams,
So various, so beautiful, so new,
Hath really neither joy, nor love, nor light,    *He thinks its negative forces.*
Nor certitude, nor peace, nor help for pain;    *Agnostic*
And we are here as on a darkling plain *(Certainty)*    35
Swept with confused alarms of struggle and flight,
Where ignorant armies clash by night.    *One thing we may cling to is one another; nothing else very despondent!*

MATTHEW ARNOLD


## THE DOLLS

A doll in the doll-maker's house
Looks at the cradle and bawls:
'That is an insult to us.'
But the oldest of all the dolls,
Who had seen, being kept for show,                          5
Generations of his sort,
Out-screams the whole shelf: 'Although
There's not a man can report
Evil of this place,
The man and the woman bring                                10
Hither, to our disgrace,
A noisy and filthy thing.'

Hearing him groan and stretch
The doll-maker's wife is aware
Her husband has heard the wretch,                    15
And crouched by the arm of his chair,
She murmurs into his ear,
Head upon shoulder leant:
'My dear, my dear, O dear,
It was an accident.'                                 20

WILLIAM BUTLER YEATS


## A GLASS OF BEER

The lanky hank of a she in the inn over there
Nearly killed me for asking the loan of a glass of beer;
May the devil grip the whey-faced slut by the hair,
And beat bad manners out of her skin for a year.

That parboiled ape, with the toughest jaw you will see   5
On virtue's path, and a voice that would rasp the dead,
Came roaring and raging the minute she looked at me,
And threw me out of the house on the back of my
    head!

If I asked her master he'd give me a cask a day;        10
But she, with the beer at hand, not a gill would
    arrange!
May she marry a ghost and bear him a kitten, and may
The High King of Glory permit her to get the mange.

JAMES STEPHENS


## JANET WAKING

Beautifully Janet slept
Till it was deeply morning. She woke then
And thought about her dainty-feathered hen,
To see how it had kept.

132

One kiss she gave her mother. 5
Only a small one gave she to her daddy
Who would have kissed each curl of his shining baby;
No kiss at all for her brother.

"Old Chucky, old Chucky!" she cried,
Running across the world upon the grass 10
To Chucky's house, and listening. But alas,
Her Chucky had died.

It was a transmogrifying bee
Came droning down on Chucky's old bald head
And sat and put the poison. It scarcely bled, 15
But how exceedingly

And purply did the knot
Swell with the venom and communicate
Its rigor! Now the poor comb stood up straight
But Chucky did not. 20

So there was Janet
Kneeling on the wet grass, crying her brown hen
(Translated far beyond the daughters of men)
To rise and walk upon it.

And weeping fast as she had breath 25
Janet implored us, "Wake her from her sleep!"
And would not be instructed in how deep
Was the forgetful kingdom of death.

JOHN CROWE RANSOM

## "DOVER BEACH"—A NOTE
## TO THAT POEM

   The wave withdrawing
Withers with seaward rustle of flimsy water
Sucking the sand down, dragging at empty shells.
The roil after it settling, too smooth, smothered . . .

After forty a man's a fool to wait in the 5
Sea's face for the full force and the roaring of

133

Surf to come over him: droves of careening water.
After forty the tug's out and the salt and the
Sea follow it: less sound and violence.
Nevertheless the ebb has its own beauty—                           10
Shells sand and all and the whispering rustle.
There's earth in it then and the bubbles of foam gone.

Moreover—and this too has its lovely uses—
It's the outward wave that spills the inward forward
Tripping the proud piled mute virginal                             15
Mountain of water in wallowing welter of light and
Sound enough—thunder for miles back. It's a fine and a
Wild smother to vanish in: pulling down—
Tripping with outward ebb the urgent inward.

Speaking alone for myself it's the steep hill and the              20
Toppling lift of the young men I am toward now,
Waiting for that as the wave for the next wave.
Let them go over us all I say with the thunder of
What's to be next in the world. It's we will be under it!

ARCHIBALD MACLEISH


## THE DOVER BITCH—A CRITICISM OF LIFE

So there stood Matthew Arnold and this girl
With the cliffs of England crumbling away behind them,
And he said to her, "Try to be true to me,
And I'll do the same for you, for things are bad
All over, etc., etc."                                              5
Well now, I knew this girl. It's true she had read
Sophocles in a fairly good translation
And caught that bitter allusion to the sea,
But all the time he was talking she had in mind
The notion of what his whiskers would feel like                    10
On the back of her neck. She told me later on
That after a while she got to looking out
At the lights across the channel, and really felt sad,
Thinking of all the wine and enormous beds
And blandishments in French and the perfumes.                      15

134

And then she got really angry. To have been brought
All the way down from London, and then be addressed
As a sort of mournful cosmic last resort
Is really tough on a girl, and she was pretty.
Anyway, she watched him pace the room                    20
And finger his watch-chain and seem to sweat a bit,
And then she said one or two unprintable things.
But you mustn't judge her by that. What I mean to say is,
She's really all right. I still see her once in a while
And she always treats me right. We have a drink          25
And I give her a good time, and perhaps it's a year
Before I see her again, but there she is,
Running to fat, but dependable as they come.
And sometimes I bring her a bottle of *Nuit d' Amour.*

ANTHONY HECHT

## THOSE BEING EATEN BY AMERICA

The cry of those being eaten by America,
Others pale and soft being stored for later eating
And Jefferson
Who saw hope in new oats
The wild houses go on                                     5
With long hair growing from between their toes
The feet at night get up
And run down the long white roads by themselves
The dams reverse themselves and want to go stand alone in the
    desert                                               10
Ministers who dive headfirst into the earth
The pale flesh
Spreading guiltily into new literatures
That is why these poems are so sad
The long dead running over the fields                    15
The mass sinking down
The light in children's faces fading at six or seven
The world will soon break up into small colonies of the saved

ROBERT BLY

135

## THE SUPERIORITY OF MUSIC

Lang has no lovewedge. The world forgot
such courtly praise for neon eyes
as roused their hurricano sighs
in knightly years. I am not
like a yacht, nor dare I to                               5
a harbor resemble thee. My tears
gully no landscapes. I have no fears
of chill disdain, nor wanly woo
pent in pantameter. My verse is ill
with marriage and commonsense                             10
constraining conceit and elegance.
Shall I sonnetize the Pill?

Nay, wife, I still with clapper tongue
proclaim that you, like any she
belied with false compare may be                          15
with hyperbolic baubles hung:
I root my ropy route among
your petal hills; I pioneerly boar
my sow of despond, salty shore,
or, as spring from pikespeak sprung,                      20
twist down melodically and clear.
I lick the jewels from corners, halt
midair nijinskywise. I sault
summerly and slobber, bucking near,

for you, my satin-saddle, gra-                            25
vey grave, my scorching wine, my squirrel.
I love you like boiled onions, girl,
buttered. You suck my spine away,
soak me. You tenderize my twigs.
I thing in orange. My tongue twitches                     30
till sundown. You invent my itches.
You look like music and taste like figs.
You are to be virtuo-solely played,
sweetly and with pizzicato,
ad libitum and obbligato,                                 35
my straddle-various, my fiddled maid.

No go. The mind in praise ties knots.
Yet when you lie there like a long smile
brownly smiling at either end a long while,
moon glazing your gullied landscape, thoughts          40
circling and settling like evening birds,
and you turn and stroke my skin with eyes
like tonic chords, and silence lies
as gently over us as music without words,
I would not then restore to love its tongue.          45
You are not like anything. No poet imagined you.
You are dreamed by the earth, wordless. You
are not to be described, but sung.

JUDSON JEROME


## LITTLE ELEGY

Here lies resting, out of breath
Out of turns, Elizabeth
Whose quicksilver toes not quite
Cleared the whirring edge of night.

Earth whose circles round us skim          5
Till they catch the lightest limb,
Shelter now Elizabeth
And for her sake trip up Death.

X. J. KENNEDY


## DADDY

You do not do, you do not do
Any more, black shoe
In which I have lived like a foot
For thirty years, poor and white,
Barely daring to breathe or Achoo.          5

Daddy, I have had to kill you.
You died before I had time—
Marble-heavy, a bag full of God,
Ghastly statue with one grey toe
Big as a Frisco seal                                    10

And a head in the freakish Atlantic
Where it pours bean green over blue
In the waters off beautiful Nauset.
I used to pray to recover you.
Ach, du.                                                15

In the German tongue, in the Polish town
Scraped flat by the roller
Of wars, wars, wars.
But the name of the town is common.
My Polack friend                                        20

Says there are a dozen or two.
So I never could tell where you
Put your foot, your root,
I never could talk to you.
The tongue stuck in my jaw.                              25

It stuck in a barb wire snare.
Ich, ich, ich, ich,
I could hardly speak.
I thought every German was you.
And the language obscene                                 30

An engine, an engine                              .
Chuffing me off like a Jew.
A Jew to Dachau, Auschwitz, Belsen.
I began to talk like a Jew.
I think I may well be a Jew.                             35

The snows of the Tyrol, the clear beer of Vienna
Are not very pure or true.
With my gypsy ancestress and my weird luck
And my Taroc pack and my Taroc pack
I may be a bit of a Jew.                                 40

I have always been scared of *you*,
With your Luftwaffe, your gobbledygoo.
And your neat moustache
And your Aryan eye, bright blue.
Panzer-man, panzer-man, O You—                          45

Not God but a swastika
So black no sky could squeak through.
Every woman adores a Fascist,
The boot in the face, the brute
Brute heart of a brute like you.                        50

You stand at the blackboard, daddy,
In the picture I have of you,
A cleft in your chin instead of your foot
But no less a devil for that, no not
Any less the black man who                              55

Bit my pretty red heart in two.
I was ten when they buried you.
At twenty I tried to die
And get back, back, back to you.
I thought even the bones would do.                      60

But they pulled me out of the sack,
And they stuck me together with glue.
And then I knew what to do.
I make a model of you,
A man in black with a Meinkampf look                    65

And a love of the rack and the screw.
And I said I do, I do.
So daddy, I'm finally through.
The black telephone's off at the root,
The voices just can't worm through.                     70

If I've killed one man, I've killed two—
The vampire who said he was you
And drank my blood for a year,
Seven years, if you want to know.
Daddy, you can lie back now.                             75

139

There's a stake in your fat black heart
And the villagers never liked you.
They are dancing and stamping on you.
They always *knew* it was you.
Daddy, daddy, you bastard, I'm through.                80

SYLVIA PLATH


## A POEM FOR BLACK HEARTS

For Malcolm's eyes, when they broke
the face of some dumb white man. For
Malcolm's hands raised to bless us
all black and strong in his image
of ourselves, for Malcolm's words,                5
fire darts, the victor's tireless
thrusts, words hung above the world
change as it may, he said it, and
for this he was killed, for saying,
and feeling, and being/ change, all                10
collected hot in his heart, For Malcolm's
heart, raising us above our filthy cities,
for his stride, and his beat, and his address
to the grey monsters of the world, For Malcolm's
pleas for your dignity, black men, for your life,                15
black men, for the filling of your minds
with righteousness, For all of him dead and
gone and vanished from us, and all of him which
clings to our speech black god of our time.
For all of him, and all of yourself, look up,                20
black man, quit stuttering and shuffling, look up,
black man, quit whining and stooping, for all of him,
For Great Malcolm a prince of the earth, let nothing in us rest
until we avenge ourselves for his death, stupid animals
that killed him, let us never breathe a pure breath if                25
we fail, and white men call us faggots till the end of
the earth.

LEROI JONES


140

*[handwritten annotations in margins:]*
*Mon. — Concise analysis (1 or 2 pgs.)*
*— tech. or formal analysis — scansion (not every line)*
*— examine meter — gen. judgement (reg., mostly reg., or what?)*
*same w/ rhyme (end or internal)*

*diction*
*sound devices*
*figures of speech*
*series of judgements follow & up?*
*suggested interp. of poem. (mood, nature) etc.*

# OLD MAN STUCKEL TALKS TO THE HOGS

Old beyond milking, his sap all gone to seed,
He moves where he moved as a boy, bringing the cows home.
On dry-stick legs he stumps through the rank sweetness
    As he did ninety summers back, eager among the barnyard
        mysteries.

Here on these acres his sons farm, in the long gloamings       5
Of his ninety-sixth summer, he leans on fencing
That creaks like his bones, and talks to the hogs.
Their lively pink noses snoof in the trough.
He tells them how it is. Good harvests, bad harvests,
Blizzards, droughts, corn-growing weather.       10
Marriages. Wars. A swamp drained,
A field gone back to birches and box elder. The old men in the
        courthouse,
Bearded like God, are slick-faced boys now,
And grandsons of girls he danced with
Stand him to beer at the Legion Club when he hitch-hikes into
        town.       15
All changed, by God. Leaning on dry-stick arms,
He tells them, by God there were women then, not skinny girls.
Real women, farm women, tossing their heads like good mares.
Real dancing, too. Polka, schottische. Moonlight and the smell
        of sweet corn.
Yards of lace. But meat on their bones, by God.       20

Stroke took his daughter-in-law during the July drought.
She lay nine days, plump hands that knew the warmth under a
        hen's breast
Palm up by her solid thighs.
The German tongue and the laughter all finished. Dying corn
Whispered in the dusty fields like old newspapers.       25

The day of the funeral it poured. Mourners scurried from car to
        church.
They brought in gusts of cool air. Scrolled incense, thick as
        cows' breath
In a frosty barn shook with the rain-sweet air.
Knocking drops from their hats with scrubbed hands

141

They muttered, "I hope it don't stop for a week."        30
After an hour of Latin they took her to the graveyard
To lie under the marble gaze of Jesus eternally dying,
To soften with the rustle of green corn.

After chores and supper, the old man told the hogs.

EDITH RYLANDER

6

# *Figurative Language and Symbolism*

The steed bit his master!
  How came this to pass?
He heard the good pastor
  Say, "All flesh is grass."

*On a Horse Who Bit a Clergyman,*
ANONYMOUS (18th century)

The preacher's literal-minded horse may be taken as representing all those people who react to the words "figurative" and "symbolism" with a nervous whinny and a strong desire to bolt. One of Ogden Nash's funniest poems criticizes poets for comparing "ladies to lilies and veal to venison"—but his tongue-in-cheek complaint that a "blanket of snow" would not be very warming is aimed as much at the everyday speaker as at the poet.

All of us use *figurative language,* language which departs from its ordinary literal meaning. "She was wearing a blue dress," is a literal statement; "She was feeling blue," is a figurative statement, in which a word normally descriptive of color is used to describe an emotional state.

Much figurative language has been so thoroughly assimilated into normal usage that it is not interpreted as figurative. Thus, if we wanted to substitute a more formal phrase for "feeling blue," we could say, "She was depressed." But a depression is a lowering, a bringing down. At the more colloquial level, we say, "She was really down," or "She

143

was feeling low." We rarely think of these expressions as being figurative, in the same way that "blanket of snow" or "eyes like limpid pools" are figurative. But they are.

Figurative language adds a dimension to poetry which it could not obtain by other means. Compare these descriptions.

Marcia Muldoon (5'8", 120, 38-24-36) is a dark-eyed, dark-haired beauty from Plunketville, majoring in animal husbandry. Her ambition is to run her own dairy farm. She was nominated for the Home-coming Queen competition by the Jolly Harvesters, after winning the title of "Miss Combine" from a field of nine other contestants.

> She walks in beauty, like the night
>   Of cloudless climes and starry skies;
> And all that's best of dark and bright
>   Meet in her aspect and her eyes:
> Thus mellowed to that tender light
>   Which heaven to gaudy day denies.

*She Walks in Beauty*, GEORGE GORDON, LORD BYRON

The first description is literal, giving us the height, weight, and measurements of the young lady. It provides a good deal of information about Miss Muldoon. The second description is figurative, all of it derived from Byron's comparison of a beautiful woman to a calm, starry night. It does not tell us the young lady's name, her place of origin, her ambitions, or her vital statistics.

How much does it tell us? Quite a lot. The "woman : starry night" comparison suggests someone with dark eyes and hair, perhaps in a black gown. Is she a bouncy, giggly, gabby little person? Byron's comparison suggests quietness—a soft voice, slow, graceful movements—and perhaps something mysterious. It tells us not only a good deal about the lady's physical appearance, but also something about her other personal qualities as they affected the poet. Of course, the appeal of rhyme, meter, sound patterns, and diction all contribute to that effect. "Walks in beauty," for instance, suggests that the lady is not only lovely herself, but carries loveli-ness with her as the night carries darkness.

The core of the poem, however, is the comparative equation "woman : starry night." This comparison is, of course, a figurative statement. The lady is not the night, nor is she like the night in every way. But she is like the night in some ways. Such a comparative statement, one using the words "like," "as," or "than" to express a resemblance, is called a *simile*.

144

Similes are one of the commonest forms of figurative expression, and they are usually not difficult to understand. "My luv is like a red, red rose" establishes the comparison "love : rose." A literalist, like the preacher-biting horse, might object that girls rarely have thorns, and do not need to be pruned, mulched, or watered. But unless we are being deliberately dense, we know what Robert Burns had in mind. He meant us to see his "luv" as radiantly beautiful and sweet. "Life, like a dome of many-colored glass/ Stains the white radiance of Eternity," is a little more difficult, because it involves two comparisons: "life : dome of many-colored glass," and "Eternity : white radiance." But once we have grasped them, these comparisons enable us to visualize two abstractions, life and eternity, in a concrete way. They also imply that what is temporal "stains" what is everlasting and prevents us from seeing it clearly.

Imagery is a term used in the discussion of literature to mean not only pictures (visual stimuli) but also descriptions which arouse our other senses. "My luv is like a red, red rose" was undoubtedly intended to convey the idea of sweet fragrance, as well as of a fresh, blooming complexion. Comparison, is frequently a very economical way of summoning up, not a single image, but a whole related group of images. Common sense might suggest that if you want to talk about a pretty girl, you should talk about the pretty girl, not about scenery such as starry nights and roses. But very frequently, talking about scenery (if you choose the right scenery and describe it with enough precision) is the best way to talk about the girl after all. Comparison, by suggesting similarities we might not have thought of, often helps us to see more clearly what was under our eyes all the time, in the same way that traveling is said to make a returning traveler look at his homeland with new eyes. If you are talking about abstractions like "life" and "eternity," you will have no concrete imagery at all unless you talk in terms of scenery, so you have no choice. If you want to move your readers, you will have to help them see and feel "love," "truth," and "eternity" as if those very large, general terms were so many apples and pears. Only through comparison can you do this.

One phrase should probably be repeated: choose the right scenery and describe it with precision. "My luv is like a blighted rose" would suggest entirely different images.

Poets use figurative language in the interests of concreteness and economy. They rarely, if ever, use it to "pretty up" their poems. In good poetry, figures of speech are part of the overall structure of the poem. Often, they *are* the overall structure of the poem. When we rephrase the poem without its figurative language, much of its "poemness" leaks out. "Marcia Muldoon, 5'8", 120, 38-24-36" is no substitute for "She walks in beauty, like the night."

145

So far, we have been concerned with the simile, that form of comparison which employs a comparative term ("like," "as," "than"). Another very common figure of speech is the *metaphor*, which is a simile with the comparative term dropped out, so that the comparison is implied rather than stated. In the lines "Life, like a dome of many-colored glass/ Stains the white radiance of eternity," the first line contains a simile, the second line a metaphor. If Burns had written "My luv *is* a red, red rose" the simile would have become a metaphor.

Many metaphors are so much a part of everyday speech that we seldom recognize them. "The hours flew" implies a comparison of time to a bird. "He would not stoop so low" speaks of moral debasement, or humiliation, as if it were a physical action. Like many familiar metaphors, this one has passed into the language, so that it summons up no mental picture. When we were discussing connotations of words, it may have occurred to you that English is full of thumbnail descriptions such as "cat," "hawk," "ham" (meaning actor) and so on. Such common metaphors, which have lost their image-evoking quality through continual use, are called dead metaphors.

A figure of speech closely related to the simile and metaphor is *personification*. A personification speaks of the nonhuman as if it were alive. "The walls have ears," "The morning smiled," and "Fate was cruel," contain personifications of "walls," "morning," and "fate." A personification may be adopted by a poet for the purposes of a particular poem, or it may be traditional. Traditional personifications often are quite elaborate. Thus, medieval poets personified fate as a woman with a wheel. The Elizabethan poets personified passionate love as Venus, the Greco-Roman goddess of love and beauty, or her son Eros (Cupid), traditionally portrayed as causing love by means of his arrows. Figures who had been objects of serious worship in an earlier culture became personifications which the poet could use for his own purposes, once they were no longer seriously believed in.

Closely related to personification is the *apostrophe*, in which the absent are addressed as though present, the dead as though living, the inanimate as though animate. Wordsworth begins one of his sonnets, "Milton! Thou should'st be living at this hour," while Shelley combines personification and apostrophe in a single line: "O wild West Wind, thou breath of autumn's being."

Another fairly common poetic figure is *metonymy*, in which something is designated, not by its own name, but by the name of a thing resembling it or closely related to it. Thus we say, "I'd like a cup," for "I'd like some coffee," and "Give me a light," instead of "Give me a match," or "Give me some fire." In Shakespeare's play,

metonymy – another name, closely related.

Synechdoche – part used to signify the whole.

*Julius Caesar*, one famous speech begins, "Friends, Romans, countrymen, lend me your ears." "Ears" in this quotation is a metonymy for "hearing." *Synechdoche* is a figure of speech, in which a part of something is used to signify the whole, or a special instance used to signify the general principle. Thus workers become "hands," and cars are sometimes called "wheels."

Another related pair of figures of speech are *hyperbole* (or overstatement) and *understatement*. Hyperbole is a fanciful exaggeration. "Her eyes shine brighter than the stars," "I could drink a gallon," and "He roared like a lion," are all examples of hyperbole. ("Roared like a lion" is also a simile. Such overlapping in figurative language is common.) While hyperbole overstates, understatement does just what the term implies. The western movie hero who confronts nine barroom toughs, all armed to the teeth, and says to his faithful sidekick, "I think we're in for a little trouble," is using understatement. A specialized form of understatement is *litotes*, in which something is affirmed by denying its opposite. A climber just down from Everest says, "It's not an easy climb." A baseball manager says of a slow outfielder, "He's no gazelle."

Finally, poets often make use of the *paradox*, a statement that seems at first sight to contradict itself. "The pen is mightier than the sword" is an absurdity if we think in terms of physical combat; like most paradoxes, it becomes comprehensible if "pen" is viewed as a metaphoric expression (technically, a synechdoche) for the power of the written word, and "sword" as a synechdoche for armed might. Many religious insights are couched in paradoxical language: "Whosoever shall save his life shall lose it: but whosoever will lose his life for my sake, the same shall save it."

All figurative language involves some deviation from literal sense, some violation of our everyday view of things. This warping of reality—or, more accurately, this recognition that reality is frequently elusive—underlies *irony*—a recognition of the discrepancy between what happens and what is expected to happen, a gap between what is said and what is intended.

But not all such discrepancy can be classified as involving irony. A mainstay of comedy is incongruity—the pompous man hit in the face with a custard pie, the clowns' car in the circus out of which come seventeen people. Often comedy plays at the edges of serious ironies, however.

Sometimes irony is verbal, the gap between what is said and what is intended. Captain Lemuel Gulliver, in Swift's satiric novel, offers the King of Brobdignag the formula for gunpowder and instructions in the manufacture of firearms. The king tells Gulliver that "he would rather lose half his kingdom than be privy to such a secret, which he commanded me, as I valued my life, never to mention any more." Captain Gulliver then says, "A strange effect of narrow principles and short views! that a prince . . . of strong parts, great wisdom, and profound learning . . . should from a nice unnecessary scruple, whereof in Europe we can have no conception, let slip such an opportunity . . . that would have made him absolute master of the lives, liberties, and the fortunes of his people." Pretty clearly, Swift, unlike Gulliver, admires the "nice unnecessary scruple" which prevents the King of Brobdignag from promoting the introduction of what was, in Swift's day, ultimate weaponry. More savagely, in "A Modest Proposal," Swift proposed that the starving Irish tenant-farmers should market their children like suckling pigs at a year of age, thus providing a source of ready cash, a general stimulus to the economy, and a better life for the unmarketed survivors.

Sometimes irony is a product of situation. In *Macbeth*, a Scots nobleman is told by witches that he will succeed to another estate, and that he will become king. When the first part of the prophecy comes true, Macbeth and his wife on their own volition murder the king in order to achieve the second part. One murder leads to others, to civil war, ultimately to Lady Macbeth's madness and Macbeth's death.

Part of the irony in *Macbeth* is at the level of verbal paradox, as when Macbeth is told by the witches that he cannot be defeated "till Birnam Wood shall come to Dunsinane." He takes this as equivalent to meaning "never." But his enemies camouflage themselves with the branches of trees, so their army looks at a distance like a moving forest, and they defeat him. The witches' speeches did not mean what Macbeth thought. But if Macbeth is fooled by the witches, he is even more fooled by himself. An honest man does not consult witches to begin with. And he does not commit murder.

In fact (and this is typical of serious literature) there are multiple ironies to *Macbeth*. Macbeth has assumed that he can rule— that is, that he can dispense justice—after committing murder. He has assumed that power, which allows us to make of life what we want of it, will make him happy, and that ultimate power (kingship) will make him ultimately happy. In fact, kingship, acquired by force, makes him miserable. By the end of the play he has committed or commanded multiple murders, and been haunted (literally and figuratively) by his victims. His wife has been driven mad by guilt and is dead. His friends have deserted him. Macbeth the faithful, trusted subject has become Macbeth the lonely, hated king.

We have given examples of irony from the novel, the essay, and the play. Irony in poems is more often implied (as in *Gulliver's Travels*) than it is dramatized (as in *Macbeth*), but it can be used in either way. Here is a poem—"The Latest Decalogue"—in which irony

148

is prominent. "Decalogue" is another word for the Ten Commandments.

> Thou shalt have one God only; who
> Would be at the expense of two?
> No graven images may be
> Worshipped, except the currency.
> Swear not at all; for, for thy curse
> Thine enemy is none the worse.
> At church on Sunday to attend
> Will serve to keep the world thy friend.
> Honor thy parents; that is, all
> From whom advancement may befall.
> Thou shalt not kill; but need'st not strive
> Officiously to keep alive.
> Do not adultery commit;
> Advantage rarely comes of it.
> Thou shalt not steal; an empty feat,
> When it's so lucrative to cheat.
> Bear not false witness; let the lie
> Have time on its own wings to fly.
> Thou shalt not covet, but tradition
> Approves all forms of competition.

ARTHUR HUGH CLOUGH

Clough is, it would appear, giving us advice on "how to succeed." Actually, he is setting up a contrast between the ethical values expressed in the original Decalogue and the actual values of many "good" churchgoing businessmen, as they reveal themselves through behavior. Each couplet begins with a paraphrase of one of the original commandments, then goes on to give the practical application of the moral teaching.

How is the reader to know that Clough does not intend all this seriously? A naive or hasty reader might conclude that Clough was a heartless hypocrite; but in fact, a hypocrite would never write such a poem, assuming he had the poetic skill to do it, because it would tell too much about him. The lack of social conscience expressed in "Thou shalt not kill; but need'st not strive/ Officiously to keep alive" would never express itself openly. In fact, Clough's cautious churchgoing, money-grubbing sinner would never write in hard, pointed little

149

couplets. One can imagine such a person writing a vaporous oration, but never a poem like "The Latest Decalogue." The decision as to whether a poem, or part of a poem, is ironically intended, has to be made by the reader on the basis of the text he has before him.

Clough's poem illustrates some of the uses of irony. Clough could have denounced the behavior of his contemporaries outright in sermonizing verse. But sermons, as "The Latest Decalogue" implies in lines 7-8, are somehow always written for other people. Irony, plus a tightly controlled structure, gives Clough the option of launching his "latest decalogue" like ten sharp darts, to deflate (if not permanently riddle) the hypocrisy at which it is aimed.

Irony, like figurative language, always involves a double sense of reality—a comparison of *what is* with *what ought to be*, or of what was expected with what actually happened. A more complex sense of reality is conveyed by *symbolism*.

A symbol, most simply defined, is anything which represents, or suggests, or is associated with something else. All of us commonly use symbols. A piece of cloth on the end of a stick can rouse our strongest feelings of loyalty and sometimes even move us to tears, providing the piece of cloth is in the color and configuration of our nation's flag. The wedding ring, the cross, the cap and gown all have cultural significance and emotional associations which go well beyond their physical qualities. Wedding rings are not always the most expensive nor the most beautiful jewelry in the world, and, viewed purely as clothing, the tasseled mortarboard of the graduating high school or college student is about as useless a garment as anybody ever devised—it is not warm, it will not keep off the rain, the style has not changed for several hundred years, and it is difficult just to keep the thing on your head. Nevertheless, the ring and the cap are valued as symbols, of marriage on the one hand, and a certain degree of education attained on the other.

Symbols of the type we have been discussing are more or less common to a broad cultural spectrum. But symbols can be limited to a certain group or class of people, such as the members of a political, religious, or fraternal group. Or they can be individual. Most of us have collections of "worthless" articles—broken jewelry, old photographs, clippings from newspapers, outworn clothing, old letters— which would be of no interest to anybody else, but which we cannot bear to part with. Defining why they are valuable to us—what part of our past they represent—might be difficult even if we were only defining it to ourselves, for ourselves; and defining it for somebody else might be just about impossible. But symbolic value they must have; otherwise why do we react so negatively when mother, spouse, or helpful roommate says, "Why don't you throw out all that old junk?"

As it functions in a poem, a symbol must be considerably more general in its comprehensibility than the box of old junk we cannot bear to part with. But let us see how symbolism functions in "Loveliest of Trees" by A. E. Housman.

> Loveliest of trees, the cherry now
> Is hung with bloom along the bough,
> And stands about the woodland ride
> Wearing white for Eastertide.
>
> Now, of my threescore years and ten,
> Twenty will not come again,
> And take from seventy springs a score,
> It only leaves me fifty more.
>
> And since to look at things in bloom,
> Fifty springs are little room,
> About the woodlands I will go
> To see the cherry hung with snow.

> from *A Shropshire Lad*

Read at the literal level, this poem presents few difficulties. It is Easter; the cherry trees are blooming; why not take a ride and look at them? The only difficulty with this reading is that it ignores stanza two and lines 9 and 10 in stanza three. If you are accustomed to reading poems for pretty pictures and lovely words, you will perhaps accept the lines on that basis. "Threescore years and ten" sounds Biblical and dignified, therefore elevated, therefore "poetic."

But poets do not customarily throw away six lines out of twelve. Therefore, presumably those six lines are there for a purpose other than demonstrating A. E. Housman's facility with rhyme and meter.

What does the poet say? The first stanza describes the beauty of the cherry trees in precise terms. "Hung with bloom along the bough" evokes visual images of the blossom clusters scattered at intervals along the branches. He tells us, moreover, where the cherry trees grow (the "woodland ride" is presumably a bridle path through the woods) and that the trees are "wearing white for Eastertide"—which gives us the color of the blossoms, plus the time of year, plus a suggestion that the trees are deliberately dressed or clothed (he has already used the word "hung") in white for Easter.

The subject of the poem in the second stanza shifts to its speaker. "Threescore years and ten" is a quotation from psalm 90, verse 10: "The days of our years are threescore years and ten: and if

151

by reason of strength, they be fourscore years, yet is their strength labour and sorrow; for it is soon cut off, and we fly away." If we assume "threescore years and ten" is a high-flown, "poetic" way of saying "seventy," the entire stanza is merely an elaborate way of telling us that the speaker is twenty. It also contains a considerable overstatement—"fifty springs are little room." In human terms, fifty years are a lot of time, after all.

But is "threescore years and ten" merely an ornamental bit of "fine writing"? Fifty springs, if certain death is at the end of them, do not seem like quite so much time. So "fifty springs are little room," which seemed at first like an overstatement, becomes an understate-ment when we think of its broader implications.

Notice too, how the blossoming cherry trees of the first stanza give way to the more generalized "things in bloom" in line 9. Cherry trees are certainly "things in bloom"; but other things besides cherries also bloom. We speak sometimes of "blooming good health." If we broaden our field of references a little further, we remember such phrases as "springtime of life." "To look at things in bloom/ Fifty springs are little room," can refer equally well to looking at blooming cherry trees, to looking at girls, traditionally compared to flowers, perhaps even to all the ardors and ambitions of youth. (Psalm 90, from which Housman drew his "threescore years and ten," also says of mankind, "They are like grass which groweth up/ In the morning it flourisheth . . . in the evening it is cut down, and withereth.")

The final two lines bring the poem back full circle, to the "woodland ride" and "the cherry hung with snow." "Snow," as a metaphor for "white blossoms," is sufficiently unusual to startle us a little. We are accustomed to saying "snowy white," but that is not the same thing as "hung with snow." The blossoms are white, like the snow, but the use of the word snow reminds us of winter, cold, perhaps even death. Also, snow melts quickly, and spring blossoms last only a few days. The reason the trees must be seen now is because their blossoms, like human life, are impermanent; they must be enjoyed quickly or not at all.

It should be clear by this time that the blossoming cherry trees in this lyric are a symbol. When we discussed figurative language, we pointed out that in using a metaphor or simile, the poet establishes this sort of equation.

my luv is like a red, red rose        luv : rose

With a symbol like the cherries, we cannot make such a simple equa-tion. Housman lets us see, in the poem, that he is using cherries as a synechdoche in this fashion.

152

cherry trees : things in bloom

But "things in bloom" can so easily be taken to mean more than the blossoming trees, that obviously it is not the end point of the equation, but a kind of middle term. The final symbolic equation Housman sets up moves from a specific, sensuously realized image (cherry trees) to a slightly more abstract image (things in bloom) to a final, unstated but implied term.

cherry trees : things in bloom : transient beauties of this world

"Enjoy the transient beauties of this world before you die" is, therefore, a partial paraphrase of "Loveliest of Trees." But only a partial paraphrase. For we have lost the woodland ride and the cherry hung with snow, which are beautiful in themselves. Housman has been talking just as much about the cherry trees as he has about the transience of life, because, like all of us, he finds the annual recurrence of "things in bloom" both beautiful and painful. The "cherry hung with snow" is not so much wrapping paper for the little hard nugget of good advice; it is part of the good advice. The poem is not "deep" or "hard," if by those words we mean obscure, difficult to understand, requiring expertise for its comprehension. It is deep, however, in the quality it has of penetrating the world, of moving from one level of reality to another. And it is hard, if we can take this word to mean that "Loveliest of Trees" faces certain inescapable facts about human existence without flinching or self-pity.

The blossoming-cherry image of "Loveliest of Trees" is symbolic because of its *ambiguity*—the fact that it can be taken to mean or represent several different things or ideas. The ambiguity of the poet is conscious, unlike the unconscious ambiguity which is the result of sloppy writing or thinking or both. The cherry tree is a successful symbol because it has an open-ended quality. It represents something more than itself, but that something is not specified and limited in the way that, say, the red cross as a symbol has become limited to representing a certain organization. The student who expects symbols and their referents to have that kind of simple, one-to-one relationship is going to find reading poetry a slippery business, like catching fish with the hands. This does not mean that poets are necessarily evasive; only that, if they are mature, they have discovered that reality, the true meaning and nature of life and experience, is a veritable ocean of slippery fish.

The open-ended quality of the symbol does not, however, mean that "anything goes," and every man's interpretation of the poem is as good as every other man's. The possible referents—the

153

life-experiences, objects, or states of mind—which the cherry tree symbol may be taken to represent are limited. It would be extremely difficult to take the image of a blossoming cherry tree as symbolic, for instance, of the domination of the machine and the destruction of natural values. The tone of the poem acts to limit the possible referents of the cherry tree symbol also. Flowers are often associated with girls, and with sexual love, but that does not mean that every blossom in every poem is secret shorthand for a love affair. While Housman's "things in bloom" might in a general way include the pleasure of love, there is no other indication in the poem itself that the cherry trees really represent an erotic relationship. For that matter, the cherry trees are "wearing white for Eastertide," the church festival that celebrates the resurrection of Christ. Does this mean the trees represent immortality? Not if we take stanza two as meaning what it says. Both Easter (a time of vegetative as well as purportedly divine resurrection) and love fall into the larger category of "things in bloom." There is no reason, on the basis of the poem, to think that Housman was either writing in praise of a girl he knew, or writing a sermon for the Church of England. There is every reason to think he was writing, simultaneously, about the beauty of the world and the inevitability of death.

Much of the above should be taken as a warning for overeager students, who, once they have been converted from "message-hunting" a poem, become obsessed with symbol hunting. And many poems do not use symbolism to any extent. The symbol is neither a *sine qua non* nor a *bête noire*. It is simply another highly useful technique that the poet can use, like meter or rhyme, another net for the slippery catch of the world.

Classifying symbols is a tricky business. In a general way, symbols tend to fall into three basic groups.

The most obvious symbols, such as the cross, the stars and stripes, the hammer and sickle, or the wedding ring, are symbolically meaningful because they grow out of some shared group experience, or out of common cultural ties. They may, then, be thought of as *culture symbols*. Culture groups may be as large as all Christendom, or as small as a neighborhood gang, though the larger and more widespread the group, the more recognized will be the symbol. A culture group may be an organized political or religious entity, like the United States of America or the Catholic Church. Or it may be linguistic (English-speaking, Spanish-speaking), occupational (farmers, policemen, professional golfers), geographic (southerners, westerners, New Englanders), educational (all college graduates, no matter how different their alma maters, will have shared certain common experiences not shared by those who never went to college), or age-determined ("teenyboppers," "senior citizens").

Obviously, everybody belongs to more than one culture group. Remembering this will help us to remember that not all cultural symbols mean the same thing to everybody. Not everyone reacts in the same way to the peace symbol, Afro hairstyles, or a policeman's badge. Also, familiar symbols may be used in poems in unfamiliar ways, and if the reader grafts his own emotional response to a familiar symbol onto a poem, he may miss what the poet is trying to say. It is not impossible, for instance, that a reader with certain kinds of expectations might read Clough's "The Latest Decalogue," which we discussed earlier, as if it were a literal-minded exhortation instead of an ironic commentary. Only reading the whole poem and reacting to it with a consciousness of your own biases can tell you what symbolic meanings, if any, the poet has built into his work.

An unreflective, careless, or biased reading can obscure the most skillfully managed symbolism. But carelessness is not limited to readers. Occasionally writers fall back on the stock response, an appeal to the emotions aroused by familiar culture symbols and situations. The irresponsible politician "waves the flag" when he has nothing concrete to offer the voters. The reprobate, hearing the chimes pealing out "Away in a Manger" on Christmas Eve, suddenly repents of his dissolute life and is miraculously restored to the company of good, clean, home-loving, churchgoing folk. Poetry which uses familiar culture symbols and stock responses in this way is sometimes spoken of as *sentimental*. This does not mean that there is anything wrong with sentiment; rather it means that sentiment should spring from the work of art at hand, not be dragged in from the outside with the wave of a flag or a peal of chimes. If the reader suspects that the poet is using this kind of arbitrary, stock-response symbolism, he has a perfect right to feel just as he would if he caught the poet using loaded dice.

One important kind of cultural symbolism utilizes figures and emblems drawn from a given body of literature. *Literary symbolism* often transcends the boundaries of national, ethnic, and even religious groups. All of Western civilization shares the mythology of the Greco-Roman world, and a reference to Venus or Mars is equally comprehensible in Athens, Greece, and in Athens, Georgia. The whole storehouse of symbols having to do with the relations of lover and beloved, which was developed in medieval literature, is very much alive today, even for people who know nothing about medieval literature. We all know about the heartless lady, Cupid with his darts (originally a god in the Greco-Roman pantheon), and the courageous knight-errant. In Cervantes' Don Quixote, the knight-errant became both more human and more funny, and he also picked up a travelling companion who could be used for all sorts of purposes, from comic relief to straight man. The dynamic duo of hero and sidekick (with or without a damsel in distress somewhere offstage) is still as lively as ever, whether hero and friend ride off into the sunset on horse, Batmobile, or motorcycle.

An important and often neglected area of literary symbolism involves folk and popular art. A literary symbol does not have to be highbrow to be effective. Artists draw on their total life experience, not just on that part of it which is collected in anthologies or finds itself on lists of "great books."

Culture symbols, whether they are literary, national, political, or religious, are the products of a given social context, a web of social relations. Thus, they are limited both spatially and historically.

Underlying our time-and-spacebound culture symbols are natural symbols. In using the term "natural," we do not mean to imply that there is anything unnatural about mankind's propensity to organize into social and political groups. Nor do we mean to limit ourselves to physical descriptions of natural objects. We are suggesting that all human beings, regardless of their social context, have in common certain experiences involving physical nature (the alternation of night and day, the succession of the seasons) and also certain life experiences (birth, sex, parenthood, death). Of course the culture groups in which we live modify and structure our responses to the natural world. Nonetheless there is a nonsocial, nonhuman, physical universe *out there* (the same sun rises over Tokyo and Topeka) and an interrelated biological universe *in here* which is common to all members of the species *homo sapiens*.

Perhaps an example will help to show what we mean when we speak of natural symbols as "underlying" culture symbols. Here is a brief poem which you may remember from its earlier use in an exercise.

> Western wind, when wilt thou blow,
> The small rain down can rain?
> Christ, if my love were in my arms,
> And I in my bed again!

As Housman, in "Loveliest of Trees," implied a symbolic relation between the "cherry hung with snow" and the larger "things in bloom," so, we think, most readers of this poem would infer a connection between the "small rain" which the western wind will bring, and the consummated sexual love implied by the final two lines of the poem. Why do we make this connection, and why did the anonymous author of many centuries ago make it?

156

One way to answer this question is to say that water, fertility, and sexual love are more-or-less constant interconnected symbols throughout much English poetry. Perhaps the poet who wrote "Western Wind" had read the very lovely scene in Chaucer's *Troilus and Criseyde* in which a rainstorm keeps Criseyde overnight at her Uncle Pandarus' house, and she and Troilus consummate their love while the "smoky rain" falls outside. On the other hand, it is equally possible that the author of "Western Wind" was a man of little or no learning who had never read Chaucer or other authors in whose work sexual fulfillment is symbolized by imagery involving water.

Another way to answer this question is to say that water, fertility, and sexual love are fairly constant interconnected symbols throughout much European culture. Anthropologists trace myths involving water and fertility far back into Greco-Roman times. But the author of "Western Wind" may have been unacquainted with the Greek legend of Aphrodite, the goddess of love, arising from the sea foam. And probably he had not read any anthropology, for not much had been written by the fifteenth century.

Still a third way to answer the question is to suggest that the author used "small rain" to symbolize a sexual reunion because the image of rain seemed "right" or "natural" in its connection with images of physical satisfaction. But *why* did it seem right to him?

The anthropologists of whom we spoke a moment ago find that many kinds of symbolic equivalences (like that of water and sexual release) occur in much the same ways in many different cultures. Some psychoanalytic theorists, notably Carl Gustav Jung (Yung) and his followers, advance the notion of a "collective unconscious"— a pool of symbolic images more or less shared throughout time by the human race. Certainly, whether one accepts the notion of a collective unconscious or not, it is hard to imagine a culture in which spring is not equated with youth, autumn with aging, winter with death, water with cleansing, renewal, and fertility, and darkness with that which is unknown.

Whether or not there is a collective unconscious, it is not hard to see why the Greek love goddess born of the waves, the "small rain" of "Western Wind," and the blues song which begins, "You never miss the water till the well runs dry,/ You never miss your baby till she says goodbye," all establish parallels between water and sexual love. To anyone who has lived on a farm or ranch during a period of extended drought, or even lived in agricultural country, the frustration of waiting for rain is very like the frustration of sexual love denied an outlet. There are also physical similarities between "climaxes" involving water (the cresting of a wave, the onset of a rainstorm) and sexual climax. Finally, both rain and sexual love are rejuvenating and fertilizing agents—rain producing an outburst of productivity in

157

plant life, sexual intercourse producing both possible pregnancy and the symbolic fertility of physical pleasure and reaffirmed intimacy. As water is related to the basic human need for survival, so sex is related to that other basic human need, reproduction.

Historically speaking, most human beings have lived in rather primitive agricultural communities and still do. It is not surprising that certain kinds of symbolic equivalence (like that of water with sexual release, or spring with youth) growing out of the common experiences of weather, plant and animal life, and human needs and desires, should be made again and again.

Many psychological investigators see familiar human emotional needs reflected and satisfied in stories like "Jack and the Bean Stalk," "Dick Whittington and His Cat," and "Cinderella." Jack, the poor farmer's son, good-hearted though a little soft in the head, wins back the family patrimony and kills a horrible, cannibalistic giant in the process. Presumably, all boys with a grudge against either their fathers (who look very large when we are children) or their bosses (the giant lives at a higher level than Jack physically as well as socially) can identify themselves with Jack; they can glory in his triumphs without having to go through the messy business of demanding *their* patrimony from either Dad or the Establishment. It may seem a long leap, but the same conflict-of-generations pattern is involved in the Greek myth of Oedipus, as well as in Shakespeare's *Hamlet.* Similarly, in "Dick Whittington and His Cat," a poor boy whose sole possession is his faithful cat becomes, through luck and hard work, a wealthy man, eventually Lord Mayor of London—and how many novels and films have been variations on that theme? "Cinderella," of course, does for poor girls (and all girls at some point in childhood feel like kitchen drudges) what "Jack and the Bean Stalk" and "Sleeping Beauty" do for boys.

In addition to culture symbols and natural symbols, there are *personal symbols*. While the equation of spring with youth has been both a natural symbol and a literary symbol for about as long as there has been such a thing as literature, at least in the Western world, the "cherry hung with snow" which Housman makes the subject of his poem does not have traditional symbolic associations. There may actually have been a "woodland ride" about which Housman was thinking when he wrote the poem, or the "woodland ride" with its cherries may have been abstracted and imagined from blossoming trees Housman had seen in other times and places. For the enjoyment of the poem, it does not matter which is true. Some poets consistently use given symbols for given emotional states, so that their work is often more comprehensible read as a whole than when it is read piecemeal. Robert Frost, for example, frequently uses "woods" as a metaphor for the life of human beings. Some poets have stated that they were writing deliberately for an educated minority, and their poems may seem obscure to you unless you share the cultural background of the poet. Most poets, however, are concerned with being understood and with moving the general reader—if those two qualities can be separated. Poetry generally tries to bring them together. Symbolism is one way of doing it.

*Exercise 1*

## THE WINDOWS

| | |
|---|---|
| Lord, how can man preach thy eternal word? | 1 |
| He is a brittle crazy glass: | 2 |
| Yet in thy temple thou dost him afford | 3 |
| This glorious and transcendent place, | 4 |
| To be a ————, through thy grace. | 5 |
| But when thou dost <u>anneal</u> in glass thy story, | 6 |
| Making thy life to ———— within | 7 |
| The holy Preachers; then the ———— and glory | 8 |
| More rev'rend grows, and more doth win: | 9 |
| Which else shows wat'rish, bleak, and thin. | 10 |
| Doctrine and life, ————, in one | 11 |
| When they combine and mingle, bring | 12 |
| A strong regard and awe: but speech alone | 13 |
| Doth vanish like a flaring thing, | 14 |
| And in the ear, not conscience ring. | 15 |

*[handwritten margin notes near lines 5–7: "anneal — to stuffen wt heath make strong"]*

1. The missing word in line 5 is (a) speaker, (b) spirit, (c) confessor, (d) window.
2. The missing word in line 7 is (a) sanctify, (b) flow, (c) exult, (d) shine.
3. The missing word in line 8 is (a) power, (b) wisdom, (c) light, (d) fear.
4. The missing phrase in line 11 is (a) colors and light, (b) all that is wise, (c) God's laws and love, (d) the gifts of God.

ANSWERS

1. The title of this poem gives us the basic metaphor around which the poem is built. Line 2 states that a preacher is a "brittle crazy

glass." Choices (a), (b), and (d) all fit the iambic tetrameter pattern established for the second, fourth and fifth lines in each stanza. Only "window," however, maintains the metaphor. Choice (d).

2. Choices (a) and (c) are ruled out by metrical considerations. Both "flow" and "shine" are acceptable semantically and syntactically. Which one of these two, though, is more relevant to the metaphor? Choice (d).

3. Metrically, only choices (c) and (d) are possible, but again the metaphor is best served by "light." Choice (c).

4. All four choices here are metrically, semantically, and syntactically possible. Only "colors and light," though, supports the metaphor. Choice (a).

## Exercise 2 √

DIRECTIONS

For each of the quotations below, choose the appropriate identifying item from the column on the right.

1. My heart is like an apple tree
   whose bough is bent with thick-set fruit.

   A. Metaphor

2. Man is a watch, wound up at first, but never wound up again.

   B. Synechdoche

3. At morn, and even, shades are longest;
   At noon, they are short, or none;
   So men at weakest, they are strongest,
   But grant us perfect, they're not known.

   C. Paradox

   D. Simile

4. Love on her breast sits panting,
   And swells with soft desire.

   E. Understatement

5. So, Buddha, beautiful! I pardon thee
   That all the All thou hadst for needy man
   Was Nothing, and thy Best of being was
   But not to be.

   F. Hyperbole

6. I see those bright, young eyes,
   Seeking my wisdom.

   G. Personification

7. Two hundred years should go to praise
   Thine eyes, and on thy forehead gaze.

   H. Apostrophe

8. The battle was but a frolic
   In May; ten thousand stared
   Blind at the sun.

   I. Metonymy

ANSWERS

1. D (see p. 144)
2. A (see p. 146)

3. C (see p. 147)
4. G (see p. 146)
5. H (see p. 146)
6. B (see p. 147)
7. F (see p. 147)
8. E (see p. 147)

*Exercise 3* ✓

from *WAR IS KIND*

*lover*

Do not weep, maiden, for war is kind.                                1
Because your lover threw wild hands toward the sky                   2
And the affrighted steed ran on alone,                               3
Do not weep.                                                         4
War is kind.                                                         5

*Personification*
*+ Synechdoche*

    Hoarse, booming drums of the regiment,                 6
    Little souls who thirst for fight,                     7
    These men were born to drill and die.                  8
    The unexplained glory flies above them,                9
    Great is the battle-god, great, and his kingdom—       10
    A field where a thousand corpses lie.                  11

*child*

Do not weep, babe, for war is kind.                                  12
Because your father tumbled in the yellow trenches,                  13
Raged at his breast, gulped and died,                                14
Do not weep.                                                         15
War is kind.                                                         16

    Swift blazing flag of the regiment,                   17
    Eagle with crest of red and gold,                     18
    These men were born to drill and die.                 19
    Point for them the virtue of slaughter,               20
    Make plain to them the excellence of killing          21
    And a field where a thousand corpses lie.             22

Mother whose heart hung humble as a button                           23
On the bright splendid shroud of your son,                           24
Do not weep.                                                         25
War is kind.                                                         26

*black*
*drips w/ sarcasm*

161

1. Specifically, what makes this poem ironic?

2. What is implied by the imagery in lines 2 and 3?

3. What figure of speech is employed in line 7? What does the poet achieve through using it?

4. What figure of speech is used in line 23? What does the poet achieve through using it?

5. To whom or to what is the fourth stanza (11. 17–22) addressed? What figure of speech is used?

6. How many different audiences does the poet speak to within the poem?

7. Is the poem sentimental? Does it call on stock responses?

## Exercise 4

1. Listen carefully to the lyrics of some popular songs. Give two examples of each of the following kinds of figurative expression used in these lyrics. Are they effectively used within the song? Why or why not?
   A. Simile
   B. Metaphor
   C. Personification
   D. Hyperbole
   E. Metonymy or synechdoche

2. Describe how irony is used in the lyrics of a specific popular song.

3. What are three symbols that occur in the lyrics of a popular song? What classification do they fall into?

4. Many of the lyrics of popular songs are ambiguous. In what line or lines do you detect ambiguity? Are the words deliberately ambiguous or accidentally so? Why do you think so?

# 6

## Poems

Huswifery
EDWARD TAYLOR (1642–1729)

*A Poison Tree*
WILLIAM BLAKE (1757–1827)

*The Sick Rose*
WILLIAM BLAKE (1757–1827)

*The Tiger*
WILLIAM BLAKE (1757–1827)

*Snowflakes*
HENRY WADSWORTH LONGFELLOW (1807–1882)

*The Chambered Nautilus*
OLIVER WENDELL HOLMES (1809–1894)

*Luke Havergal*
EDWIN ARLINGTON ROBINSON (1869–1935)

*The Silken Tent*
ROBERT FROST (1874–1963)

*Disillusionment of Ten O'Clock*
WALLACE STEVENS (1879–1955)

*The Negro Speaks of Rivers*
LANGSTON HUGHES (1902–1967)

*90 North*
RANDALL JARRELL (1914–1965)

*The U.S. Sailor with the Japanese Skull*
WINFIELD TOWNLEY SCOTT (1910–1968)

*A Light and Diplomatic Bird*
GWENDOLYN BROOKS (B. 1917)

*In Defense of Felons*
ROBERT MEZEY (B. 1935)

163

## HUSWIFERY

Make me, O Lord, thy Spin[n]ing Wheele compleat;
    Thy Holy Worde my Distaff make for mee.
Make mine Affections thy Swift Flyers neate,
    And make my Soule thy holy Spoole to bee.
    My Conversation make to be thy Reele,         5
    And reele the yarn thereon spun of thy Wheele.

Make me thy Loome then, knit therein this Twine:
    And make thy Holy Spirit, Lord, winde quills:
Then weave the Web thyselfe, The yarn is fine.
    Thine Ordinances make my Fulling Mills.        10
    Then dy the same in Heavenly Colours Choice,
    All pinkt with Varnish't Flowers of Paradise.

Then cloath therewith mine Understanding, Will,
    Affections, Judgment, Conscience, Memory;
My Words and Actions, that their shine may fill     15
    My wayes with glory and thee glorify.
    Then mine apparell shall display before yee
    That I am Cloathd in Holy robes for glory.

EDWARD TAYLOR

## A POISON TREE

I was angry with my friend:
I told my wrath, my wrath did end.
I was angry with my foe:
I told it not, my wrath did grow.

And I watered it in fears,         5
Night and morning with my tears;
And I sunned it with smiles,
And with soft deceitful wiles.

And it grew both day and night,
Till it bore an apple bright;         10
And my foe beheld it shine,
And he knew that it was mine,

164

And into my garden stole
When the night had veiled the pole:
In the morning glad I see
My foe outstretched beneath the tree.    *He stole the apple & I*    15
                                          *killed him.*

WILLIAM BLAKE


## THE SICK ROSE

O Rose, thou art sick!
The invisible worm,
That flies in the night,
In the howling storm,

Has found out thy bed                                    5
Of crimson joy;
And his dark secret love
Does thy life destroy.

WILLIAM BLAKE


## THE TIGER

Tiger! Tiger! burning bright
In the forests of the night,
What immortal hand or eye
Could frame thy fearful symmetry?

In what distant deeps or skies                           5
Burnt the fire of thine eyes?
On what wings dare he aspire?
What the hand dare seize the fire?

And what shoulder, and what art,
Could twist the sinews of thy heart?                     10
And when thy heart began to beat,
What dread hand? and what dread feet?

What the hammer? what the chain?
In what furnace was thy brain?
What the anvil? what dread grasp                          15
Dare its deadly terrors clasp?


165

When the stars threw down their spears,
And water'd heaven with their tears,
Did he smile his work to see?
Did he who made the Lamb make thee?                    20

Tiger! Tiger! burning bright
In the forests of the night,
What immortal hand or eye,
Dare frame thy fearful symmetry?

WILLIAM BLAKE


## SNOWFLAKES

*[handwritten: personification 1st stanza]*

Out of the bosom of the Air,      *[handwritten: apostrophe]*
    Out of the cloud-folds of her garments shaken,
Over the woodlands brown and bare,
    Over the harvest-fields forsaken,
        Silent, and soft, and slow                    5
        Descends the snow.

Even as our cloudy fancies take   *[handwritten: reinforcement of above stanza]*
    Suddenly shape in some divine expression,
*[handwritten: similie]* Even as the troubled heart doth make
    In the white countenance confession,             10
*[handwritten: personification]* {The troubled sky reveals   *[handwritten: "pathetic fallacy" — giving to nature (or object) human feelings.]*
                                 {The grief it feels.
This is the poem of the air,
    Slowly in silent syllables recorded;
This is the secret of despair,     *[handwritten: melancholy at the essence of things]*   15
    Long in its cloudy bosom hoarded,
        Now whispered and revealed
        To wood and field.

HENRY WADSWORTH LONGFELLOW


## THE CHAMBERED NAUTILUS

This is the ship of pearl, which, poets feign,
    Sails the unshadowed main,—


166

The venturous bark that flings
On the sweet summer wind its purpled wings
In gulfs enchanted, where the Siren sings,                    5
    And coral reefs lie bare,
Where the cold sea-maids rise to sun their streaming hair.

Its webs of living gauze no more unfurl;
    Wrecked is the ship of pearl!
    And every chambered cell,                                10
Where its dim dreaming life was wont to dwell,
As the frail tenant shaped his growing shell,
    Before thee lies revealed,—
Its irised ceiling rent, its sunless crypt unsealed!

Year after year beheld the silent toil                       15
    That spread his lustrous coil;
    Still, as the spiral grew,
He left the past year's dwelling for the new,
Stole with soft step its shining archway through,
    Built up its idle door,                                  20
Stretched in his last-found home, and knew the old no
        more.

Thanks for the heavenly message brought by thee,
    Child of the wandering sea,
    Cast from her lap, forlorn!
From thy dead lips a clearer note is born                    25
Than ever Triton blew from wreathèd horn!
    While on mine ear it rings,
Through the deep caves of thought I hear a voice that
        sings:—

Build thee more stately mansions, O my soul,
    As the swift seasons roll!                               30
    Leave thy low-vaulted past!
Let each new temple, nobler than the last,
Shut thee from heaven with a dome more vast,
    Till thou at length art free,
Leaving thine outgrown shell by life's unresting sea!        35

OLIVER WENDELL HOLMES

## LUKE HAVERGAL

Go to the western gate, Luke Havergal,
There where the vines cling crimson on the wall,
And in the twilight wait for what will come.
The leaves will whisper there of her, and some,
Like flying words, will strike you as they fall;                    5
But go, and if you listen she will call.
Go to the western gate, Luke Havergal—
Luke Havergal.

No, there is not a dawn in eastern skies
To rift the fiery night that's in your eyes;                       10
But there, where western glooms are gathering,
The dark will end the dark, if anything:
God slays Himself with every leaf that flies,
And hell is more than half of paradise.
No, there is not a dawn in eastern skies—                          15
In eastern skies.

Out of a grave I come to tell you this,
Out of a grave I come to quench the kiss
That flames upon your forehead with a glow
That blinds you to the way that you must go.                        20

Yes, there is yet one way to where she is,
Bitter, but one that faith may never miss.
Out of a grave I come to tell you this—
To tell you this.

There is the western gate, Luke Havergal,                          25
There are the crimson leaves upon the wall.
Go, for the winds are tearing them away,—
Nor think to riddle the dead words they say,
Nor any more to feel them as they fall;
But go, and if you trust her she will call.                        30
There is the western gate, Luke Havergal—
Luke Havergal.

EDWIN ARLINGTON ROBINSON

## THE SILKEN TENT

She is as in a field a silken tent
At midday when a sunny summer breeze
Has dried the dew and all its ropes relent,
So that in guys it gently sways at ease,
And its supporting central cedar pole,                    5
That is its pinnacle to heavenward
And signifies the sureness of the soul,
Seems to owe naught to any single cord,
But strictly held by none, is loosely bound
By countless silken ties of love and thought              10
To everything on earth the compass round,
And only by one's going slightly taut
In the capriciousness of summer air
Is of the slightest bondage made aware.                   15

ROBERT FROST


## DISILLUSIONMENT OF TEN O'CLOCK

The houses are haunted
By white night-gowns.
None are green,
Or purple with green rings,
Or green with yellow rings,                               5
Or yellow with blue rings.
None of them are strange,
With socks of lace
And beaded ceintures.
People are not going                                      10
To dream of baboons and periwinkles.
Only, here and there, an old sailor,
Drunk and asleep in his boots,
Catches tigers
In red weather.                                           15

WALLACE STEVENS

169

## THE NEGRO SPEAKS OF RIVERS

I've known rivers:
I've known rivers ancient as the world and older than the
      flow of human blood in human veins.

My soul has grown deep like the rivers.

I bathed in the Euphrates when dawns were young.
I built my hut near the Congo and it lulled me to sleep.    5
I looked upon the Nile and raised the pyramids above it.
I heard the singing of the Mississippi when Abe Lincoln
      went down to New Orleans, and I've seen its
      muddy bosom turn all golden in the sunset.

I've known rivers:
Ancient, dusky rivers.

My soul has grown deep like the rivers.    10

LANGSTON HUGHES

## 90 NORTH

At home, in my flannel gown, like a bear to its floe,
I clambered to bed, up the globe's impossible sides
I sailed all night—till at last, with my black beard,
My furs and my dogs, I stood at the northern pole.

There in the childish night my companions lay frozen,    5
The stiff furs knocked at my starveling throat,
And I gave my great sigh: the flakes came huddling,
Were they really my end? In the darkness I turned to my rest.

—Here, the flag snaps in the glare and silence
Of the unbroken ice. I stand here,    10
The dogs bark, my beard is black, and I stare
At the North Pole . . .
                 And now what? Why, go back.

Turn as I please, my step is to the south.
The world—my world spins on this final point    15
Of cold and wretchedness: all lines, all winds
End in this whirlpool I at last discover.

170

And it is meaningless. In the child's bed
After the night's voyage, in that warm world
Where people work and suffer for the end                    20
That crowns the pain—in that Cloud-Cuckoo-Land    *fantasy world*

I reached my North and it had meaning.    *paradox*
Here at the actual pole of my existence,
Where all that I have done is meaningless,
Where I die or live by accident alone—                      25
Where, living or dying, I am still alone;
Here where North, the night, the berg of death
Crowd me out of the ignorant darkness,
I see at last that all the knowledge

I wrung from the darkness—that the darkness flung me—  30
Is worthless as ignorance: nothing comes from nothing,
The darkness from the darkness. Pain comes from the darkness
And we call it wisdom. It is pain.

RANDALL JARRELL


## THE U.S. SAILOR WITH THE JAPANESE SKULL

Bald-bare, bone-bare, and ivory yellow: skull
Carried by a thus two-headed U.S. sailor
Who got it from a Japanese soldier killed
At Guadalcanal in the ever-present war: our

Bluejacket, I mean, aged 20, in August strolled            5
Among the little bodies on the sand and hunted
Souvenirs: teeth, tags, diaries, boots; but bolder still
Hacked off this head and under a Ginkgo tree skinned it:

Peeled with a lifting knife the jaw and cheeks, bared
The nose, ripped off the black-haired scalp and gutted      10
The dead eyes to these thoughtful hollows: a scarred
But bloodless job, unless it be said brains bleed.

Then, his ship underway, dragged this aft in a net
Many days and nights—the cold bone tumbling
Beneath the foaming wake, weed-worn and salt-cut           15
Rolling safe among fish and washed with Pacific;

171

Till on a warm and level-keeled day hauled in
Held to the sun and the sailor, back to a gun-rest,
Scrubbed the cured skull with lye, perfecting this:
Not foreign as he saw it first: death's familiar cast.          20

Bodiless, fleshless, nameless, it and the sun
Offend each other in strange fascination
As though one of the two were mocked; but nothing is in
This head, or it fills with what another imagines

As: here were love and hate and the will to deal          25
Death or to kneel before it, death emperor,
Recorded orders without reasons, bomb-blast, still
A child's morning, remembered moonlight on Fujiyama:

All scoured out now by the keeper of this skull
Made elemental, historic, parentless by our          30
Sailor boy who thinks of home, voyages laden, will
Not say, "Alas! I did not know him at all."

WINFIELD TOWNLEY SCOTT


## A LIGHT AND DIPLOMATIC BIRD

A light and diplomatic bird
Is lenient in my window tree.
A quick dilemma of the leaves
Discloses twist and tact to me.

Who strangles his extremist need          5
For pity of my imminence
On utmost ache and lacquered cold
Is prosperous in proper sense:

He can abash his barmecides;
The fantoccini of his range          10
Pass over. Vast and secular
And apt and admirably strange.

Augmented by incorrigible
Conviction of his symmetry,
He can afford his sine die.          15
He can afford to pity me

172

Whose hours at best are wheats or beiges
Lashed with riot-red and black.
Tabasco at the lapping wave.
Search-light in the secret crack.                          20

Oh open, apostolic height!
And tell my humbug how to start
Bird balance, bleach: make miniature
Valhalla of my heart.

GWENDOLYN BROOKS


## IN DEFENSE OF FELONS

Winter will not let go of earth. The lust
Of a listless sun finds April difficult,
Weakly astonished that frost fights so hard.
The black earth still is tough in my back yard,
The brittle stubble has not begun to melt,          5
And in the shed, my frozen spade turns rust.

Possibly Winter is afraid of what
The softening soil might turn up to the sight—
Perhaps my spade would scrape against a bone,
Perhaps some half-starved animal would moan,        10
Having endured the long, relentless night—
Possibly Winter is ashamed of that.

How many stiff-furred bodies has she buried,
How many coverts converted into graves
About my house? All that I want to know            15
Is underground or underneath of snow.
But circumstantial icicles plunge from the eaves.
I know that Winter is at large, and worried.

Well, late or soon, the sun will have his day
And drive her into hiding, in the north.           20
And when that trouble's over, there will come
Swallows venturing back to their summer home,
And many citizen flowers will step forth
In the green wake of Winter's getaway.

173

And what of this felon who is doomed to be                    25
The hack and executioner of Time?
Her cruel hands are sweet, and death is worth
The green and giant labor of the earth—
I call her conscience clear, her breath sublime,
Striving with heat for balance, harmony.                      30

Sometime, not now, in bloody boot and glove,
Stirred by compulsive memories, she will turn
Back to these fields, again and again, until
The earth be driven against heaven's will
To its old asylum, where the sun would burn                   35
Winter and earth to ashes with its love.

ROBERT MEZEY

# 7

## Lining and Stanzaic Writing

Why is poetry written in lines? This is the sort of question
most of us rarely ask. Poetry is just "that way." We accept the
line in poetry, as we accept the sentence in prose, without
questioning its function. Inept oral readings of poetry seem
nearly always to proceed from the assumption that the line
is all-important, with the reader coming down hard on the word
at the end of the line and making a full stop there before
he continues.

Historically, we can understand how the line
developed. In its beginning, poetry was most often sung or
chanted, often to accompany a dance or ritual or game.
This meant a fairly regular rhythmic pattern, with frequent
breath pauses—in other words, lines of poetry, rather than
the more irregular unpatterned structures of sentence and
paragraph. The "timekeeping" function of the line is still
important today, even if nobody is dancing or tapping his feet.
The breath-pause function of the line would seem rather less
important, since poetry most often is read silently. But in fact
many, perhaps most, poets still think of poetry as primarily
oral art. And a considerable number of contemporary poets
who have rejected traditional forms use the breath pause as a
structural technique in their work.

In addition to its timekeeping and breath-pause
functions, the line as a structuring technique has some other
advantages. While few of us are wandering minstrels, and even
those who are usually do not have to depend on their memories alone, it remains true that it is easier to memorize regular,
fairly small word units, like lines, than the much more

175

irregular and variable word groups of prose. While "rememberability" is not quite the same as memorability, the two characteristics are certainly related.

The line also gives the poet structural advantages. The positions of greatest emphasis in the English sentence are, in order of emphasis, the end and the beginning. The same tends to be true also in the line, since the line is usually heard or read as a single sound unit. (Even if one line runs into the next without a break, producing a line which is *run on* or *enjambed*, there is still a longer pause between lines than between words, simply because it takes the eye more time to swing back to the other side of the page.) Therefore any word at the end of a line is an emphasis word. The poet can reduce the degree of emphasis by various metrical techniques, such as ending the line on an unaccented syllable. But often he wants emphasis. Positioning his key words at the ends of lines can give him that emphasis.

As we suggested, the line is often felt to be more or less equivalent to the sentence—that is, prose is written in sentences, poetry in lines. But of course this is not quite accurate, for poetry is nearly always written simultaneously in lines *and* sentences. The poet can build his lines so that sentence and line, or phrase and line, coincide, to make verse which is *end stopped*. Or he can, if he wishes, build his poems so that many of his lines are enjambed. In other words, he can parallel grammatical structure with line structure, or he can set up a counterpart (part logical, part rhythmic) between grammatical structure and line structure. Thus the line, whether or not it is written in a traditional form, gives the poet both a technique for emphasizing key words and a technique for varying his rhythms. The expressive possibilities which result from the double presence of the sentence and the line probably explain why free verse poets, who have rejected most conventional techniques, still retain the line, and why poems like Karl Shapiro's "The Dirty Word" (Chapter 9), in which lining is abandoned for prose-like sentence structure, are quite rare.

Poetry which is primarily end stopped has a contained quality, as if the poet were moving forward one step at a time. By contrast, poetry in which there is considerable enjambment is more fluid, less static. As with all poetic devices, the choice of end stopping or enjambment is related to the overall meaning of the poem as it expresses itself through its structure.

Consider the use of end stopping in this poem by Sir Richard Blackmore:

If casual concourse did the world compose,
And things from hits fortuitous arose,
Then anything might come from anything;

For how from chance can constant order spring?
The forest oak might bear the blushing rose,
And fragrant myrtles thrive in Russian snows;
The fair pom'granate might adorn the pine,
The grape the bramble, and the sloe the vine;
Fish from the plains, birds from the floods, might rise,
And lowing herds break from the starry skies.

*The Creation*, Book III

If this seriously intended poem seems slightly ridiculous to
you, it is not only because of its absurd imagery ("lowing herds break
from the starry skies"), but also because, with its end-stopped lines,
balanced sentence structures, and largely unvaried meter, it is such an
extraordinarily orderly poem. Blackmore describes total chaos
through line structures which approximate total order.

Compare the accommodation of line structure to sense in this
passage from Shakespeare's *The Winter's Tale*.

I would I had some flower o' the spring that might
Become your time of day; and yours, and yours,
That wear upon your virgin branches yet
Your maidenheads growing: O Proserpina,
For the flowers now, that frighted thou let'st fall
From Dis's waggon! daffodils,
That come before the swallow dares, and take
The winds of March with beauty; violets dim,
But sweeter than the lids of Juno's eyes
Or Cytherea's breath; pale primroses,
That die unmarried, ere they can behold
Bright Phoebus in his strength, a malady
Most incident to maids; bold oxlips and
The crown imperial; lilies of all kinds
The flower-de-luce being one!

Notice how much more flowing this verse is than Blackmore's.
In part, this is the result of very free, skillful metrical variation,
including the substitution of a tetrameter line, plus manipulation of
the caesura (pause within a line) so that it is rarely in the same posi-

177

tion two lines running. Enjambment here is used very freely; six out of these fourteen lines are run on. This gives Shakespeare a fluid, at times almost breathless line, which beautifully parallels the rush of growth implied in his succession of flowers. Where Blackmore's line orchestrates chaos to the tinkle of a Swiss music box, Shakespeare's line supports and expands his meaning.

Lines in English poetry are almost always grouped together. These groups are called stanzas. Some writers use the term "stanza" to mean only regularly recurring groups of lines of the same number, and prefer the term "verse paragraph" or something like it for less strictly patterned parts of poems. For our purpose, a *stanza* is any group of lines set off typographically from the poem as a whole. In long poems, of course, where line groupings may run for several printed pages without a break, the term "stanza" would be inappropriate. In such cases, we would probably speak of a "section" or "division." Often the poet solves our nomenclature problem for us by calling the divisions within his poem "books" or "cantos."

There are a large number of traditional stanzas in English poetry. Identifying them, and knowing something about their history, will help you to get inside poems in which they are written. In Chapter 8 we will discuss traditional stanza forms, turning our attention in Chapter 9 to nontraditional forms.

Before we begin considering how and why the major English stanzas came into being, perhaps we should ask ourselves the same questions about the stanza that we have asked about the line. Why do we have them? What functions do the stanzas serve?

One reason we have stanzas, presumably, is that poets have assimilated them through their reading and have then employed these familiar forms in their own poems. To some extent this is true, but another reason is that each stanza form has certain formal possibilities, and those stanza forms which have been widely enough used to be named and readily recognizable have demonstrated their potential expressiveness. But to talk about writing in stanzas is rather like saying, "We play on musical instruments." There are, after all, many kinds of instruments. The tuba is not a piccolo, nor is the technique of the violinist especially useful in playing the kettledrum. In other words, stanzas differ. They differ in what they can give the poet. They differ, also, in what the poet must put into them.

But let us turn to a concrete example. Here is a poem— "I Kissed Pa Twice After His Death"—written in one of the two or three most common stanzaic patterns in English, the four-line stanza or *quatrain*. The quatrains are in the form known as *ballad meter*— alternating lines of iambic tetrameter and iambic trimeter, rhymed *xaxa*.

I kissed dear Pa at the grave,
   Then soon he was buried away;
Wreaths were put on his tomb,
   Whose beauty soon decay.

I lay down and slept after the burial;—
   I had started to school, I dreamed,
But had left my books at home,
   Pa brought them it seemed.

I saw him coming stepping high
   Which was of his walk the way;
I had stopped at a house near by—
   His face was pale as clay.

When he lay under a white sheet
   On the morning after his decease,
I kissed his sad and sunken cheek,
   And hoped his spirit had found peace.

When he was having convulsions
   He feared he would hurt me;
Therefore told me to go away.
   He had dug artichokes for me.

Pa dug artichokes on that day,
   He never will dig anymore;
He has only paid the debt we owe.
   We should try to reach the shining shore.

MATTIE J. PETERSON

This is not intended as a parody, but as a serious poem. Undoubtedly Miss Peterson wrote from the heart, but that truth does not keep the poem from being a failure, which it is on almost every score possible. But if we consider some of the ways in which "I Kissed Pa Twice . . ." fails, perhaps we can go on to look at the demands of stanzaic writing with a more informed eye.

There are plenty of things wrong with "I Kissed Pa Twice . . ." besides the stanzaic pattern, but for the moment, let us limit ourselves to that. Miss Peterson was undoubtedly aiming for the alternating tetrameter and trimeter of ballad meter, though she misses as often as she hits. Furthermore, when a poet uses a four-line stanza, he sets up the expectation in the reader's mind that he will say something in four-line units. Successful four-line poems, like "Loveliest of Trees," do this. So do Keats's "La Belle Dame sans Merci," Suckling's "The Constant Lover," Johnson's "A Short Song of Congratulation," and a good many other poems included in this text. But Miss Peterson really does not know what to do with her stanzas. The first stanza seems almost like a warming-up exercise, since the decaying beauty of the funeral wreaths (a clichéd sentiment) is not developed in this poem. The next two stanzas are full of garbled time relations, perhaps the result of rhyme hunting. "His face was pale as clay" probably belongs to the dream sequence, but could just as well belong to stanza four. The final line of stanza five ("He had dug artichokes for me") has nothing to do with the three lines that have come before it. And halfway through stanza six, the author finds that she has run out of poem material with half a quatrain still to write. Either that, or the finality of "he never will dig anymore" seems downbeat and unchristian. In any case, the poem ends with a final two-line slosh of hymnal clichés, like a thick decorative layer of margarine over Pa's honest artichokes.

It may seem belaboring the obvious to discuss at such length why a bad poem is bad. But it is worth saying that what is wrong with this poem is that form and content are not combined. If it is hard to read "I Kissed Pa Twice . . ." while keeping a straight face, that is the fault of the execution, not the content.

There is nothing intrinsically funny about the events narrated in "I Kissed Pa Twice. . . ." What is wrong is that rhyme, meter, metaphor, diction, tone, and stanza form, instead of meshing so that they give an effect of wholeness and inevitability, all pull in different directions. The only things holding the poem together are its subject matter and its conformation on the page.

Amateur and beginning poets often think of the stanza as a kind of jug into which the syrup of verse is poured. Poets of a somewhat higher metrical competence than Miss Peterson (Edgar A. Guest, for instance) can, if necessary, water the syrup in mid-quatrain if they see they are running out. This is "fitting content to form" all right; but it is not the same as meshing content and form. Every form has its own imperatives, and often a certain kind of content seems to call for a certain kind of form. This is as true of nontraditional stanzas as it is of traditional ones.

For contrast, let us turn now to two poems in which, we believe, the possibilities of stanza form have been exploited to the fullest—poems in which the stanza form is not a jug but an instrument of which the poet demonstrates his mastery. Both of them are in the traditional accentual-syllabic form called the *sonnet*.

Though the name "sonnet" originally meant "little song," and was used during the Elizabethan era for a number of stanzaic forms,

*The Sonnet*

since that time it has been usually restricted to poems fourteen lines
in length, written in iambic pentameter, and using one of a handful
of accepted rhyme patterns. The sonnet has a long and interesting
history, which in some ways is almost a capsule history of changing
poetic tastes and ideals, and it has a number of variations; but for the
moment, let us limit our attention to the two major forms in which
it is written.

The older of these historically is called the *Italian sonnet*
(from its country of origin) and also the *Petrarchan sonnet* (from its
use in the work of the Italian poet Petrarch). The younger and more
popular form is called the *English sonnet* (because it was adapted by
English poets during the Elizabethan era) and also the *Shakespearean
sonnet* (because of Shakespeare's mastery in the form). In both
forms, the stanza is invariably fourteen lines, and is constructed in
what we might call a "question-answer" or a "tension-release"
pattern.

The Petrarchan sonnet is a two-part form, the first section
consisting of an eight-line *octave* rhyming *abbaabba*. The second part
of the Petrarchan sonnet (sometimes separated in print from the first
by extra space, sometimes not) is the six-line *sestet*, which is rhymed
*cdecde* or *cdcdcd* in Italian, but frequently rhymed *cdcdee* in English.
An important characteristic of the sonnet is what is called the *turn*—
the point at which the poet moves from doubt to faith, from abstract
to concrete, or from question to answer. In the traditional Petrarchan
form the turn occurs at the beginning of the sestet.

Here is the way John Keats used the traditional Petrarchan
form in "On First Looking Into Chapman's Homer."

Much have I travell'd in the realms of gold,
And many goodly states and kingdoms seen;
Round many western islands have I been
Which bards in fealty to Apollo hold.
Oft of one wide expanse had I been told
That deep-brow'd Homer ruled as his demesne;
Yet did I never breathe its pure serene
Till I heard Chapman speak out loud and bold:

Then felt I like some watcher of the skies
When a new planet swims into his ken;
Or like stout Cortez when with eagle eyes
He star'd at the Pacific—and all his men
Look'd at each other with a wild surmise—
Silent, upon a peak in Darien.

181

Chapman was an Elizabethan translator of Homer, whose presentation Keats clearly found more to his taste than the currently popular translation by Alexander Pope. The reference in the sestet to the Pacific refers to Cortez' sighting the Pacific after crossing the Isthmus of Panama. (Balboa, not Cortez, was the first European to cross the isthmus. Perhaps Keats meant to imply a parallel between Balboa, the first explorer, and Chapman, who "explored" Homer before Keats did—whose exploration, in fact, made Keats's possible.)

A single metaphor is used throughout the entire poem—that of travel. But it takes on a different dimension at the turn. The "realms of gold" are "goodly states and kingdoms"; settled, known places, as if, in his previous readings, Keats was taking a Cook's tour of literature. But with "Then felt I like some watcher of the skies" the metaphor shifts slightly. The tourist is suddenly an explorer, finding a new world and a new, immensely larger, ocean. In the octave, expressions such as "rule" and "fealty" underline the notion of something controlled, known; in the sestet, we have "new planet," "star'd," "wild surmise," and "silent upon a peak in Darien"—the men are too astounded at the vastness even to speak. "Peak" suggests emotional and literary heights as much as physical ones, and "Darien" is an exotic word, or was to a nineteenth-century Englishman. The sonnet has moved us from the beautiful and suggestive but rather abstract "realms of gold" to a final three lines in which appreciation for Chapman's skill as a translator has been transmuted into a vision of a little cluster of men on a mountaintop in a strange country, gazing at a strange sea.

"On First Looking Into Chapman's Homer" is a traditional Petrarchan sonnet handled in a traditional way by a man who realized the possibilities of the stanza form. The first quatrain of the octave develops the literature-travel metaphor; the second tells us that Homer's "demesne" remained a matter of hearsay until Keats read Chapman's translation. In other words, the first quatrain states the theme, the second develops and complicates it, a very common pattern in the Petrarchan sonnet.

Then with the turn we move to a new and heightened level of poetic intensity. John Keats, the armchair traveler, becomes, in a mere six lines, first an astronomer or navigator discovering a new world, then an explorer of what had been a new world to Chapman's century and was still a frontier to Keats, then the discoverer of a new ocean. All of this development—statement of theme in the first quatrain, development in the second, turn at the first line of the sestet, concrete development in the sestet of what has been more abstractly suggested in the octave—is quite conventional. Yet this is a stunning poem. There is no sense at all that Keats is slavishly following a preset form, because form and content are one. In fact, there is no straining anywhere, at least no straining we are conscious of.

It would be possible to spend a good deal more time on this poem alone; but let us briefly touch some of its high points. Notice the way the diction of the octave prepares for the sestet, especially "western islands" and "realms of gold." (The new world was quite literally a realm of gold for Cortez.) "Wide expanse" and "pure serene," which seem relatively abstract in the octave, become an actual ocean in the sestet; we can almost breathe in the salt air. Notice, too, the nice balance of "loud and bold" (the description of Chapman's style) with "silent" (the effect of the translation on the reader).

The point of all the above discussion is not that the reader of "On First Looking Into Chapman's Homer" is likely to spend much time sitting around thinking, "What beautifully chosen diction!" or "What a masterful use of caesura in the last three lines"—though these are things another poet might notice—but that, working together, they make a whole in which form and content, matter and manner, are well-nigh indivisible. We will not, at this point, suggest that the reader look back and reread "I Kissed Pa Twice . . . ." The point should be clear, however. Stanzas are not jugs. Without the sonnet form, Keats might have written a poem called "On First Looking Into Chapman's Homer," but it would have been a very different poem. "I Kissed Pa Twice . . ." (and many another more sophisticated effort) is a poem written in stanzas, but it is not stanzaically written. "On First Looking Into Chapman's Homer" is stanzaic writing of a high order.

The Petrarchan sonnet, we said earlier, is the oldest sonnet form in English, but not the most popular. From the beginning, there was a tendency to vary the Italian rhyme ending (*cdecde* or *cdcdcd*) with a terminal couplet, so that the rhyme ran *cdcdee*. Wyatt, who wrote the first sonnets in English, often used the terminal couplet. There was also the difficulty that the octave, in the Italian form, runs only on two rhymes. To find that many unworn rhyme words in English is difficult. The Shakespearean sonnet solved the rhyme problem by combining a more varied rhyme scheme with the terminal couplet. Instead of being divided into an octave and a sestet, the Shakespearean sonnet consists of three quatrains, each rhymed separately, and a concluding couplet. The meter is iambic pentameter, as in the Petrarchan sonnet, and the rhyme scheme is *ababcdcdefefgg*. Here is a sonnet of Shakespeare's.

> Let me not to the marriage of true minds
> Admit impediments; love is not love
> Which alters when it alteration finds

Or bends with the remover to remove.
O, no, it is an ever-fixed mark
That looks on tempests and is never shaken;
It is the star to every wand'ring bark,
Whose worth's unknown, although his height be taken.
Love's not Time's fool, though rosy lips and cheeks
Within his bending sickle's compass come;
Love alters not with his brief hours and weeks,
But bears it out even to the edge of doom.
    If this be error, and upon me proved,
    I never writ, nor no man ever loved.

*Sonnet 116*

As Keats's sonnet was typical in its development of the Petrarchan model, so "Sonnet 116" typifies the Shakespearean sonnet at its best. Notice the organizational difference between the octave-sestet arrangement and the three quatrains and concluding couplet. Here, instead of the Petrarchan pattern (statement of theme in quatrain one, development in quatrain two, turn at line 9 and metaphoric resolution) we have the Shakespearean pattern. Each quatrain in the body of the sonnet develops its own metaphoric content, though all are interrelated. The first quatrain tells us that neither change in the beloved nor physical absence can alter "the marriage of true minds." Love, in the second quatrain, becomes a mariner's landmark, or the star by which navigators steer. ("Although his height be taken" is a reference to the use of stars in navigation.) Finally, in stanza three, we are told that even age cannot destroy love. Lines 9–10 personify time in the traditional way, as a reaper, but the phrase "sickle's compass" reminds us also of the mariner's compass. "Love alters not" refers us back to "Which alters when it alteration finds" in quatrain one.

Then the turn and the resolution—and where Keats had six lines to resolve in, Shakespeare has only two. Therefore (again typical of the Shakespearean sonnet) the resolution is dependent upon verbal double-meaning and irony. "If this be error, and upon me proved/ I never writ, nor no man ever loved." (The final line can be read as meaning either "no man ever loved anyone," or "I never loved a man.")

A cynic, reading that final couplet, might conclude that indeed no man ever loved. But since "Sonnet 116" (with its predecessors and followers in the sequence) was written by William Shakespeare, at least half the statement must be true. In fact the concluding couplet is likely to make us shake our heads and reread the sonnet, especially if we have taken "marriage of true minds" as a metaphor for romantic love. As a close reading of the sonnet shows, Shakespeare is talking about ideal love, the "ever-fixéd mark" which inspires lovers to "bear it out even to the edge of doom." He may—scholars are not certain of this point—be talking about friendship between two men, and not necessarily a homosexual friendship either. Are the "tempests" storms of passion or argument between lovers, friends, husband and wife? They could be. But the very metaphors which underline the "ever-fixéd" nature of ideal love also indicate very graphically just about everything that can go wrong with human love—change, separation, disagreement. While suggesting that ideal love can bear it out "even to the edge of doom," the images of storms and lost ships suggest how near the edge of doom can be. Finally, the beauty of the ideal in no way diminishes the beauty of "rosy lips and cheeks." The poignancy of the couplet lies in its recognition that much which passes as love is not love, and that, in fact, "no man ever loved" ideally—to the extent and in the way that Shakespeare suggests. But if we feel tempted to reject the ideal as too hard, in the same moment Shakespeare's image of an "ever-fixéd mark," undimmed and undestroyed by our human deficiencies, draws us back to the ideal again. Simultaneously, Shakespeare suggests the difficulty of the ideal and its importance to us. For without that "ever-fixéd mark," we would not have even our imperfect human love, nor any excuse for the courage that "bears it out even to the edge of doom," nor any impulse to write in the difficult, demanding sonnet form as if it were easy—as if any lover could do it.

In this chapter we have compared three poems: one very bad poem, two which almost any reader would regard as great. We are not suggesting that Mattie J. Peterson could have written as well as John Keats or William Shakespeare, if she had only learned how to handle the stanza. For "handling the stanza," like handling metrical variation or choice of rhyme or diction choice or imagery or symbolism, widens out to include all the other skills the poet needs. But we hope we have demonstrated that the poet does not choose his stanzas arbitrarily, and that the interrelation between stanza form and poetic accomplishment is of more than passing interest. As we go on in the next chapter to discuss traditional stanza forms, bear in mind the ways in which Keats and Shakespeare adapted their chosen stanza form to themselves, and themselves to their form. But remember, also, that there must be thousands of abysmally bad sonnets in the language. Some techniques used in poetry have historically been more successful than others. But ultimately it is what the poet does with the technique that counts.

185

## Exercise 1

## ON HIS BLINDNESS

When I consider how my light is spent,           1
     Ere half my days, in this dark world and wide,      2
     And that one talent which is death to hide,        3
     Lodged with me useless, though my soul more bent    4
To serve therewith my Maker, and present           5
     My true account, lest he returning chide,         6
     "Doth God exact day-labour, light denied?"       7
     I fondly ask; But patience to prevent          8
That murmur, soon replies, "God doth not need     9
     Either man's work or his own gifts, who best     10
     Bear his mild yoke, they serve him best. His state   11
     Is kingly. Thousands at his bidding speed      12
     And post o'er land and ocean without rest:     13
     They also serve who only stand and wait."     14

1. The "turn" of this sonnet occurs in (a) line 7, (b) line 8, (c) line 11, (d) line 12.
2. The rhyme scheme of this sonnet indicates that it is (a) Italian, (b) English, (c) Petrarchan, (d) Shakespearean.
3. The basic foot of this sonnet is the (a) iamb, (b) trochee, (c) anapest, (d) dactyl.
4. The meter of this poem is (a) trimeter, (b) tetrameter, (c) pentameter, (d) hexameter.

ANSWERS

1. The question asked in line 7 is syntactically tied to "I fondly ask" in line 8; therefore the "turn" does not occur within line 7. Both lines 11 and 12 continue the argument begun earlier. Nothing signals a turn in logic, emotion, or approach. Looking back to line 8, then, we see the conjunction "But" which indicates the beginning of a counter argument, or the "turn" of this sonnet.
2. The rhyme scheme is *abba abba cde cde*. While the sestet's rhyme scheme (*cde cde*) is sometimes varied (*cdc cdc* or *cde dce*), both the rhyme scheme and the structural division tell us that this is an Italian or Petrarchan sonnet. Both (a) and (c) are correct.
3. This sonnet, as do nearly all sonnets, employs the iambic foot. Choice (a). Notice, however, the artful substitution of spondees— "dark world" in line 2 and "man's work" and "own gifts" in line

10. The inversions are noteworthy, too. "Lodged with me use . . ." in line 4 powerfully emphasizes the several ways in which "lodge" works in the poem.

4. Again, this sonnet is pentameter as are most sonnets: choice (c). Iambic pentameter is so irreversibly associated with the sonnet form that it is almost impossible to write a successful sonnet in any other foot or meter.

*Exercise 2*

# TO THE VIRGINS, TO MAKE MUCH OF TIME

Gather ye rose-buds while ye may, old time is still
a-flying; and this same flower that smiles today,
tomorrow will be dying. The glorious lamp of heaven,
the Sun, the higher he's a-getting the sooner will
his race be run, and nearer he's to setting. That
age is best which is the first, when youth and blood
are warmer; but being spent, the worse, and worst
times, still succeed the former. Then be not coy,
but use your time; and while ye may, go marry: for
having lost but once your prime, you may forever tarry.

1. How many lines are there in this poem? (a) 8, (b) 12, (c) 16, (d) 24.
2. How many stanzas are there in this poem? (a) 2, (b) 4, (c) 6, (d) 8.
3. What is the rhyme scheme of this poem?
4. What clue or clues did you use for determining the number of stanzas? (a) punctuation, (b) rhyme scheme, (c) rhetorical divisions within the poem, (d) intuition.

ANSWERS

1. Your reading of these lines should quickly give you an easy iambic flow. The punctuation of the first complete sentence gives you natural pauses after "may," "a-flying," "today," "dying." A check of these lines indicates alternating lines of tetrameter and trimeter, with an extra unaccented syllable in the trimeter lines. Following this principle, then, the answer is choice (c).
2. The answer here is choice (b), and the reasons will be discussed in question 4.
3. As was indicated in the discussion of question 1, lines 1 and 3, 2 and 4, rhyme, so the rhyme scheme is *abab, cdcd,* etc.

4. While intuition is a valuable commodity to possess when
approaching poetry, the proper information and analytic skills
can be useful too. For example, enjambed stanzas are not common in nonmodern poetry—and the diction should have told you
that this poem is not modern. There are four complete sentences
in the poem, so the sentence punctuation provides a clue. The
*abab* rhyme scheme is another. These clues when combined with
the rhetoric of the poem make the stanza divisions inevitable.
Stanza 1 (through "dying") addresses "ye" and urges her to pick
flowers while she still has time. Stanza 2 ("The glorious . . .
setting") compares the life and life span of the girl to that of the
sun. Stanza 3 ("that age . . . former") points out that for humans,
life is best in early maturity and that while life continues after
that, it gets successively worse. Stanza 4 ("Then be not . . . tarry")
again directly addresses the girl, urging her to immediately begin
enjoying life to the fullest. Each stanza, then, has a specific
function. Choices (a), (b), (c)—and (d), too.

*Exercise 3*

*Note:* The stanzas are not in proper order, except the first.

## THE ARROW AND THE SONG

| | |
|---|---|
| I shot an arrow into the air, | 1 |
| It fell to earth, I knew not where; | 2 |
| For, so swiftly it flew, the sight | 3 |
| Could not follow it in its flight. | 4 |
| | |
| Long, long afterward, in an oak | 5 |
| I found the arrow, still unbroke; | 6 |
| | |
| For who has sight so keen and strong, | 7 |
| That it can follow the flight of song? | 8 |
| | |
| And the song, from beginning to end, | 9 |
| I found again in the heart of a friend. | 10 |
| | |
| I breathed a song into the air, | 11 |
| It fell to earth, I knew not where; | 12 |

1. Stanza 2 begins with (a) Long, (b) For, (c) And, (d) I breathed.
2. Stanza 3 begins with (a) Long, (b) For, (c) And, (d) I breathed.
3. Which two couplets make up stanza 2?
4. Which two couplets make up stanza 3?

188

*Exercise 4*

*Note:* The first two stanzas are in order; the next three are not.

## THE SNAKE

| | |
|---|---|
| Daylong, light, gold, leans on the land. | 1 |
| You stroke the tractor. You *gee* and *haw*. | 2 |
| You feed the thresher's gap-toothed maw. | 3 |
| Then on a load-top, high, you stand | 4 |
| And see your shadow black as law, | 5 |
| | |
| Stretch far now on the gold stubble. | 6 |
| By now breath's short. Sweat stings the eyes. | 7 |
| Blue denim is sweat-black at the thighs. | 8 |
| If you make a joke, you waste your trouble. | 9 |
| In that silence the ———— with surprise. | 10 |
| | |
| Defiant, tall in the blast of day. | 11 |
| Now eye for eye, he swaps his stare. | 12 |
| His outrage glitters on the air. | 13 |
| ———————————— | 14 |
| Yes, they are men, and a stone is there. | 15 |
| | |
| Against the wounded evening matched, | 16 |
| Snagged high on a pitchfork tine, he will make | 17 |
| Slow arabesque till the bullbats wake. | 18 |
| An old man, ————, detached, | 19 |
| Spits once, says, "Hell, just another snake." | 20 |
| | |
| When you wreck a shock, the spot below | 21 |
| Is damp and green with a vernal gloom, | 22 |
| ———————————— | 23 |
| | |
| And you scarcely notice how they go. | 24 |
| But a black snake rears big in his ————. | 25 |

1. The third stanza should begin with (a) line 16, (b) line 11, (c) line 21.
2. The fourth stanza should begin with (a) line 16, (b) line 11, (c) line 21.
3. The fifth stanza should begin with (a) line 16, (b) line 11, (c) line 21.

189

4. The missing phrase in line 10 is (a) shout rings, (b) quiet comes, (c) noise thunders, (d) scream shrieks.

5. The missing line 14 is (a) Women scream and run around; the snakes at bay. (b) He's circled round; his eyes are only glare. (c) All yell and jump and at his flesh do tear. (d) Men shout, ring around. He can't get away.

6. The missing phrase in line 19 is (a) standing stooped, (b) bent over, (c) bending low, (d) standing rigid.

7. The missing line 23 is (a) Field mouse or rabbit flees its doom, (b) Animals run as shadows loom, (c) Mice chatter to a deathly tune, (d) Far off one hears the cry of a loon.

8. The missing phrase in line 25 is (a) broken room (b) ruined room, (c) shattered room, (d) Eden tomb.

*Note:* The poems for this chapter have been combined with those at the end of Chapter 8.

# 8

# Traditional Stanza Forms

Stanzas in English are organized in one of three ways. The simplest of these forms of organization to discuss (though not necessarily the easiest to write) is the *additive* stanza.

Additive stanzas are built up one line at a time. There is no precommitment by the poet to end the stanza at a given number of lines. The poem may be as long, or as short, as the poet wishes. If it is divided into stanzas, these too may be any length the poet wants. Additive stanzas are most often written in *blank verse* (unrhymed iambic pentameter), *heroic couplets* (rhymed iambic pentameter couplets) or free verse. Tennyson's "Ulysses" (blank verse) and the selection from Pope's *Essay on Criticism* (heroic couplets) are good examples of additive organization. (Unless otherwise noted, all the poems cited in this chapter will be found at its conclusion.) We will discuss free verse technique in Chapter 9.

Poems in *open* stanzas are composed in stanzaic units of the poet's choice, using any number of stanzas the poet wishes. In other words, a poem in quatrains may contain any number of stanzas; but they will normally all be quatrains. William Wordsworth's "I Wandered Lonely as a Cloud," Edgar Allen Poe's "To Helen," and John Crowe Ransom's "Here Lies a Lady" are all written in open stanzas.

Finally, poems are written in *closed* stanzas—stanzaic forms in which the number of lines, and, usually, the meter and rhyme scheme are limited and specified in advance. The sonnet is the best known and the most widely practiced of these closed forms; but there are some others which we will discuss.

191

In addition to its structural dimension, which is fairly obvious—we can count the lines in a poem and analyze its rhyme scheme—each poem carries with it a certain historical dimension. Just as words carry with them their connotations, often the product of past history, so any traditional stanza form has a certain structural connotativeness. A sonnet, just by being a sonnet (a form with courtly, aristocratic associations), arouses different expectations in the reader than a ballad; unless we know something about the history of the sonnet and the other traditional forms, we cannot really understand everything the poet is trying to give us.

Perhaps you remember our discussion, in the chapter on meter, of the way in which accentual-syllabic meter developed out of a merger of Old English and Norman French poetic techniques. Some of our most common stanzaic forms grew out of that merger, so it is worth looking at in a little more depth.

Old English verse was written in *accentual* measure. Each line contained four heavily stressed syllables in combination with any number of unstressed syllables. This heavy accentual "beat" was reinforced by concentrated alliterative effects. The Old English four-stress line was invariably divided into hemistiches, or half-lines, each (usually) containing two stresses. We can get some idea of what Old English poetry sounded like by reading some lines from Richard Wilbur's poem "Junk." Wilbur, a contemporary poet, uses Old English verse technique to write about a frequent Old English subject, the power of good workmanship. Another beautiful touch is that Wilbur uses a nearly obsolete prosody in order to write about objects which are themselves obsolete and considered useless. His choice of meter and stanza pattern reinforce references to Wayland, the magician and blacksmith of Teutonic mythology, and Hephaestus, the lame blacksmith-god of the Greeks.

> The sun shall glory
>       in the glitter of glass-chips,
> Forseeing the salvage
>       of the prisoned sand,
> And the blistering paint
>       peel off in patches,
> That the good grain
>       be discovered again.
> Then burnt, bulldozed,
>       they shall all be buried
> To the depth of diamonds
>       in the making dark

Where halt Hephaestus
    keeps his hammer
And Wayland's work
    is worn away.

Most Teutonic languages, including English, are accentual in nature, and their poetry uses primarily accentual meters. Romance languages (like French) are much less accentual. In their poetry, and that of some other languages, stress is ignored. The meter of a line is determined by the number of syllables which it contains. This kind of meter is called *syllabic*.

Out of the tension between the two forms, accentual-syllabic meter evolved; but there were numerous experiments along the way in pure accentualism and pure syllabism. Syllabic verse is particularly difficult in English because we are accustomed to paying attention to stress patterns (not only in poetry, but in other writing) and not accustomed to counting syllables. Though fine accentual poetry (like "Junk") and fine syllabic poetry (some of which we will discuss in Chapter 9) has been written in the twentieth century, for most of the period between the fourteenth and twentieth centuries both accentual and syllabic meters were assimilated into the prevailing accentual-syllabic meter. In some historic periods, English verse is heavily stressed; in others, smooth and regular, depending on the extent to which the taste of the time favors accentualism or syllabism.

Out of the confusion and experimentation which produced a common language (English) and a common meter (accentual-syllabic) came also our two chief stanzaic forms. Ballad stanza (quatrains of alternating iambic tetrameter and trimeter, rhymed *xaxa*) became a common vehicle for folk expression. The sixteenth century saw the development of blank verse, with its flexible line and movable caesura.

The Tudor and Elizabethan periods in England saw a great proliferation of poetic forms. Many continental stanzas were introduced, most notably the sonnet. At this time, too, the first of many attempts was made to write English poems in *quantitative* meter. Quantitative meter is meter in which the structure of the line is based on the durations of individual syllables—the length of time they take to say—rather than on patterns of stress. But attempts to transplant the meters of classical Greek and Latin to English have been largely unproductive. As with syllabic verse, the heavy stresses of English fight against a nonaccentual norm. In addition, English has many more vowel and consonant sounds than Latin or Greek, so English "quantities" (the "longness" or "shortness" of a given sound) never seem fixed as they do in the classical tongues.

The experimentalism of the sixteenth and early seventeenth centuries, which produced an enormously flexible, varied line in

Shakespeare's late plays and a sometimes deliberately rough metric in the poems of John Donne, was beginning by the middle of the seventeenth century to subside in favor of a smoother, less accentual, more syllabic line. The poems of John Milton show the beginnings of the change. Milton substitutes very freely in his verse, but his iambic pentameter lines are predominantly ten-syllable as well as five-stress.

In eighteenth-century poetry, smoothness reigned supreme. The *elisions* (words with dropped letters or fused sounds, such as "ne'er," "o'er," "Heav'n") which you encounter in the poetry of men like John Dryden and Alexander Pope, are not just "poeticisms," but a tightening-up of the language, a tightening deemed necessary by poets to whom a substitution in any but duple meter would have been a gross breach of artistic taste. This Age of Reason, as it is sometimes called, glorified urbanity, good taste, restraint, civilized behavior, rationality, wit. It saw the poet less as a seer, more as a wise commentator on human frailties and foibles, with the intent of correcting them. Much of its best work was satiric.

Though other poetic forms were used, the real soul of the age is in the heroic couplet. Rhymed iambic pentameter couplets were first used, and well used, by Geoffrey Chaucer in the late fourteenth century; and they had been used periodically in one form or another before the eighteenth century. In fact, virtually all English rhyming forms are combinations of couplets and quatrains, in one variation or another. But the eighteenth century polished and refined the closed iambic pentameter couplet, called "heroic" because of its use by Dryden and Pope in their translations of Virgil and Homer, and turned it into a supreme instrument of wit and rationality. The taste of the age ran to balance and antithesis, often used to comic effect.

> Not louder shrieks to pitying Heaven are cast,
> When husbands, or when lap-dogs breathe their last.
>
> ... There heroes' wits are kept in ponderous vases,
> And beaux' in snuff-boxes and tweezer cases.
> There broken vows and death-bed alms are found,
> And lovers' hearts with ends of riband bound,
> The courtier's promises, and sick man's prayers,
> The smiles of harlots, and the tears of heirs.
>
> from *The Rape of the Lock,* ALEXANDER POPE

Notice the balancing both of ideas and sentence structure, and the self-contained, epigrammatic quality. The heroic couplet is also

194

eminently suited for didactic poetry, as in the selection from Pope's *Essay on Criticism* at the end of this chapter. Much of the spirit of the age can be summed up in his, "Know then thyself, presume not God to scan,/ The proper study of mankind is man."

As eighteenth-century poetry reacted against what it often saw as the excesses of the too-exuberant Elizabethans, so the poetry of the early nineteenth century challenged the values of the Age of Reason. The Romantic movement, which some would argue is still going on, was identified generally with a challenging of fixed institutions and ideas and with the movement of authority away from the court and the *beau monde* to the individual. In the nineteenth century a cool, orderly, hierachical world began to disintegrate (from the viewpoint of people who like orderly hierachies) or to expand (from the viewpoint of people who like their life experience more-or-less free form). The man on the street might have remained untouched by the revolutionary fervor and individualism of Byron and Shelley, but the mental structure of his world could not indefinitely withstand the undermining effect of Darwin, Marx, Freud, and their followers. There would be—there were and still are—frequent retreats from the huge untidiness of the world into national, religious, political, or artistic parochialism. But it seems unlikely that anyone will ever again be able to say, with the conviction of an Alexander Pope, "Whatever is, is right."

Much poetic technique which we think of as "modern" began in the nineteenth century. The strict accentual-syllabism of the heroic couplet yielded to a looser, more strongly accentual verse. Triple-meter substitutions were once more permitted. A tide of formal experimentation revived many Elizabethan forms, and the Romantic enthusiasms for that which was "natural" and uncivilized had the good effect of preserving many fine old ballads, along with a certain amount of "ye olde tea shoppe" sham. Folk forms were used for serious literary purposes. But this was only the beginning. By the 1850's Emily Dickinson was experimenting with slant rhyme and Walt Whitman published *Leaves of Grass*, which shocked by its manner (free verse) as much as by its matter (frank celebration of physical being and sexual love). Formal experimentation has continued both in England and America straight through the first seventy years of the twentieth century and shows no signs of subsiding today.

Now that we have at least a general notion of the ways in which poetry changes and is changed by the taste of the age which produced it, let us discuss briefly the major English stanza forms. We have already analyzed the additive forms (blank verse, heroic couplet, and free verse) so let us begin with the open stanzas.

## COUPLETS

Lines rhymed in pairs are common in English poetry. We have already discussed the heroic couplet, but couplets are written in all meters and all line lengths. Occasionally a poem will be written in unrhymed couplets, or with the couplets rhymed, but composed of metrically uneven lines.

## THREE-LINE STANZAS

These are quite rare in English. If a three-line stanza rhymes *aaa*, it is called a *triplet;* if it rhymes in any other pattern, it is called a *tercet*.

Two forms are sufficiently important to deserve mention. The first, *terza rima,* is the stanza of Dante's *Divine Comedy.* The meter in Italian is iambic pentameter with an extra syllable, but English-speaking poets have used various meters. The rhyme is interlocking, rhyming *aba, bcb, cdc,* and so on. Probably the most famous *terza rima* poem in English is Shelley's "Ode to the West Wind." The interlocking rhyme gives great structural density, but it is hard for an English poet to find enough rhymes for a *terza rima* poem of any length. Philip Booth's "North," a fine contemporary example of *terza rima,* solves the rhyme problem by using slant rather than full rhyme.

The second three-line stanza of any importance is the *blues stanza.* While song forms such as the ballad, the work song, and the spiritual are an important element in the cultural heritage upon which poets draw, especially American poets, most of them are written in stanza forms of English origin. But the blues stanza is uniquely Afro-American, possibly with West African antecedents.

Though blues stanzas approximate tetrameter or pentameter, it is most sensible to think of them prosodically as four-beat accentual lines, written to the measure of the characteristic twelve-bar musical form to which they are usually sung. Langston Hughes' poem "Evenin' Air Blues" is divided into six-line stanzas, but transcribers of sung blues most frequently use three-line stanzas, each stanza rhymed independently. The rhyming pattern is *aaa, bbb* and so forth, with the first and second lines identical, or nearly so. (A repeated line of this type is called a *refrain.*) The best blues are characterized by pungent, earthy, colloquial language and a tough-minded stoicism which is often very moving.

## QUATRAIN

The quatrain is by all odds the commonest stanza form in English. The most familiar form is the ballad stanza, alternating iambic tetrameter and trimeter lines. The most common rhyme pattern is *xaxa,* but the pattern *abab* also occurs. The "*In Memoriam*" stanza (so-called from Tennyson's use of it in the poem-sequence of that name and quoted below) is an iambic tetrameter quatrain rhyming *abba*.

> Our little systems have their day;
>> They have their day and cease to be;
>> They are but broken lights of thee,
> And thou, O Lord, art more than they.

Another tetrameter quatrain form is the *Rubaiyyat stanza*, devised by Edward Fitzgerald for his translation of Omar Khayyam's Persian poem. The rhyme scheme is *aaxa*. Other occasional tetrameter quatrains also occur.

The term *heroic quatrain* is sometimes used for an iambic pentameter quatrain rhyming *abab*. Its most familiar use, probably, is in Thomas Gray's "Elegy Written in a Country Church Yard."

> The curfew tolls the knell of parting day;
>> The lowing herd winds slowly o'er the lea;
> The ploughman homeward plods his weary way,
>> And leaves the world to darkness and to me.

John Crowe Ransom, in "Here Lies a Lady," uses the five-stress line and rhyme scheme of the heroic quatrain, but subtly alters its rhythmic pattern by freely using dactylic and anapestic substitutions.

Quatrains are written in a variety of line lengths, meters, and rhyme schemes, in addition to those we have discussed.

## Five-line Stanzas

There are numerous five-line stanzas. The most common rhyme scheme is *ababb*, which is of course an alternating-rhyme quatrain with one extra line. Poe's "To Helen" is written in this pattern. But line lengths, rhyme schemes, and meters vary.

The best-known five-line stanza is the *limerick*, of which lines 1, 2, and 5 are anapestic trimeter, lines 3 and 4 anapestic dimeter, with a rhyme scheme of *aabba*. The verse is often irregular, the rhymes intentionally comic, the subject matter humorous when it is not scatological. Here is a familiar printable limerick.

> There was on old man of Nantucket
> Who kept all his cash in a bucket;
>> But his daughter, named Nan,

197

Ran away with a man,
And as for the bucket, Nantucket.

## SIX-LINE STANZAS

Common six-line stanza forms include three grouped couplets rhyming *aabbcc,* or a quatrain-couplet combination rhyming *ababcc.* The quatrain-couplet combination is called a *stave of six.* It is the form Wordsworth uses in "I Wandered Lonely as a Cloud," and Donald Justice uses in "In Bertram's Garden."

## SEVEN-LINE STANZAS

The only seven-line stanza (septet) with much traditional standing is *rhyme royal,* also called Chaucerian stanza. It is iambic pentameter rhyming *ababbcc.*

> Without the bed her other fair hand was
> On the green coverlet; whose perfect white
> Show'd like an April daisy on the grass,
> With pearly sweat resembling dew of night.
> Her eyes, like marigolds, had sheath'd their light,
> And canopied in darkness sweetly lay,
> Till they might open to adorn the day.

from *The Rape of Lucrece,* WILLIAM SHAKESPEARE

## EIGHT-LINE STANZAS

Just as it is easy to make a six-line stanza by fusing three couplets, or a quatrain and a couplet, so it is easy to make an eight-line stanza by various combinations of quatrains and couplets, in various meter and rhyme schemes. The best known of the eight-line stanzas is *ottava rima.* Its history is of the kind that makes editors cautious about generalizations.

As the name suggests, *ottava rima* is an Italian importation, like *terza rima.* Widely practiced during the Renaissance, it was abandoned till Byron took it as the stanza for his long, discursive poem, *Don Juan. Ottava rima* is iambic pentameter rhyming *abababcc* and in Byron's hands it is racy, witty, humorous, and debunking.

> What are the hopes of man? Old Egypt's King
>     Cheops erected the first pyramid
> And largest, thinking it was just the thing
>     To keep his memory whole, and mummy hid:

But somebody or other rummaging
   Burglariously broke his coffin's lid.
Let not a monument give you or me hopes,
Since not a pinch of dust remains of Cheops.

   *Don Juan,* Canto I

The marriage of Byron's lightly satiric manner with the
*ottava rima* stanza seemed to fix it permanently as a semihumorous,
satiric verse form—in fact, as the stanza in which Byron wrote
*Don Juan.* Then William Butler Yeats began writing this kind of
*ottava rima.*

I dream of a Ledaen body, bent
Above a sinking fire, a tale that she
Told of a harsh reproof, or trivial event
That changed some childish day to tragedy—
Told, and it seemed that our two natures blent
Into a sphere from youthful sympathy,
Or else, to alter Plato's parable,
Into the yolk and white of the one shell.

   from *Among School Children*

This is poetry of high seriousness and gravity. More than
once, some stanza or technique has been cast in a certain role deemed
"appropriate" for it, till a poet of different sensibility saw that it
had other possibilities.

## NINE-LINE STANZAS

The only named nine-line stanza is the *Spenserian stanza.* The rhyme
pattern is *ababbcbcc,* with the first eight lines in iambic pentameter,
the last in hexameter. Edmund Spenser invented this form for his
long allegory *The Faery Queene,* but some of the loveliest Spenserian
stanzas in the world occur in John Keats's "Eve of St. Agnes."

Full on this casement shone the wintry moon,
And threw warm gules on Madeline's fair breast,
As down she knelt for heaven's grace and boon;
Rose-bloom fell on her hands, together prest,
And on her silver cross soft amethyst,
And on her hair a glory, like a saint:

She seemed a splendid angel, newly drest,
    Save wings, for heaven:—Prophyro grew faint:
She knelt, so pure a thing, so free from mortal taint.

Though stanzas longer than nine lines are not uncommon
in English, none of them has been of sufficiently frequent occurrence
to acquire a name, except for some of the closed forms.

*Closed stanzas,* as we mentioned earlier, are stanza forms
like the sonnet, in which the number of lines employed and, usually,
the rhyme scheme and meter are specified in advance. The sonnet
itself is the only closed form of really common occurrence. Introduced
during the Elizabethan era in its Petrarchan or Italian form (the
rhyme scheme used by Keats in "On First Looking Into Chapman's
Homer"), it was even more widely practiced in the English or
Shakespearean form, as in "Sonnet 116." Elizabethan sonnets are
typically parts of sonnet sequences, groups of related sonnets written
to the poet's real, desired, or imagined mistress. Donne and Milton
later turned the intensity of the sonnet to religious subjects. Donne's
deliberately rough metrics disrupted the smoothness of the "sugared"
style, and Milton's fondness for enjambment produced what is
sometimes called the *Miltonic* sonnet—a Petrarchan sonnet with the
octave spilling over into the sestet, and the turn occurring in the middle
of the ninth line, or even later. The eighteenth century, with its
rationalizing, satiric forms, did not excel at the sonnet, but Romantic
poets like Wordsworth, Keats, and Shelley revived it, and their
sonnets are among the finest in the language. Later in the nineteenth
century, George Meredith created a sixteen-line sonnet, now called
the *Meredithian* sonnet. Gerard Manley Hopkins, who wrote in
the late nineteenth century but was not published until 1913, wrote
both conventional sonnets and an abbreviated form he invented
called the *curtal* sonnet. In twentieth-century America, fine traditional
sonnets were written by Edwin Arlington Robinson and Robert Frost,
and interesting experimental sonnets by e. e. cummings.

In addition to the sonnet, a number of other closed stanza
forms, most of them French in origin, are occasionally used in English.
All of them are somewhat complicated and artificial and some of
them are quite rare.

Probably the form most often turned to serious purposes,
at least in the twentieth century, is the *villanelle.* It consists of
five three-line stanzas rhyming *aba,* and a concluding stanza of four
lines rhyming *abaa.* The first and third lines of the opening tercet
are repeated alternately as a refrain closing the succeeding stanzas
and are joined as the concluding couplet of the quatrain. In other

words, line 1 is repeated as lines 6, 12, and 18, line 3 repeated as lines 9, 15, and 19. While many villanelles are light and playful, Dylan Thomas' "Do Not Go Gentle Into That Good Night" demonstrates the serious possibilities of this form.

The *sestina* consists of six six-line pentameter stanzas and a concluding pentameter tercet. Instead of some rhyme scheme, the stanzas are tied together by a pattern of repetition in which the line endings of each stanza repeat, in a different and pre-determined pattern, the end words of the first stanza. The usual arrangement is *abcdef, faebdc, cfdabe, ecbfad, daecfb, bdfeca, eca.* Notice that Rudyard Kipling's "Sestina of the Tramp Royal" adds an extra fillip by incorporating the *b, d,* and *f* line-end words at midline positions in the final tercet. Kipling has also combined an elaborate, highly structured and formalized Italianate form with cockney dialect.

The *ballade* is a French form, of which Chaucer is said to have written the first examples in English. It consists of three stanzas of eight or ten lines each and a concluding envoy (or dedicatory stanza) of from four to six lines. The entire poem runs on three or four rhymes, but no rhyme word may be repeated, and the last line of the first stanza becomes the concluding line for all other stanzas and the envoy. The commonest rhyme scheme is *ababbcbc.* Dante Gabriel Rosetti's translation of Francois Villon's "*Ballade des Dames du Temp Jadis*" is probably the most famous post-Chaucerian ballade. Rosetti called his ballade "The Ballad of Dead Ladies." Nevertheless it *is* a ballade, not a ballad.

The *rondeau* is typically fifteen lines using but two rhymes; the first word or opening phrase of the first line is repeated as a refrain after the eighth, and again after the fourteenth line. The usual stanzaic grouping is *aabba, aabR, aabbaR,* ("R" representing the refrain") and the tone is nearly always light and playful. Paul Lawrence Dunbar's "We Wear the Mask," however, is a serious poem. Dunbar very effectively uses the slightly stilted, artificial quality of the form to parallel the "mask" which blacks often feel they must wear in white society.

The *rondel* is usually a poem of fourteen lines using but two rhymes; the first two lines are repeated verbatim as lines 7 and 8 and again as lines 13 and 14. However, the pattern can be varied. Louise Townsend Nicholl uses a slight variation from the norm quite effectively in "Rondel for Middle Age."

The smallest and tightest of the French closed forms is the *triolet,* usually an eight-line tetrameter stanza rhyming *abaaabab.* Lines 1, 4, and 7 are identical, as are lines 2 and 8. Obviously it is very difficult to write a triolet that really says anything, and a good many triolets are devoted to discussions of the form in which they are written, subject matter presumably of little interest to anyone but triolet fans. However, Robert Bridges' "When First We Met" turns the tightness and repetition of the form to good use.

Unlike the French forms, which advertise their difficulty in their limited rhymes and complex repetitions, the Japanese form called the *haiku* often looks, at first sight, as if anybody could dash one off. In fact, teachers who would hesitate to assign a sonnet to a class of high school students or college students will instruct them all to write haiku. A haiku is only seventeen syllables long (in Japanese; English translators do not always abide by the seventeen-syllable limitation) and certainly anybody can produce seventeen syllables. But the apparent simplicity of the form should suggest its difficulty. In fact, the haiku is grounded in a tradition quite as complex as that which gave rise to the sonnet, and a good deal less accessible to the Western reader. The haiku we have selected can be enjoyed purely for their pictorial images and verbal felicities, but they will yield more to the student who is willing to approach them contemplatively, perhaps with some knowledge of the Zen Buddhist doctrine which so many of them reflect.

One poetic form which does not fit neatly into any category, but which is far too important to be ignored, is the *ode*. The *Pindaric ode* is a very elaborate form derived originally from the odes of Pindarus or Pindar, a Greek poet who died in 443 B.C. A Pindaric ode consists of three stanzas called, respectively, the "strophe," or turn, the "antistrophe," or counterturn, and the "epode" or stand. Pindar wrote his odes for public performance by a chorus; the terminology by which the stanzas are described probably referred to the movements of the chorus. As the Greek form was adapted in English by Ben Jonson and others, the first two stanzas are identical in pattern except for rhyme sounds, while the third stanza uses a different stanzaic pattern. Meters, line lengths, and rhyme patterns are determined by the poet within this somewhat loose framework.

Perhaps more important than the stanzaic form is the tone of the ode. Pindar wrote his odes to commemorate victories in the great traditional Greek games, which were as much religious exercises as they were athletic events. English odes, whether Pindaric or not, are almost invariably poems of high seriousness, elevated in both rhetoric and spirit, addressed in an oracular style to a public audience. As might be expected, the very seriousness associated with the ode has sometimes encouraged poets to produce parodies or burlesque treatments of the ode as a form. Indeed, sometimes the parody is unintentional.

The only ode with a relatively fixed form is the Horatian ode, patterned after the odes of the Roman poet Horace. The *Horatian ode* is written in quatrains, which may be rhymed *aabb* or unrhymed. Lines 3 and 4 are shorter than lines 1 and 2. William

Collins "Ode to Evening," of which a stanza follows, is probably the most well-known Horatian ode in English.

Now air is hushed, save where the weak-eyed bat
With short, shrill shriek, flits by on leathern wing;
    Or where the beetle winds
    His small but sullen horn . . .

The freest of the English ode forms is the *Cowleian ode,* named after the seventeenth-century poet Abraham Cowley. All Cowleian odes use rhyme and meter in some fashion, but in all other ways the form is entirely free. Notice the structural complexity of these stanzas from Wordsworth's "Ode on Intimations of Immortality from Recollections of Early Childhood."

1

There was a time when meadow, grove, and stream,
The earth, and every common sight
    To me did seem
    Apparelled in celestial light,
The glory and the freshness of a dream.
It is not now as it hath been of yore;—
    Turn wheresoe'er I may,
    By night or day,
The things which I have seen I now can see no more.

2

    The rainbow comes and goes,
    And lovely is the rose;
    The moon doth with delight
Look round her when the heavens are bare;
    Waters on a starry night
    Are beautiful and fair;
    The sunshine is a glorious birth;
    But yet I know, where'er I go,
That there hath past away a glory from the earth.

3

Now, while the birds thus sing a joyous song,
    And while the young lambs bound
    As to the tabor's sound,

To me alone there came a thought of grief:
A timely utterance gave that thought relief,
  And I again am strong.
The cataracts blow their trumpets from the steep,—
No more shall grief of mine the season wrong:
I hear the echoes through the mountains throng.
The winds come to me from the fields of sleep,
  And all the earth is gay;
    Land and sea
  Give themselves up to jollity,
    And with the heart of May
  Doth every beast keep holiday;—
    Thou child of joy,
Shout round me, let me hear thy shouts, thou happy
  Shepherd-boy!

The effect is one of great richness and complexity, in part derived from a formally ordered structure which constantly violates its own formality, only to return to it. Later Romantic poets used the term 'ode' for poems in almost any stanzaic structure—for instance, Shelley's "Ode to the West Wind" (sonnet sequence in *terza rima*) and Keats' "To Autumn" and "Ode on Melancholy," both written in ten-lined stanzas, with rhyme variations that are pretty clearly related to the sonnet.

In addition to providing a model for some magnificent seventeenth, eighteenth, and nineteenth-century poems, the many variations of the ode provided an example of a poetic mode which was at once formal and free. Right through the Age of Reason, with its emphasis on control and rationality, and its closed couplets, the ode, with its emotional emphasis and symphonic effects, was not only written, but written by such masters of the closed couplet as John Dryden. Clearly, the freeness of the ode was a natural outlet for the emotionalism of the Romantics. And it is not hard to see a connection between Wordsworth's freely varied line lengths and freely changing rhyme patterns, and the symphonic free verse of Walt Whitman. In fact, many of today's poets owe a large historic debt to the early practitioners of the ode. Freedom is never an instant invention.

Before leaving traditional stanza forms behind and moving on to recent developments, we should make two generalizations, which have been implied in what we have said so far about stanzaic writing. The first is that a stanza exists to fulfill a function. Stanzas grow out of the tastes of poets, out of their need for a vehicle of

204

expression, out of the taste of the age in which they write. Other poets accept, reject, or alter the poetic forms they inherit.

The other generalization, which has considerable bearing on the whole question of traditionalism versus modernism, is that the past and the present are not separated by a vast gulf. As we have seen, the six-hundred years during which English poets have employed accentual-syllabic meter and developed our traditional stanzaic forms have seen multiple revolutions in technique and taste. The battle between the modernists, who want change, and the traditionalists, who want to stand pat, is on-going. This century's Revolutionary is frequently next century's Grand Old Man.

## Exercise 1

### DIRECTIONS

Match the stanza definitions on the right with their correct descriptions on the left.

1. blank verse
2. heroic couplet
3. tercet
4. "In Memoriam" stanza
5. heroic quatrain
6. Rubaiyyat stanza
7. limerick
8. stave of six
9. rhyme royal
10. ottava rima

A. two lines, iambic pentameter, rhyming *aa*
B. four lines, iambic tetrameter, rhyming *abba*
C. four lines, iambic pentameter, rhyming *aaxa*
D. five lines, light verse, rhyming *aabba*
E. six lines, rhyming *ababcc*
F. unrhymed iambic pentameter
G. six lines, rhyming *abccba*
H. three lines, rhyming *axa*
I. seven lines, iambic pentameter, rhyming *ababbcc*
J. eight lines, iambic pentameter, rhyming *abababcc*
K. four lines, iambic pentameter, rhyming *abab*

### ANSWERS

1-F  (see p. 191)      6-C  (see p. 197)

2-A  (see p. 191)      7-D  (see p. 197-198)

3-H  (see p. 196)      8-E  (see p. 198)

4-B  (see p. 196)      9-I  (see p. 198)

5-K  (see p. 197)      10-J  (see p. 198)

205

## Exercise 2

DIRECTIONS

Match the description of the closed form on the right with its name on the left.

1. Shakespearean sonnet
2. Petrarchan sonnet
3. villanelle
4. sestina
5. rondeau
6. rondel
7. triolet
8. haiku
9. ode

A. 19 lines, only two rhymes, repeated lines
B. 14 lines, two rhymes, repeated lines
C. 17 syllables, usually three lines of 5, 7, and 5 syllables each
D. 14 lines, rhyming *abba, abba cdecde*
E. 6 six-line stanzas, plus 1 of three lines
F. lengthy, usually serious, many varieties
G. 9 lines, rhyming *aba bcb cca*
H. 14 lines, rhyming *abab cdcd efef gg*
I. 5 lines, first line repeated as last
J. 8 lines, many repeated lines
K. 13 lines, two rhymes, refrain

ANSWERS

1-H (see p. 181)   6-B (see p. 201)
2-D (see p. 181)   7-J (see p. 201-202)
3-A (see p. 200)   8-C (see p. 202)
4-E (see p. 201)   9-F (see p. 202-204)
5-K (see p. 201)

## Exercise 3

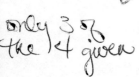
*only 3 of the 4 given*

1. Write at least six lines of blank verse. Try to use some meaningful metrical variations.
2. Write an heroic couplet which could serve as an epitaph for yourself, your instructor, or the authors of this text.
3. Write a Rubaiyyat stanza. Try to capture the wistful, melancholy feeling that Fitzgerald did in his translation.
4. Try to invent a short stanza form in rhymed verse. Write at least two such stanzas.

## Exercise 4

1. Write one of the following: haiku, limerick, or triolet.
2. Write, in order, the nineteen rhyming words of the villanelle that you intend to write some day.

3. Write, in order, the fourteen rhyming words of either a Shakespearean or a Petrarchan sonnet. Try to find rhymes that give you the feeling that a poem lurks behind them.

4. In a few sentences, indicate the divisions of an idea which could be developed into a sonnet, either Petrarchan or Shakespearean.

# 7 and 8

## Poems

*My Mistress' Eyes*
WILLIAM SHAKESPEARE (1564–1616)

*The Flea*
JOHN DONNE (1573–1631)

*The Good Morrow*
JOHN DONNE (1573–1631)

*On the Late Massacre in Piedmont*
JOHN MILTON (1608–1674)

*The Critic's Task*
ALEXANDER POPE (1688–1744)

*I Wandered Lonely as a Cloud*
WILLIAM WORDSWORTH (1770–1850)

from *Don Juan,* Canto I
GEORGE GORDON, LORD BYRON (1788–1824)

*Ode to the West Wind*
PERCY BYSSHE SHELLEY (1792–1822)

*To Helen*
EDGAR ALLEN POE (1809–1849)

from the *Rubaiyyat* of Omar Khayyam
EDWARD FITZGERALD (1809–1883)

*Ulysses*
ALFRED, LORD TENNYSON (1809–1892)

*The Ballad of Dead Ladies*
DANTE GABRIEL ROSSETTI (1828–1882)

*Pied Beauty*
GERARD MANLEY HOPKINS (1844–1889)

209

## MY MISTRESS' EYES

My Mistress' eyes are nothing like the sun;
Coral is far more red than her lips' red;
If snow be white, why then her breasts are dun;
If hairs be wires, black wires grow on her head.
I have seen roses damasked, red and white,                    5
But no such roses see I in her cheeks;
And in some perfumes is there more delight
Than in the breath that from my mistress reeks.
I love to hear her speak, yet well I know
That music hath a far more pleasing sound;                    10
I grant I never saw a goddess go;
My mistress, when she walks, treads on the ground:
   And yet, by heaven, I think my love as rare
   As any she belied with false compare.

WILLIAM SHAKESPEARE


## THE FLEA

Mark but this flea, and mark in this
How little that which thou deny'st me is;
It sucked me first, and now sucks thee,
And in this flea our two bloods mingled be;
Thou know'st that this cannot be said                         5
A sin, nor shame, nor loss of maidenhead;
   Yet this enjoys before it woo,
   And pampered swells with one blood made of two,
   And this, alas, is more than we would do.

Oh stay, three lives in one flea spare,                       10
Where we almost, yea, more than married are.
This flea is you and I, and this
Our marriage bed, and marriage temple is;
Though parents grudge, and you, we are met
And cloistered in these living walls of jet.                  15
   Though use make you apt to kill me,
   Let not to that, self-murder added be,
   And sacrilege, three sins in killing three.

210

Cruel and sudden, hast thou since
Purpled thy nail in blood of innocence?          20
Wherein could this flea guilty be,
Except in that drop which it sucked from thee?
Yet thou triumph'st and say'st that thou
Find'st not thyself, nor me the weaker now.
    'Tis true. Then learn how false fears be:         25
      Just so much honor, when thou yield'st to me,
      Will waste, as this flea's death took life from thee.

JOHN DONNE

# THE GOOD MORROW

I wonder, by my troth, what thou and I
Did till we loved? Were we not weaned till then,
But sucked on country pleasures, childishly?
Or snorted we in the Seven Sleepers' den?
'Twas so; but this, all pleasures fancies be.         5
If ever any beauty I did see,
Which I desired, and got, 'twas but a dream of thee.

And now good morrow to our waking souls,
Which watch not one another out of fear;
For love all love of other sights controls,         10
And makes one little room an everywhere.
Let sea-discoverers to new worlds have gone;
Let maps to other, worlds on worlds have shown;
Let us possess one world; each hath one, and is one.

My face in thine eye, thine in mine appears,         15
And true plain hearts do in the faces rest;
Where can we find two better hemispheres
Without sharp north, without declining west?
Whatever dies was not mixed equally;
If our two loves be one, or thou and I         20
Love so alike that none do slacken, none can die.

JOHN DONNE

211

## ON THE LATE MASSACRE IN PIEDMONT

Avenge, O Lord, thy slaughtered saints, whose bones
Lie scattered on the Alpine mountains cold;
Even them who kept thy truth so pure of old,
When all our fathers worshipped stocks and stones,
Forget not: in thy book record their groans       5
Who were thy sheep, and in their ancient fold
Slain by the bloody Piedmontese, that rolled
Mother with infant down the rocks. Their moans
The vales redoubled to the hills, and they
To heaven. Their martyred blood and ashes sow       10
O'er all the Italian fields, where still doth sway
The triple tyrant; that from these may grow
A hundredfold, who, having learnt thy way,
Early may fly the Babylonian woe.

JOHN MILTON

## THE CRITIC'S TASK

A little learning is a dang'rous thing;
Drink deep, or taste not the Pierian spring:
There shallow draughts intoxicate the brain,
And drinking largely sobers us again.
Fir'd at first sight with what the Muse imparts,       5
In fearless youth we tempt the heights of Arts,
While from the bounded level of our mind
Short views we take, nor see the lengths behind;
But more advanc'd, behold with strange surprise
New distant scenes of endless science rise!       10
So pleas'd at first the tow'ring Alps we try,
Mount o'er the vales, and seem to tread the sky,
Th' eternal snows appear already past,
And the first clouds and mountains seem the last:
But, those attain'd, we tremble to survey       15
The growing labours of the lengthen'd way,
Th' increasing prospect tires our wand'ring eyes.
Hills peep o'er hills, and Alps on Alps arise!
A perfect Judge will read each work of Wit

With the same spirit that its author writ:  20
Survey the Whole, nor seek slight faults to find
Where nature moves, and rapture warms the mind;
Nor lose, for that malignant dull delight,
The gen'rous pleasure to be charm'd with Wit.
But in such lays as neither ebb, nor flow,  25
Correctly cold, and regularly low,
That shunning faults, one quiet tenour keep;
We cannot blame indeed—but we may sleep.
In Wit, as Nature, what affects our hearts
Is not th' exactness of peculiar parts;  30
'Tis not a lip, or eye, we beauty call,
But the joint force and full result of all.
Thus when we view some well-proportion'd dome
(The world's just wonder, and ev'n thine, O Rome!)
No single parts unequally surprise,  35
All comes united to th' admiring eyes;
No monstrous height, or breadth, or length appear;
The Whole at once is bold, and regular.

from *The Essay on Criticism*, ALEXANDER POPE

# I WANDERED LONELY AS A CLOUD

I wandered lonely as a cloud
That floats on high o'er vales and hills,
When all at once I saw a crowd,
A host, of golden daffodils,
Beside the lake, beneath the trees,  5
Fluttering and dancing in the breeze.

Continuous as the stars that shine
And twinkle on the milky way,
They stretch'd in never-ending line
Along the margin of a bay:  10
Ten thousand saw I at a glance
Tossing their heads in sprightly dance.

The waves beside them danced, but they
Out-did the sparkling waves in glee:—
A Poet could not but be gay  15

In such a jocund company!
I gazed—and gazed—but little thought
What wealth the show to me had brought;

For oft, when on my couch I lie
In vacant or in pensive mood,                                    20
They flash upon that inward eye
Which is the bliss of solitude;
And then my heart with pleasure fills
And dances with the daffodils.

WILLIAM WORDSWORTH

## from *DON JUAN*, Canto I

In Seville was he born, a pleasant city,
   Famous for oranges and women—he
Who has not seen it will be much to pity,
   So says the proverb—and I quite agree;
Of all the Spanish towns is none more pretty,                    5
   Cadiz perhaps—but that, you soon may see;—
Don Juan's parents lived beside the river,
A noble stream, and call'd the Guadalquivir.

His father's name was José—*Don*, of course,
   A true Hidalgo, free from every stain                    10
Of Moor or Hebrew blood, he traced his source
   Through the most Gothic gentlemen of Spain;
A better cavalier ne'er mounted horse,
   Or, being mounted, e'er got down again,
Than José, who begot our hero, who                               15
Begot—but that's to come—Well, to renew:

His mother was a learnéd lady, famed
For every branch of every science known—
In every Christian language ever named,
   With virtues equalled by her wit alone:                  20
She made the cleverest people quite ashamed,
   And even the good with inward envy groan,
Finding themselves so very much exceeded,
In their own way, by all the things that she did.

GEORGE GORDON, LORD BYRON

214

## ODE TO THE WEST WIND

1

O wild West Wind, thou breath of Autumn's being,
Thou, from whose unseen presence the leaves dead
Are driven, like ghosts from an enchanter fleeing,

Yellow, and black and pale, and hectic red,
Pestilence-stricken multitudes: O thou,           5
Who chariotest to their dark wintry bed

The winged seeds, where they lie cold and low,
Each like a corpse within its grave, until
Thine azure sister of the Spring shall blow

Her clarion o'er the dreaming earth, and fill      10
(Driving sweet buds like flocks to feed in air)
With living hues and odours plain and hill:

Wild Spirit, which art moving everywhere;
Destroyer and preserver; hear, oh hear!

2

Thou on whose stream, mid the steep sky's commotion.   15
Loose clouds like earth's decaying leaves are shed,
Shook from the tangled boughs of Heaven and Ocean,

Angels of rain and lightning: there are spread
On the blue surface of thine aëry surge,
Like the bright hair uplifted from the head      20

Of some fierce Maenad, even from the dim verge
Of the horizon to the zenith's height,
The locks of the approaching storm. Thou dirge

Of the dying year, to which this closing night
Will be the dome of a vast sepulchre,      25
Vaulted with all thy congregated might

Of vapours, from whose solid atmosphere
Black rain, and fire, and hail will burst: oh hear!

3

Thou who didst waken from his summer dreams
The blue Mediterranean, where he lay,      30
Lulled by the coil of his crystalline streams,

Beside a pumice isle in Baiae's bay,
And saw in sleep old palaces and towers
Quivering within the wave's intenser day,

All overgrown with azure moss and flowers          35
So sweet, the sense faints picturing them! Thou
For whose path the Atlantic's level powers

Cleave themselves into chasms, while far below
The sea-blooms and the oozy woods which wear
The sapless foliage of the ocean, know          40

Thy voice, and suddenly grow gray with fear,
And tremble and despoil themselves: oh, hear!

4

If I were a dead leaf thou mightest bear;
If I were a swift cloud to fly with thee;
A wave to pant beneath thy power, and share          45

The impulse of thy strength, only less free
Than thou, O uncontrollable! If even
I were as in my boyhood, and could be

The comrade of thy wanderings over Heaven,
As then, when to outstrip thy skiey speed          50
Scarce seemed a vision; I would ne'er have striven

As thus with thee in prayer in my sore need.
Oh, lift me as a wave, a leaf, a cloud!
I fall upon the thorns of life! I bleed!

A heavy weight of hours has chained and bowed          55
One too like thee; tameless, and swift, and proud.

5

Make me thy lyre, even as the forest is:
What if my leaves are falling like its own!
The tumult of thy mighty harmonies

Will take from both a deep, autumnal tone,          60
Sweet though in sadness. Be thou, Spirit fierce,
My spirit! Be thou me, impetuous one!

Drive my dead thoughts over the universe
Like withered leaves to quicken a new birth!
And by the incantation of this verse,          65

Scatter, as from an unextinguished hearth
Ashes and sparks, my words among mankind!
Be through my lips to unawakened earth

The trumpet of a prophecy! O, Wind,
If Winter comes, can Spring be far behind?                    70

PERCY BYSSHE SHELLEY


## TO HELEN

Helen, thy beauty is to me
   Like those Nicéan barks of yore,
That gently, o'er a perfumed sea,
   The weary, way-worn wanderer bore
   To his own native shore.                               5

On desperate seas long wont to roam,
   Thy hyacinth hair, thy classic face,
Thy Naiad airs have brought me home
   To the glory that was Greece,
And the grandeur that was Rome.                               10

Lo! in yon brilliant window-niche
   How statue-like I see thee stand,
   The agate lamp within thy hand!
Ah, Psyche, from the regions which
   Are Holy Land!                                          15

EDGAR ALLEN POE


## from the RUBAIYYAT OF OMAR KHAYYAM

Awake! for Morning in the Bowl of Night
Has flung the Stone that puts the Stars to Flight:
   And Lo! the Hunter of the East has caught
The Sultan's Turret in a Noose of Light.

Come, fill the Cup, and in the Fire of Spring                 5
The Winter Garment of Repentance fling:
   The Bird of Time has but a little way
To fly—and Lo! the Bird is on the Wing.

217

Here with a Loaf of Bread beneath the Bough,
A Flask of Wine, a Book of Verse—and Thou 10
   Beside me singing in the Wilderness—
And Wilderness is Paradise enow.

'How sweet is mortal Sovranty'—think some:
Others—'How blest the Paradise to come!'
   Ah, take the Cash in hand and waive the Rest; 15
Oh, the brave Music of a *distant* Drum!

They say the Lion and the Lizard keep
The Courts where Jamshyd gloried and drank deep;
   And Bahrám, that great Hunter—the Wild Ass
Stamps o'er his Head, and he lies fast asleep. 20

Ah, make the most of what we yet may spend,
Before we too into the Dust descend;
   Dust into Dust, and under Dust, to lie,
Sans Wine, sans Song, sans Singer, and—sans End!

Alike for those who for To-DAY prepare, 25
And those that after a To-MORROW stare,
   A Muezzin from the Tower of Darkness cries
'Fools! your Reward is neither Here nor There!'

Why, all the Saints and Sages who discuss'd
Of the Two Worlds so learnedly, are thrust 30
   Like foolish Prophets forth; their Words to Scorn
Are scatter'd, and their Mouths are stopt with Dust.

Oh, come with old Khayyám, and leave the Wise
To talk; one thing is certain, that Life flies;
   One thing is certain, and the Rest is Lies; 35
The Flower that once has blown for ever dies.

I think the Vessel, that with fugitive
Articulation answer'd, once did live,
   And merry-make; and the cold Lip I kiss'd
How many Kisses might it take—and give! 40

For in the Market-place, one Dusk of Day,
I watch'd the Potter thumping his wet Clay:
   And with its all obliterated Tongue
It murmured—'Gently, Brother, gently, pray!'

The moving Finger writes; and, having writ,    45
Moves on: nor all thy Piety nor Wit
   Shall lure it back to cancel half a Line,
Nor all thy Tears wash out a Word of it.

And that inverted Bowl we call The Sky,
Whereunder crawling coop't we live and die,    50
   Lift not thy hands to *It* for help—for it
Rolls impotently on as Thou or I.

*Tamam Shod*

EDWARD FITZGERALD

## ULYSSES

*[handwritten: unrhymed iambic pentameter (blank verse) — Shakespeare uses " " esp. in his Tragedies]*

*[handwritten left margin: Desire to move on & seek new adventures. This is his last voyage]*

It little profits that an idle king,
By this still hearth, among these barren crags,
Matched with an agèd wife, I mete and dole
Unequal laws unto a savage race,
That hoard, and sleep, and feed, and know not me.    5
I cannot rest from travel; I will drink
Life to the lees. All times I have enjoyed
Greatly, have suffered greatly, both with those
That loved me, and alone; on shore, and when
Through scudding drifts the rainy Hyades    10
Vext the dim sea. I am become a name;
For always roaming with a hungry heart
Much have I seen and known,—cities of men
And manners, climates, councils, governments,
Myself not least, but honoured of them all,—    15
And drunk delight of battle with my peers,
Far on the ringing plains of windy Troy.
I am a part of all that I have met;
Yet all experience is an arch wherethrough
Gleams that untravelled world whose margin fades    20
For ever and for ever when I move.
How dull it is to pause, to make an end,
To rust unburnished, not to shine in use!
As though to breathe were life! Life piled on life

*dramatic monogule — 1 person Speaking, you listening in a scene! He speaks to a group*

Were all too little, and of one to me                                    25
Little remains; but every hour is saved
From that eternal silence, something more,
A bringer of new things; and vile it were
For some three suns to store and hoard myself,

*redpage image* → And this grey spirit yearning in desire                30
To follow knowledge like a sinking star,
Beyond the utmost bound of human thought.
    This is my son, mine own Telemachus,
To whom I leave the sceptre and the isle,
Well-loved of me, discerning to fulfill                                   35
This labour, by slow prudence to make mild
A rugged people, and through soft degrees
Subdue them to the useful and the good.
Most blameless is he, centred in the sphere
Of common duties, decent not to fail                                     40
In offices of tenderness, and pay
Meet adoration to my household gods,
When I am gone. He works his work, I mine.
    There lies the port; the vessel puffs her sail;
There gloom the dark, broad seas. My mariners,                           45
Souls that have toiled, and wrought, and thought with me,
That ever with a frolic welcome took
The thunder and the sunshine, and opposed
Free hearts, free foreheads—you and I are old;
Old age hath yet his honour and his toil.                                50
Death closes all; but something ere the end,
Some work of noble note, may yet be done,
Not unbecoming men that strove with Gods.
The lights begin to twinkle from the rocks;

*He can't get enough of life's experience*
The long day wanes; the slow moon climbs; the deep    55
Moans round with many voices. Come, my friends,
'T is not too late to seek a newer world.
Push off, and sitting well in order smite
The sounding furrows; for my purpose holds
To sail beyond the sunset, and the baths                                 60
Of all the western stars, until I die.
It may be that the gulfs will wash us down;
It may be we shall touch the Happy Isles,

220

And see the great Achilles, whom we knew.
Though much is taken, much abides; and though          65
We are not now that strength which in old days
Moved earth and heaven; that which we are, we are,
One equal temper of heroic hearts,
Made weak by time and fate, but strong in will
To strive, to seek, to find, and not to yield.          70

ALFRED, LORD TENNYSON


## THE BALLAD OF DEAD LADIES

Tell me now in what hidden way is
     Lady Flora the lovely Roman?
Where's Hipparchia, and where is Thaïs,
     Neither of them the fairer woman?
     Where is Echo, beheld of no man,          5
Only heard on river and mere—
     She whose beauty was more than
          human? . . .
But where are the snows of yester-year?

Where's Héloïse, the learned nun,
     For whose sake Abeillard, I ween,          10
Lost manhood and put priesthood on?
     (From Love he won such dule and teen!)
     And where, I pray you, is the Queen
Who willed that Buridan should steer
     Sewed in a sack's mouth down the
          Seine? . . .          15
But where are the snows of yester-year?

White Queen Blanche, like a queen of lilies,
     With a voice like any mermaiden—
Bertha Broadfoot, Beatrice, Alice,
     And Ermengarde the lady of Maine—          20
     And that good Joan whom Englishmen
At Rouen doomed and burned her there—
     Mother of God, where are they then? . . .
     But where are the snows of yester-year?

221

Nay, never ask this week, fair lord,                                    25
    Where they are gone, nor yet this year,
Except with this for an overword—
    But where are the snows of yester-year?

DANTE GABRIEL ROSSETTI
*The Ballad of Dead Ladies* is a translation
of *Ballade des Dames du Temp Jadis* by François Villon.


## PIED BEAUTY

Glory be to God for dappled things—
    For skies of couple-colour as a brinded cow;
      For rose-moles all in stipple upon trout that swim;
Fresh-firecoal chestnut-falls; finches' wings;
    Landscape plotted and pieced—fold, fallow, and plough;  5
      And áll trádes, their gear and tackle and trim.

All things counter, original, spare, strange;
    Whatever is fickle, freckled (who knows how?)
      With swift, slow; sweet, sour; adazzle, dim;
He fathers-forth whose beauty is past change:
        Praise him.                                    10

*oxymoron*

GERARD MANLEY HOPKINS


## WHEN FIRST WE MET

When first we met we did not guess
That Love would prove so hard a master;
Of more than common friendliness
When first we met we did not guess.
Who could foretell this sore distress,                                  5
This irretrievable disaster
When first we met?—We did not guess
That Love would prove so hard a master.

ROBERT BRIDGES

## SESTINA OF THE TRAMP-ROYAL

Speakin' in general, I 'ave tried 'em all,
The 'appy roads that take you o'er the world.
Speakin' in general, I 'ave found them good
For such as cannot use one bed too long,
But must get 'ence, the same as I 'ave done,       5
An' go observin' matters till they die.

What do it matter where or 'ow we die,
So long as we've our 'ealth to watch it all—
The different ways that different things are done,
An' men an' women lovin' in this world—       10
Takin' our chances as they come along,
An' when they ain't, pretendin' they are good?

In cash or credit—no, it ain't no good;
You 'ave to 'ave the 'abit or you'd die,
Unless you lived your life but one day long,       15
Nor didn't prophesy nor fret at all,
But drew your tucker some'ow from the world,
An' never bothered what you might ha' done.

But, Gawd, what things are they I 'aven't done?
I've turned my 'and to most, an' turned it good,       20
In various situations round the world—
For 'im that doth not work must surely die;
But that's no reason man should labour all
'Is life on one same shift; life's none so long.

Therefore, from job to job I've moved along.       25
Pay couldn't 'old me when my time was done,
For something in my 'ead upset me all,
Till I 'ad dropped whatever 'twas for good,
An', out at sea, be'eld the dock-lights die,
An' met my mate—the wind that tramps the world.       30

It's like a book, I think, this bloomin' world,
Which you can read and care for just so long,
But presently you feel that you will die
Unless you get the page you're readin' done,
An' turn another—likely not so good;       35
But what you're after is to turn 'em all.

Gawd bless this world! Whatever she 'ath done—
Excep' when awful long—I've found it good.
So write, before I die, " 'E liked it all!"

RUDYARD KIPLING

## WE WEAR THE MASK

We wear the mask that grins and lies,
It hides our cheeks and shades our eyes,—
This debt we pay to human guile;
With torn and bleeding hearts we smile,
And mouth with myriad subtleties.                   5
Why should the world be overwise,
In counting all our tears and sighs?
Nay, let them only see us, while
    We wear the mask.

We smile, but, O great Christ, our cries           10
To thee from tortured souls arise.
We sing, but oh the clay is vile
Beneath our feet, and long the mile;
But let the world dream otherwise,
    We wear the mask!                                  15

PAUL LAWRENCE DUNBAR

## HERE LIES A LADY

Here lies a lady of beauty and high degree.
Of chills and fever she died, of fever and chills,
The delight of her husband, her aunt, an infant of three,
And of medicos marveling sweetly on her ills.

For either she burned, and her confident eyes would blaze,   5
And her fingers fly in a manner to puzzle their heads—
What was she making? Why, nothing; she sat in a maze
Of old scraps of laces, snipped into curious shreds—

Or this would pass, and the light of her fire decline
Till she lay discouraged and cold, like a stalk white
    and blown,                                                  10

224

And would not open her eyes, to kisses, to wine;
The sixth of these states was her last; the cold settled down.

Sweet ladies, long may ye bloom, and toughly I hope ye may
    thole,
But was she not lucky? In flowers and lace and mourning,
In love and great honor we bade God rest her soul          15
After six little spaces of chill, and six of burning.

JOHN CROWE RANSOM


# LADIES AND GENTLEMEN THIS LITTLE GIRL

    ladies and gentlemen this little girl
    with the good teeth and small important breasts
    (is it the Frolic or the Century whirl?
    one's memory indignantly protests)
    this little dancer with the tightened eyes          5
    crisp ogling shoulders and the ripe quite too
    large lips always clenched faintly, wishes you
    with all her fragile might to not surmise
    she dreamed one afternoon
                    . . . . or maybe read?          10
    of a time when the beautiful most of her
    (this here and This, do you get me?)
    will maybe dance and maybe sing and be
    absitively posolutely dead,
    like Coney Island in winter          15

    E. E. CUMMINGS


# RONDEL FOR MIDDLE AGE

    We play now very lightly, on the strings,
    Meticulous, with infinite finesse.
    Love was a symphony, the wind and brass
    Throwing the thunder wide with stripéd wings,
    But storm has softened into murmurings,          5
    The careful modulations of caress:

We play now very lightly, on the strings,
Meticulous, with infinite finesse.

The bright bouquet of sound has lingerings
Of pastel tint and wildflower tenderness,                    10
Hepatica, anemone, or less.
Love is returning to its earliest springs,
We play now very lightly, on the strings.

LOUISE T. NICHOLL


## EVENIN' AIR BLUES

Folks, I come up North
Cause they told me de North was fine.
I come up North
Cause they told me de North was fine.
Been up here six months—                                     5
I'm about to lose my mind.

This mornin' for breakfast
I chawed de mornin' air.
This mornin' for breakfast
Chawed de mornin' air.                                       10
But this evenin' for supper,
I got evenin' air to spare.

Believe I'll do a little dancin'
Just to drive my blues away—
A little dancin'                                             15
To drive my blues away,
Cause when I'm dancin'
De blues forgets to stay.

But if you was to ask me
How de blues they come to be,                                20
Says if you was to ask me
How de blues they come to be—
You wouldn't need to ask me:
Just look at me and see!

LANGSTON HUGHES


226

*The 1st time*
*Ever I saw your*
*Face ...*
*Ever I heard your*
*Voice*

## THE WAKING

I wake to sleep, and take my waking slow.
I feel my fate in what I cannot fear.
I learn by going where I have to go.

We think by feeling. What is there to know?
I hear my being dance from ear to ear.      5
I wake to sleep, and take my waking slow.

Of those so close beside me, which are you?
God bless the Ground! I shall walk softly there,
And learn by going where I have to go.

Light takes the Tree; but who can tell us how?      10
The lowly worm climbs up a winding stair;
I wake to sleep, and take my waking slow.

Great Nature has another thing to do
To you and me; so take the lively air,
And, lovely, learn by going where to go.      15

This shaking keeps me steady. I should know.
What falls away is always. And is near.
I wake to sleep, and take my waking slow.
I learn by going where I have to go.

THEODORE ROETHKE

## DRUG STORE

*I do remember an apothecary,*
*And hereabouts 'a dwells*

It baffles the foreigner like an idiom,
And he is right to adopt it as a form
Less serious than the living-room or bar;
    For it disestablishes the cafe,
Is a collective, and on basic country.      5

Not that it praises hygiene and corrupts
The ice-cream parlor and the tobacconist's
Is it a center; but that the attractive symbols
    Watch over puberty and leer
Like rubber bottles waiting for sick-use.      10

Youth comes to jingle nickels and crack wise;
The baseball scores are his, the magazines
Devoted to lust, the jazz, the Coca-Cola,
    The lending-library of love's latest.
He is the customer; he is heroized.                15

And every nook and cranny of the flesh
Is spoken to by packages with wiles.
"Buy me, buy me," they whimper and cajole;
    The hectic range of lipsticks pouts,
Revealing the wicked and the simple mouth.         20

With scarcely any evasion in their eye
They smoke, undress their girls, exact a stance;
But only for a moment. The clock goes round;
    Crude fellowships are made and lost;
They slump in booths like rags, not even drunk.      25

KARL SHAPIRO

## DO NOT GO GENTLE INTO THAT GOOD NIGHT

Do not go gentle into that good night,
Old age should burn and rave at close of day;
Rage, rage against the dying of the light.

Though wise men at their end know dark is right,
Because their words have forked no lightning they      5
Do not go gentle into that good night.

Good men, the last wave by, crying how bright
Their frail deeds might have danced in a green bay,
Rage, rage against the dying of the light.

Wild men who caught and sang the sun in flight,      10
And learn, too late, they grieved it on its way,
Do not go gentle into that good night.

Grave men, near death, who see with blinding sight
Blind eyes could blaze like meteors and be gay,
Rage, rage against the dying of the light.             15

And you, my father, there on the sad height,
Curse, bless, me now with your fierce tears, I pray.
Do not go gentle into that good night.
Rage, rage against the dying of the light.

DYLAN THOMAS

## JUNK

> Huru Welandes
>
> worc ne geswiceð
>
> monna aenigum
>
> óara óe Mimming can
>
> heardne gehealdan.
>
> WALDERE

An axe angles
            from my neighbor's ashcan;
It is hell's handiwork,
               the wood not hickory,
The flow of the grain
            not faithfully followed.
The shivered shaft
           rises from a shellheap
Of plastic playthings,
           paper plates,             5
And the sheer shards
           of shattered tumblers
That were not annealed
            for the time needful.
At the same curbside,
           a cast-off cabinet
Of wavily-warped
           unseasoned wood
Waits to be trundled
           in the trash-man's truck.      10
Haul them off! Hide them!
           The heart winces
For junk and gimcrack,
           for jerrybuilt things

And the men who make them
                            for a little money,
Bartering pride
                    like the bought boxer
Who pulls his punches,
                            or the paid-off jockey                    15
Who in the home stretch
                            holds in his horse.
Yet the things themselves
                            in thoughtless honor
Have kept composure,
                            like captives who would not
Talk under torture.
                        Tossed from a tailgate
Where the dump displays
                            its random dolmens,              20
Its black barrows
                    and blazing valleys,
They shall waste in the weather
                            toward what they were.
The sun shall glory
                    in the glitter of glass-chips,
Foreseeing the salvage
                    of the prisoned sand,
And the blistering paint
                            peel off in patches,                25
That the good grain
                    be discovered again.
Then burnt, bulldozed,
                        they shall all be buried
To the depth of diamonds,
                            in the making dark
Where halt Hephaestus
                        keeps his hammer
And Wayland's work
                    is worn away.                            30

RICHARD WILBUR

## IN BERTRAM'S GARDEN

Jane looks down at her organdy skirt
As if *it* somehow were the thing disgraced,
For being there, on the floor, in the dirt,
And she catches it up about her waist,
Smooths it out along one hip,                           5
And pulls it over the crumpled slip.

On the porch, green-shuttered, cool,
Asleep is Bertram, that bronze boy,
Who, having wound her around a spool,
Sends her spinning like a toy                           10
Out to the garden, all alone,
To sit and weep on a bench of stone.

Soon the purple dark will bruise
Lily and bleeding-heart and rose,
And the little Cupid lose                               15
Eyes and ears and chin and nose,
And Jane lie down with others soon
Naked to the naked moon.

DONALD JUSTICE

## NORTH

North is weather, winter, and change:
a wind-shift, snow, and how ice ages
shape the moraine of a mountain range.

At tree line the chiseled ledges
are ragged to climb; wind-twist trees                  5
give way to the thrust of granite ridges,

peaks reach through abrasive centuries
of rain. The worn grain, the sleet-cut,
is magnified on blue Northwest days

where rock slides, like rip-tide, break out            10
through these geologic seas. Time
in a country of hills is seasonal light:

231

alpenglow, Northern lights, and tame
in October: Orion, cold hunter of stars.
Between what will be and was, rime                           15

whites the foothill night and flowers
the rushes stilled in black millpond ice.
The dark, the nightfall temperatures

are North, and the honk of flyway geese
high over valley sleep. The woodland                          20
is evergreen, ground pine, spruce,

and deadwood hills at the riverbend.
Black bear and mink fish beaver streams
where moose and caribou drink: beyond

the forests there are elk. Snowstorms                         25
breed North like arctic birds that swirl
downhill, and in a blind wind small farms

are lost. At night the close cold is still,
the tilt world returns from sun to ice.
Glazed lichen is North, and snowfall                          30

at five below. North is where rockface
and hoarfrost are formed with double grace:
love is twice warm in a cold place.

PHILLIP BOOTH

# JAPANESE HAIKU

Tremendous forces . . .
    Stone-piled fence all tumbled down
  By two cats in love
        —Shiki

Yes: the young sparrows
  If you treat them tenderly                          5
    Thank you with droppings
        —Issa

Planted rows of beans
   And random clumps of lilies
  Prosperous islet!
        —Shiki

Night is darkening . . .                            10
   Silent in the paddy
Shines the milky way
        —Izen

That night when I had
   Sold my lower field . . .
I lay wakeful from frog-calls.                15
        —Hokushi

translated by PETER BEILENSON

# 9

## Free Verse and Self-devised Forms

Most discussions of poetry proceed from the assumption that all those poems which do not lend themselves naturally to dumping into a bin marked "traditional metrics" must belong in a bin marked "free verse." Historically, the second bin is a fairly recent addition to the critic's desk. Long after Whitman, Stephen Crane, and other free-verse pioneers had demonstrated the possibilities offered by a break with metrical tradition, some teachers and critics were still maintaining that only one bin existed—one marked "poetry"—and that only metered verse was eligible. Nonmetered verse belonged in a bin marked "prose," if it did not in fact belong (along with nonrepresentational painting, atonal music, short skirts, and women's suffrage) in a large loathesome trash can marked "decadent modernism." While it is not impossible that, here and there, a diehard traditionalist still hangs on, the attitude which made "meter" and "poetry" synonymous has now largely been discarded.

Unfortunately, a kind of psychic hangover remains as a result of the Battle of the Bins, which still affects the thinking of many students and not a few critics. Perhaps such a critical headache is implicit in the terminology we will be using in this chapter. For words, as we pointed out in Chapter 5, have connotations as well as denotations, and words like "free" and "traditional" carry a fairly heavy load of connotational freight. Their political, social, and philosophical implications are likely to carry over into discussions of poetic form, and even into expectations about poetic form. Some students approach nontraditional verse with the expectation that it will

234

be "far out" or obscure, while others are ready to condemn all traditional forms unread as square old "de-dum de-dum" stuff. For those readers whose hearts leap up when they behold an irregular right-hand margin, as well as for those who heave a great sigh of relief at the sound of rhyme and wrap themselves in iambic pentameter as if it were a soul security blanket, let us suggest that reaction on the basis of form alone is not usually a very informed reaction. The bare minimum necessary to deciding whether you like or dislike a poem ought to be a reading of the poem that actually exists on the page, not a projection onto the page of your own prejudgments.

Before we go further in our discussion of nontraditional poetry, perhaps we should define what we mean by "traditional metrics" and "free verse." Traditional metrics is based on that body of metrical practice which we have inherited from the past. Dominating the field almost to the exclusion of other forms is accentual-syllabic meter. But the older, pre-Norman conquest, four-stress accentual measure of *Beowulf* has been used with some success by modern poets such as Richard Wilbur and W. H. Auden and certainly comes within our definition of traditional metrics. Finally, though they have left no very prominent memorials behind them, the efforts of those poets who attempted to reproduce the quantitative measures of Greek and Latin poetry in English should not be ignored.

So traditional verse in English is verse written to a regular metrical pattern. In addition, it often (though not always) employs rhyme, full or slant, and is written in traditional stanzas. By contrast, *free verse* is not limited by any regularizing pattern. It employs freely varied line lengths and irregular rather than patterned stanzas.

One fairly obvious thing which ought to be said about free verse is that no verse is wholly "free," if by free one means entirely spontaneous. The act of writing involves making choices. And any poem will have been subjected to criticism by the poet himself and probably by others before it reaches print. Any memorable art has form. If the free verse poet frees himself from the traditional demands of rhyme, meter, and so on, he takes on the job of inventing a form which will, ideally, be as rhythmically satisfying and as memorable as traditional verse. This is not an easy task.

Of course the very unfamiliarity of free verse forms can be an advantage in generating reader interest. There is an undeniable exhilaration to the poet and to many readers in deliberately violating convention. Here, for instance, is Walt Whitman, invoking that three-thousand-year-old literary convention, the Muse, on his own terms.

Come Muse migrate from Greece and Ionia,
Cross out please those immensely overpaid accounts,

That matter of Troy and Achilles' wrath, and Aeneas',
    Odysseus' wanderings,
Placard "removed" and "To Let" on the rocks of your snowy
    Parnassus,
Repeat at Jerusalem, place the notice high on Jaffa's gate
    and on Mount Moriah,
The same on the walls of your German, French, and Spanish
    castles, and Italian collections,
For know a better, fresher, busier sphere, a wide, untried
    domain awaits, demands you.

. . . I say I see, my friends, if you do not, the illustrious
    emigré, (having it is true in her day, although the same,
    changed, journey'd considerable,)
Making directly for this rendezvous, vigorously ·clearing a
    path for herself, striding through the confusion,
By thud of machinery and shrill steam-whistle undismay'd,
Bluff'd not a bit by drain-pipe, gasometers, artificial
    fertilizers,
Smiling and pleas'd with palpable intent to stay,
She's here, install'd amid the kitchen ware!

    from *Song of the Exposition*

Notice that, though the "illustrious emigre" is invited to
abandon not only the traditional subject matter of poetry (Greek
mythology, chivalry, and so forth), but also by implication its manner
("By thud of machinery and shrill steam-whistle undismay'd"),
Whitman assumes sufficient knowledge of these traditions on the part
of the reader to make the lines meaningful. The full effectiveness of the
Muse "install'd amid the kitchen ware" is greatest for those readers
who have read enough earlier poetry to remember, for instance,
Milton's invocation in *Paradise Lost*.

    Sing, Heavenly Muse, that on the secret top
    Of Oreb, or of Sinai, didst inspire
    The shepherd who first taught the chosen seed
    In the beginning how the heavens and earth
    Rose out of Chaos.

Much of the early vitality of free verse came from the conviction of its practitioners that they were smashing open old, jammed,

dusty windows, and letting in some good fresh air. At least in its early days, there was a frequent smashing which went beyond form—a demand that poetry should outgrow the timid mental habits and archaic niceties of a suffocating genteel tradition. That impulse is obvious in Whitman, in Stephen Crane, in the 'twenties experimentalists, notably Ezra Pound, T. S. Eliot, Carl Sandburg, and e. e. cummings, and in the work of the Beat poets such as Allen Ginsberg. But convention smashing can only function in the presence of a smashable convention. When all the glass is out of the windows, you can heave bricks all day without raising so much as a tinkle.

In any case, good free verse has always had something more than shock value to offer. We have, in our earlier chapters, considered at some length the techniques which practitioners of traditional metrics have used to give their work memorability and intensity. Let us look now at some of the techniques employed in free verse. Here is a passage from Section 42 of Whitman's *Leaves of Grass.*

> Ever the hard unsunk ground,
> Ever the eaters and drinkers, ever the upward and downward
>     sun, ever the air and the ceaseless tides,
> Ever myself and my neighbors, refreshing, wicked, real,
> Ever the old inexplicable query, ever that thorn'd thumb,
>     that breath of itches and thirsts,
> Ever the vexer's hoot! hoot! till we find where the sly one
>     hides and bring him forth,
> Ever love, ever the sobbing liquid of life,
> Ever the bandage under the chin, ever the trestles of death.

Whitman's "Muse install'd amid the kitchen-ware" here sings with great lyric power. What techniques does she use?

Perhaps the most notable thing about this passage is the pattern of repetition. The single word "ever" (which, we realize as we read the poem, has tremendous implications of inevitability and recurrence built into it) performs much of the function which rhyme might fulfill in a traditionally patterned stanza. The use of parallel phrasing, which results in repeated cadences, is also of great importance.

Sound qualities are also of considerable importance. The effect of specific phonemes and combinations of phonemes is essentially the same in poetry, whether that poetry is traditional or free verse. In either case the poet needs to find those sounds which complement his other poetic materials. In this passage Whitman employs alliteration and assonance extensively. Nearly every line contains alliteration.

237

Lines 2 and 3 repeat the /iy/ phoneme four times (*eaters, ceaseless, refreshing, real*). Line 5 is especially noteworthy for its repetition of /ay/ in "find," "sly," and "hides," three words with obvious semantic affinities, which become all the more prominent when their assonance ties them together.

The effect of these sound devices is to create a richer texture for the entire passage than would result were the lines devoid of them. Whitman's use of assonance weaves together words and ideas, acting to intensify semantic binds which otherwise might not have been established.

While he does not employ any conventional metrical pattern, Whitman does manipulate stresses in the passage in a controlled and artful manner. We have marked stress patterns here, not with any intention of detecting nonexistent metrical norms, but to indicate how important the aspect of controlled rhythm is, even in free verse.

Ever the hard unsunk ground,                                                     1
Ever the eaters and drinkers, ever the upward and                               2
    downward sun, ever the air and the ceaseless tides,
Ever myself and my neighbors, refreshing, wicked, real,                         3
Ever the old inexplicable query, ever that thorn'd thumb,                       4
    that breath of itches and thirsts.
Ever the vexer's hoot! hoot! till we find where the sly one                     5
    hides and bring him forth,
Ever love, ever the sobbing liquid of life,                                     6
Ever the bandage under the chin, ever the trestles of death.                    7

In effect, Whitman comes close to establishing a normative pattern. Certainly lines 4 and 5, with their heavy stress clusters, break in upon the musical earlier cadence. Then in lines 6 and 7, the earlier cadence is reestablished, as Whitman brings his imagery full circle, since the "hard unsunk ground" of line 1 will receive the man who has died. Notice, also, Whitman's diction choices, especially "refreshing, wicked, real"—an extraordinary cluster of qualities to admit in oneself and one's neighbors—"thorn'd thumb," and "sobbing liquid of life"— presumably semen, but "sobbing" suggests tears, carrying out the imagery of birth, love, death as a continuous process.

Obviously this is highly controlled language, densely inter- weaving imagery, sound quality, diction choices, and stress patterns into a moving whole. From our vantage point, one hundred and seven- teen years after the first edition of *Leaves of Grass*, it is difficult to see why the Battle of the Bins, to which we referred in our opening paragraphs, was ever necessary. But it was a real battle, and it left a legacy of combativeness which still causes some practitioners of free verse to behave as if they had to do battle with a live enemy instead of a straw man. This antitraditional saber-rattling has, we think, obscured some important developments in the poetry which has been written since free verse became an accepted mode of composition.

First of all, the metrical verse of the 1970's is not the metrical verse of 1850, or even 1900. The same experimental thrust which led to free-verse development is also reflected in the work of every major twentieth-century poet writing in traditional forms. Traditional poets, such as William Butler Yeats and Robert Frost, tightened up a line which, by the late Victorian period, had run into excesses of sweetness for sweetness' sake. Both were expert manipulators of traditional forms, but both assimilated the idioms and voice patterns of their own time to the uses of poetry. Yeats in particular developed an enormously flexible metric. In an earlier chapter, we analyzed his skillful use of slant rhyme. Many contemporary poets move freely from traditional verse to free verse, sometimes within the context of a single composition.

In addition, we believe that the two bins—one marked "traditional metrics," one marked "free verse"—are now clearly inadequate. Midway between traditional metrics and free verse, an impressively large body of work has been growing which has some of the qualities of both but which can properly be classified with neither. While recognizing that any system of classification will create some problems as it solves others, we suggest that future classifications of poetic work add a third bin to the classifier's desk—a bin labeled self-devised forms.

In a sense this label is misleading, for any good free-verse poem has a satisfying form which the poet has chosen, and, as we have seen, the traditional forms allow a large amount of leeway for individual choice on the part of the poet, most notably the initial choice of meter and stanza form. What we mean by a self-devised form is verse limited by some regularizing nontraditional pattern.

Let us illustrate by example. Here are three poems, all successfully realized on their own terms, concerning a somewhat similar theme. The first is "Channel Firing," by Thomas Hardy.

> That night your great guns, unawares,
> Shook all our coffins as we lay,
> And broke the chancel window-squares,
> We thought it was the judgment-day.
>
> And sat upright. While drearisome
> Arose the howl of wakened hounds:
> The mouse let fall the altar-crumb,
> The worms drew back into the mounds,

The glebe cow drooled. Till God called, "No;
It's gunnery practice out at sea
Just as before you went below;
The world is as it used to be:

All nations striving strong to make
Red war yet redder. Mad as hatters
They do no more for Christés sake
Than you who are helpless in such matters.

That this is not the judgment-hour
For some of them's a blessed thing,
For if it were they'd have to scour
Hell's floor for so much threatening . . .

Ha, ha. It will be warmer when
I blow the trumpet (if indeed
I ever do; for you are men,
And rest eternal sorely need.)

So down we lay again. "I wonder,
Will the world ever saner be,"
Said one, "than when He sent us under
In our indifferent century!"

And many a skeleton shook his head.
"Instead of preaching forty year,"
My neighbor Parson Thirdly said,
"I wish I had stuck to pipes and beer."

Again the guns disturbed the hour,
Roaring their readiness to avenge,
As far inland as Stourton Tower,
And Camelot, and starlit Stonehenge.

This is a traditional poem—iambic tetrameter quatrains,
rhymed *abab*, the form sometimes called long ballad meter.
Here is our second poem—"Grass," by Carl Sandburg:

Pile the bodies high at Austerlitz and Waterloo.
Shovel them under and let me work—
    I am the grass; I cover all.

240

And pile them high at Gettysburg
And pile them high at Ypres and Verdun.
Shovel them under and let me work.
Two years, ten years, and the passengers ask the conductor:

What place is this?
Where are we now?

I am the grass.
Let me work.

Here we have free verse. Although the repetitions, and especially the twice-repeated phrase, "I am the grass," may remind us of traditional forms such as the rondeau and villanelle in which repeated lines play an important part, essentially the repetitions in this poem provide structural density. The stanzas have irregular numbers of lines; the lines themselves vary in length; and there is no pronounced rhythmic pulse. The language is deliberately flat and conversational, to underscore Sandburg's ironic message. The poem is well made; it is certainly not "formless," anymore than Whitman's "Ever the hard unsunk ground" is formless; but there is no sense of a regularizing norm underlying the verse form which Sandburg wrote.
Finally, let us consider the poem "My Tribe," by John Ciardi.

Everyone in my tribe hates
everyone in your tribe.

Every girl in my tribe wants to
be there when we bring in anyone
from your tribe. Our girls save faggots
in their hope chests for you.

Every boy in my tribe has a peg
from which to hang the scalp of
anyone in your tribe. Our boys
hone knives in their dreams of you.

Everyone in my tribe is proud of
our boys and their dreams, of our
girls and their trousseaus. Our lives
have dear goals across which we

shall all finally kick all of your
heads. We are united.

Visually, this poem is considerably closer in structure to "Channel Firing" than it is to "Grass" or the two Whitman selections which we discussed earlier in the chapter. The stanzas, though rhymeless, are not loosely organized, like the stanzas in "Grass," but patterned in a traditional way: introductory couplet, three quatrains, closing couplet. There is some variation in line length, but it is no greater than the possible range of variation within a poem in metered verse. On the other hand, while there is a strong rhythmic element in these lines, it is not a rhythm which we can describe in any traditional way. It is not accentual-syllabic, and the heavy stresses are irregularly distributed. (In fact, its rough, hacking effect is not unlike the effect of a football yell, just as its approach to war and patriotism might be summed up as, "Give 'em the ax!") Attempts to find a pattern in these lines on the basis of syllable count are equally doomed to failure.

We defined free verse as "verse not limited by any regularizing pattern." But, while there is no normative rhythmic or syllabic pattern employed here, other traditional normative patterns—patterns of line length and stanzaic organization—are employed. So "My Tribe" seems to us suited neither for the "traditional verse" bin, nor the "free-verse" bin.

If you are still unconvinced of the need for a "self-devised form" bin, consider this poem by William Carlos Williams "The Red Wheelbarrow."

so much depends

upon

a red wheel
barrow

glazed with rain
water

beside the white
chickens.

This cannot be anything but poetry written to a pattern. There is both a visual pattern and a word-count pattern (three words in lines 1, 3, 5, and 7; one word in lines 2, 4, 6 and 8), and if we take the trouble of marking stresses, we find that there is an accentual pattern of alternating two- and one-stress lines. This is not only a patterned poem, it is as tightly patterned, in its own way, as a sonnet or a sestina. It is not free verse. It is equally not traditional verse. It is, we would suggest, a fine example of a self-devised form.

What have we gained by establishing a third bin? For one thing, we have provided a language with which we can talk intelligently about the poetry of our own time. We have made it possible to recognize that twentieth-century poetry is not schizophrenically torn between the proponents of order, rationality, and traditional beauty on the one hand, and the advocates of spontaneity, freedom, and the cultural revolution on the other. Human beings write poetry. If it is good poetry they write it out of their deepest experiences. Their deep experiences rarely lend themselves to either-or formulation. Historically, a number of influential poets, among whom William Carlos Williams is prominent, have sought in their work to establish a new kind of metric. While most of the poems which we would classify as self-devised forms are probably *nonce forms*—patterns devised for a particular poem—it should be pointed out that all poetic forms, including the familiar metrical stanzas, were nonce forms once. Some of the new metrists, if we may call them that, find patterns which are satisfying enough to be used extensively throughout a considerable body of their work.

Prominent among these experimenters was Gerard Manley Hopkins, who wrote in the nineteenth century but was not published till the twentieth. Hopkins used an accentual metric which he called "sprung rhythm," characterized by a heavy use of juxtaposed stresses. The peculiar tension and broken music of his lines, while productive of great beauty in his hands, has not become established in the work of others as a regular pattern. But his work probably contributed to the intensification of the twentieth-century line and to freer use of spondees and pyrrhics.

Two very good and very different modern poets have used syllabic verse. Marianne Moore combines syllable count with elaborate stanzaic patterning and rhyme. Dylan Thomas, who also wrote masterfully in accentual-syllabic meter, composed some of his finest poems, such as "Fern Hill," in syllabic verse. All his poetry is characterized by an extremely dense sound texture.

The theories and practice of Williams, Hopkins, Moore, and Thomas, in addition to being embodied in some very lovely poems, are of interest because they have influenced large numbers of other poets. Williams, in particular, has many disciples on the American scene, and his quest for a "new metric" goes on in their work. To discuss in detail the theories and contributions of any of these major experimental figures would be beyond the compass of our discussion here. No one of them, it may be said, has as yet established a norm which seems close to replacing accentual-syllabism as a means of ordering rhythm within poems. This does not mean such a norm may not develop, and for all we know it may be in the process of developing. Any new mode of perception, including new ways of perceiving rhythm, takes a period of time to develop.

Where no clear rhythmic norm exists, variation is not possible, since the reader cannot tell the variant measure from the normative measure. As Gerard Manley Hopkins said of his own sprung rhythm, "Sprung rhythm cannot be counterpointed." To the extent that free-verse poets and poets working within self-devised forms look for expressive rhythmic possibilities, often they fall back on underlying, historically ingrained techniques borrowed from accentual-syllabism. The day may come, however, when a new rhythmic measure of some kind will replace accentual-syllabism; but at the present time, verse in free, self-devised, and accentual-syllabic forms is being created in about equal quantities and with about equal degrees of skill and commitment on the part of the creators.

We have suggested a number of ways in which self-devised forms are patterned—stanzaically, or by limiting the line length accentually (Williams), syllabically (Moore, Thomas) or visually (as in James Dickey's "The Bee," where line lengths vary in what is certainly a patterned way). One rare but interesting category of verse we have not discussed in the *shaped* poem, a poem patterned to make an identifiable shape on the page, usually a shape associated with its subject matter. Shaped poems have been written in traditional meters. May Swenson's "Night Practice" is a shaped poem in which subject-shape becomes compositional form. A special form of shaped poetry is concrete poetry, in which a minimum of letters, words, or other symbols are combined in visually evocative patterns. Nearly all concrete poetry relies on sight rather than hearing for its effect.

The chart below shows in concise form the similarities and differences between the forms of poetry we have discussed in this chapter.

Many of the poems which we regard as self-devised forms probably "grew" into the forms they would take; similarly, a poet with a traditional orientation often finds that he has "grown" himself into a sonnet. But once a poet has used a patterning technique and found that it works for him—that it achieves the effects he wants—then he is likely to repeat it.

Of course all bin classification ultimately falls down. There are always borderline poems, about which people will differ. What matters is not so much agreement as to whether a poem goes into bin *A*, bin *B*, or bin *C*, as the recognition that form is, in a curious way, both superficial and fundamental: superficial because there is, in fact, no great gulf between a Richard Wilbur and an Allen Ginsberg, at least no gulf on the basis of form alone; important in that, without discussing form, we cannot really come to grips with the "poemness" of the poem. Unfortunately, it often seems easier for teacher and student both to discuss subject matter, imagery, diction, and symbolism, and in a pinch to fall back on the biography of the poet, especially if he was a particularly picturesque figure. But, though form may be only the bones

244

| POETIC DEVICE OR TECHNIQUE | TRADITIONAL POEMS | SELF-DEVISED POEMS | FREE-VERSE POEMS |
|---|:---:|:---:|:---:|
| Meter (iambic, trochaic, etc.) | + | v | − |
| Metrical Variation (substitution, etc.) | + | v | − |
| Nonmetrical Rhythms | − | v | + |
| Full End Rhymes | + | v | − |
| Slant End Rhyme | v | + | − |
| Internal Rhyme | + | + | + |
| Alliteration (initial, medial, final) | + | + | + |
| Assonance | + | + | + |
| Caesura | + | + | + |
| Imagery, Symbolism | + | + | + |
| Historic (metrical) Lining | + | v | − |
| Accentual Lining | v | v | − |
| Syllabic Lining | v | v | − |
| Rhetorical Lining | − | v | + |
| Historic Stanzas (quatrains, etc.) | + | v | − |
| Self-created Stanzas | − | v | + |
| Historic Forms (sonnet, etc.) | + | − | − |
| Visually Shaped Forms | v | + | − |
| Figurative Language (Personification, metaphor, simile, etc.) | + | + | + |

Key:
+ Typically or always used
v Occasionally used
− Rarely or never used

of the poem, without the form the poem would be simply loose meat in a slack skin.

We began this text with the infant on his mother's knee, rocking and crowing to "Humpty Dumpty." In a sense the poet always retains the infant's eye—the capacity to experience directly. The infant's eye alone is not enough, for it is the nature of life to grow, to expand, to complicate. But at the center of any artistic vision—at the center of the *Divine Comedy*, of *King Lear*, of any lasting poetry one chooses to name—there is always a single human voice saying, in Walt Whitman's phrase, "I am the man, I suffered, I was there." Amazingly, the things poetry is "about," if we can ever separate form from content to that extent, are remarkably the same from age to age, from country to country. Perhaps there is only one permanent message: that to be alive, to be human, to experience the world, is, for good or evil, a memorable thing. In a world where man seems often a kind of clumsy, badly-made machine, so much more difficult to manufacture and expensive to repair than those made on assembly lines, the poet's message is perhaps more necessary today than it ever was.

*Exercise 1*

## SIMPLE AND FRESH AND FAIR

Simple and fresh and fair from _____ close emerging,    1

As if no artifice of fashion, business, politics, had ever been,   2

Forth from its _____ nook of shelter'd grass—
    innocent, golden,                                           3

_____,                                                          4

The spring's first _____ shows its trustful face.            5

1. The missing word in line 1 is (a) summer, (b) winter, (c) spring, (d) fall.

2. The missing word in line 3 is (a) hidden, (b) sunny, (c) bedazzling, (d) crooked.

3. The missing words in line 4 are (a) radiant as the moon, (b) calm as the dawn, (c) suffused with love, (d) pretty as a picture.

4. The missing word in line 5 is (a) bluebell, (b) daffodil, (c) tulip, (d) dandelion.

ANSWERS

1. A little knowledge of northern hemisphere botany is needed here. When do the first flowers of the year appear? Choices (c) and (d) should be easy to rule out. And by summer, choice (a), most flowers have already appeared. The only answer, then, is (b).

2. Neither metrical nor rhythmic approaches offer us much help here, as all four choices would seem possible. Phonemic analysis likewise is not productive since each of the four possibilities blends into the line. Look at the diction that pervades the poem: "simple," "fresh," "innocent," and "trustful." Neither choice (c) nor (d) seem to fit the pattern. Both choice (a) and (b) are possibilities, but (b) was the poet's choice, because it is more accurate in terms of the growing habits of the flower mentioned in line 5.

3. Here again diction provides the major clue. It is a quiet, unpretentious little poem, and both choices (a) and (c) are too strong. Choice (d) is, as we hope you have noted, the type of cliché that genuine poets avoid. Choice (b), in addition to maintaining the desired level of diction, also provides a pleasantly unobstrusive repetition of the vowel in "calm" and "dawn."

4. The last word in line 3 tells us the color of the flower; therefore choice (a) is not a possibility. Daffodils, tulips, and dandelions, however, can be golden. Tulips, though, are cultivated flowers, and the poem seems clearly to be about a natural, uncultivated flower, which daffodils sometimes are and dandelions always are. The word "nook," though, in line 3 provides us with the needed clue. Dandelions grow in such a way that they form their own "nook," their own sun-space, as the broad leaves spread out to form a cup for the developing flower. (d) was Whitman's choice.

*Exercise 2*

## LXVI

| | |
|---|---:|
| If I should cast off this ―――――― coat, | 1 |
| And go free into the mighty sky; | 2 |
| ―――――――――― | 3 |
| But a vast blue, | 4 |
| Echoless, ――――― ― | 5 |
| What then? | 6 |

1. The missing word in line 1 is (a) pretty, (b) abraided, (c) gorgeous, (d) tattered.
2. Line 3 is (a) And find nought there, (b) Finding nothing in it, (c) If I should find nothing there, (d) Discovering nothing.

247

3. The missing word in line 5 is (a) ignorant, (b) silent, (c) bereft, (d) irrational.

ANSWERS

1. Does the condition of the coat seem particularly relevant to the sense of the poem? If not, then the adjective modifying "coat" is probably chosen for its phonemic pattern, a pattern which will through repetition of other phonemes in the line bind the line tightly together. Choice (a) does repeat the /t/, and choice (b) repeats the /d/. Choice (c) echoes only the /s/. Choice (d) repeats not only the /t/ and /d/ phonemes of cast and coat, but it also has the /a/ vowel in common with cast. Choice (d) is the poet's choice.

2. In our discussion of free verse, the importance of parallelism was stressed. In lines 1 and 2 we get an "If . . . and" structure which is paralleled by the "If . . . but" structure of lines 3 and 4. Choice (c).

3. The sense of the poem dictates a word which indicates a mindless, purposeless universe. There is no life beyond human, worldly life, speculates the poet. All choices, on this basis, seem reasonable. Therefore, we need to choose that word which is most rhythmically or phonetically apt. Stephen Crane's choice was (a) probably because it repeats the DUM di di pattern of "echoless."

*Exercise 3*

## TO A STEAM ROLLER

| | |
|---|---|
| The illustration | 1 |
| is nothing to you without the application. | 2 |
|     You lack half wit. You crush all the particles down | 3 |
| into close conformity, and then walk back and forth on them. | 4 |
| Sparkling chips of rock | 5 |
| are crushed down to the level _____. | 6 |
|     Were not 'impersonal judgement in aesthetic | 7 |
|       matters, a metaphysical impossibility," you | 8 |
| _____ achieve | 9 |
| it. As for butterflies, I can hardly _____ | 10 |
| of one's attending upon you, but to question | 11 |
| the congruence of the complement is vain, _____. | 12 |

248

1. The missing words in line 6 are (a) of chalk, (b) of base emetic, (c) of the parapatetic, (d) of the parent block.
2. The missing word(s) in line 9 is/are (a) might, (b) could, imperceptibly, (c) could decently, (d) might fairly.
3. The missing word in line 10 is (a) conceive, (b) think, (c) imagine, (d) mention.
4. The missing word(s) in line 12 is/are (a) period, (b) if it exists, (c) unless predictable, (d) useless vanity.

## Exercise 4

1. Using the same basic theme or subject matter, write three variants of a poem, at least eight lines long, following the prin ciples of traditional verse, self-devised verse, and free verse.
2. Transcribe several lines of advertising from radio or television. What prosodic principles have been employed by the advertising copywriter?
3. Find a passage in a short story, or novel that you feel is especially effective or moving. Line it so that it looks like poetry. What, if any, prosodic principles are evident in your revision?
4. Write a brief scene for a play in which two poets meet and talk (poetically, of course). You might choose contrasting types, such as Emily Dickinson and Walt Whitman, or you might choose poets from different eras, such as William Shakespeare and Allen Ginsberg.
5. Choose a short poem in traditional form. Rewrite it as free verse. What has been lost?
6. Choose a short self-devised or free verse poem. Rewrite it in a traditional form. What have you gained or lost?

# 9

## Poems

250

## WHAT IS THE GRASS?

A child said, What is the grass? fetching it to me with full
    hands;
How could I answer the child? . . . . I do not know what it
    is any more than he.

I guess it must be the flag of my disposition, out of hopeful
    green stuff woven.

Or I guess it is the handkerchief of the Lord,
A scented gift and remembrancer designedly dropped    5
Bearing the owner's name someway in the corners, that we
    may see and remark, and say Whose?

Or I guess the grass is itself a child . . . . the produced babe
    of the vegetation.
Or I guess it is a uniform hieroglyphic,
And it means, Sprouting alike in broad zones and narrow
    zones,
Growing among black folks as among white,    10
Kanuck, Tuckahoe, Congressman, Cuff, I give them the
    same, I receive them the same.

251

. . .

I wish I could translate the hints about the dead young
    men and women,
And the hints about old men and mothers, and the
    offspring taken soon out of their laps.

What do you think has become of the young and old men?
And what do you think has become of the women and
    children?                                       15

They are alive and well somewhere;
The smallest sprout shows there is really no death,
And if ever there was it led forward life, and does not wait
    at the end to arrest it,
And ceased the moment life appeared.

All goes onward and outward . . . . and nothing collapses,   20
And to die is different from what any one supposed, and
    luckier.

WALT WHITMAN


## A MAN SAID TO THE UNIVERSE

A man said to the universe:
"Sir, I exist!"
"However, replied the universe,
"The fact has not created in me
A sense of obligation."                                    5

STEPHEN CRANE


## SHOULD THE WIDE WORLD ROLL AWAY

Should the wide world roll away,
Leaving black terror,
Limitless night,
Nor God, nor man, nor place to stand
Would be to me essential                               5
If thou and thy white arms were there,
And the fall to doom a long way.

STEPHEN CRANE

## THE DANCE

In Breughel's great picture, The Kermess,
the dancers go round, they go round and
around, the squeal and the blare and the
tweedle of bagpipes, a bugle and fiddles
tipping their bellies (round as the thick-      5
sided glasses whose wash they impound)
their hips and their bellies off balance
to turn them. Kicking and rolling about
the Fair Grounds, swinging their butts, those
shanks must be sound to bear up under such     10
rollicking measures, prance as they dance
in Breughel's great picture, The Kermess.

WILLIAM CARLOS WILLIAMS

## SHINE, PERISHING REPUBLIC

While this America settles in the mould of its vulgarity,
    heavily thickening to empire,
And protest, only a bubble in the molten mass, pops and
    sighs, out, and the mass hardens,
I sadly smiling remember that the flower fades to make
    fruit, the fruit rots to make earth.
Out of the mother; and through the spring exultances, ripe-
    ness and decadence; and home to the mother.
You make haste on decay: not blameworthy; life is good,
    be it stubbornly long or suddenly      5
A mortal splendor: meteors are not needed less than moun-
    tains: shine, perishing republic.
But for my children, I would have them keep their distance
    from the thickening center; corruption
Never has been compulsory, when the cities lie at the
    monster's feet there are left the mountains.
And boys, be in nothing so moderate as in love of man, a
    clever servant, insufferable master.
There is the trap that catches noblest spirits, that caught—
    they say—God, when he walked on earth.      10

ROBINSON JEFFERS

253

## THE FISH

wade
through black jade.
   Of the crow-blue mussel-shells, one keeps
   adjusting the ash-heaps;
      opening and shutting itself like         5

an
injured fan.
   The barnacles which encrust the side
   of the wave, cannot hide
      there for the submerged shafts of the      10

sun,
split like spun
   glass, move themselves with spotlight swiftness
   into the crevices—
      in and out, illuminating         15

the
turquoise sea
   of bodies. The water drives a wedge
   of iron through the iron edge
      of the cliff; whereupon the stars,      20

pink
rice-grains, ink-
   bespattered jelly-fish, crabs like green
   lilies, and submarine
      toadstools, slide each on the other.     25

All
external
   marks of abuse are present on this
   defiant edifice—
      all the physical features of        30

ac-
cident—lack
   of cornice, dynamite grooves, burns, and
   hatchet strokes, these things stand
      out on it; the chasm-side is       35

dead.
Repeated
   evidence has proved that it can live
   on what can not revive
      its youth. The sea grows old in it.          40

MARIANNE MOORE

## *THE DIRTY WORD*

The dirty word hops in the cage of the mind like the Pondi-
cherry vulture, stomping with its heavy left claw on the
sweet meat of the brain and tearing it with its vicious beak,
ripping and chopping the flesh. Terrified, the small boy
bears the big bird of the dirty word into the house, and   5
grunting, puffing, carries it up the stairs to his own room in
the skull. Bits of black feather cling to his clothes and his
hair as he locks the staring creature in the dark closet.

   All day the small boy returns to the closet to examine
and feed the bird, to caress and kick the bird, that now  10
snaps and flaps its wings savagely whenever the door is
opened. How the boy trembles and delights at the sight of
the white excrement of the bird! How the bird leaps and
rushes against the walls of the skull, trying to escape from
the zoo of the vocabulary! How wildly snaps the sweet  15
meat of the brain in its rage.

   And the bird outlives the man, being freed at the man's
death-funeral by a word from the rabbi.

   But I one morning went upstairs and opened the door
and entered the closet and found in the cage of my mind  20
the great bird dead. Softly I wept it and softly removed it
and softly buried the body of the bird in the hollyhock garden of the house I lived in twenty years before. And out of
the worn black feathers of the wing have I made pens to
write these elegies, for I have outlived the bird, and I have  25
murdered it in my early manhood.

KARL SHAPIRO

255

## FERN HILL

Now as I was young and easy under the apple boughs
About the lilting house and happy as the grass was green,
   The night above the dingle starry,
    Time let me hail and climb
Golden in the heydays of his eyes,                 5
And honoured among wagons I was prince of the apple towns
And once below a time I lordly had the trees and leaves
    Trail with daisies and barley
   Down the rivers of the windfall light.

And as I was green and carefree, famous among the barns   10
About the happy yard and singing as the farm was home,
   In the sun that is young once only,
    Time let me play and be
Golden in the mercy of his means,
And green and golden I was huntsman and herdsman,
   the calves                            15
Sang to my horn, the foxes on the hills barked clear and cold,
    And the sabbath rang slowly
   In the pebbles of the holy streams.

All the sun long it was running, it was lovely, the hay
Fields high as the house, the tunes from the chimneys, it
     was air                           20
   And playing, lovely and watery

    And fire green as grass.
    And nightly under the simple stars
As I rode to sleep the owls were bearing the farm away,
All the moon long I heard, blessed among stables, the
     nightjars                       25
   Flying with the ricks, and the horses
    Flashing into the dark.

And then to awake, and the farm, like a wanderer white
With the dew, come back, the cock on his shoulder: it was all
   Shining, it was Adam and maiden,           30
    The sky gathered again
   And the sun grew round that very day.

So it must have been after the birth of the simple light
In the first, spinning place, the spellbound horses walking
    warm
      Out of the whinnying green stable              35
        On to the fields of praise.

And honoured among foxes and pheasants by the gay house
Under the new made clouds and happy as the heart was long,
    In the sun born over and over,
        I ran my heedless ways,                40
    My wishes raced through the house high hay
And nothing I cared, at my sky blue trades, that time allows
In all his tuneful turning so few and such morning songs
    Before the children green and golden
        Follow him out of grace,             45

Nothing I cared, in the lamb white days, that time would take
    me
Up to the swallow thronged loft by the shadow of my hand,
    In the moon that is always rising,
        Nor that riding to sleep
    I should hear him fly with the high fields      50
And wake to the farm forever fled from the childless land.
Oh as I was young and easy in the mercy of his means,
    Time held me green and dying
    Though I sang in my chains like the sea.

DYLAN THOMAS

## DREAM SONGS: 16

Henry's pelt was put on sundry walls
where it did much resemble Henry and
them persons was delighted.
Especially his long & glowing tail
by all them was admired, and visitors.      5
They whistled: This is *it*!

Golden, whilst your frozen daiquiris
whir at midnight, gleams on you his fur
& silky & black.
Mission accomplished, pal.                                          10
My molten yellow & moonless bag,
drained, hangs at rest.

Collect in the cold depths barracuda. Ay,
in Sealdah Station some possessionless
children survive to die.                                           15
The Chinese communes hum. Two daiquiris
withdrew into a corner of the gorgeous room
and one told the other a lie.

JOHN BERRYMAN


## DREAM SONGS: 76 (HENRY'S CONFESSION)

Nothin very bad happen to me lately.
How you explain that?—I explain that, Mr Bones,
terms o' your bafflin odd sobriety.
Sober as man can get, no girls, no telephones,
what could happen bad to Mr Bones?                                 5
—If life is a handkerchief sandwich,

in a modesty of death I join my father
who dared so long agone leave me.
A bullet on a concrete stoop
close by a smothering southern sea                                 10
spreadeagled on an island, by my knee.
—You is from hunger, Mr Bones,

I offers you this handkerchief, now set
your left foot by my right foot,
shoulder to shoulder, all that jazz,                               15
arm in arm, by the beautiful sea,
hum a little, Mr Bones.
—I saw nobody coming, so I went instead.

JOHN BERRYMAN

## NIGHT PRACTICE

*fighting to live & to live the life she wants to.*

```
                          I
                        will
                     remem-
                   ber with
                my breath to
             make a moun-                    5
           tain, with my
        sucked-in breath a val-
       ley, with my pushed-out
     breath a mountain. I will make
   a valley wider than the whisper,        10
 I will make a higher mountain than
   the cry; will with my will breathe a
 mountain, I will with my will breathe a
 valley. I will push out a mountain, suck in
 a valley, deeper than the shout YOU MUST   15
 DIE, harder, heavier, sharper, a mountain than the
 truth YOU MUST DIE. I will remember. My breath will
 make a mountain. My will will remember to will. I, suck-
 ing, pushing, I will breathe a valley, I will breathe a mountain.
```

MAY SWENSON  *a "shaped" poem*

## THE BEE

*To the football coaches of Clemson College, 1942*

One dot
Grainily shifting    we at roadside and
The smallest wings coming    along the rail fence out
Of the woods    one dot    of all that green. It now
Becomes flesh-crawling    then the quite still        5
Of stinging. I must live faster for my terrified
Small son    it is on him. Has come. Clings.

Old wingback, come
To life. If your knee action is high
Enough, the fat may fall in time    God damn        10
You, Dickey, *dig*    this is your last time to cut

And run    but you must give it everything you have
Left, for screaming near your screaming child is the sheer
Murder of California traffic: some bee hangs driving
Your child                                                    15
Blindly onto the highway. Get there however
Is still possible. Long live what I badly did
At Clemson    and all of my clumsiest drives
For the ball    all of my trying to turn
The corner downfield    and my spindling explosions        20
Through the five-hole over tackle. O backfield
Coach Shag Norton,

Tell me as you never yet have told me
To get the lead out    scream whatever will get
The Slow-motion of middle age off me    I cannot          25
Make it this way    I will have to leave
My feet    they are gone    I have him where
He lives    and down we go singing with screams into
The dirt,
Son-screams of fathers    screams of dead coaches turning   30
To approval    and from between us the bee rises screaming
With flight    grainily shifting    riding the rail fence
Back into the woods    traffic blasting past us
Unchanged, nothing heard through the air-
conditioning glass    we lying at roadside full             35
Of the forearm prints
Of roadrocks    strawberries on our elbows as from
Scrimmage with the varsity    now we can get
Up    stand    turn away from the highway    look straight
Into trees. See, there is nothing coming out    no          40
Smallest wing    no shift of a flight-grain    nothing
Nothing. Let us go in, son, and listen
For some tobacco-
mumbling voice in the branches    to say "That's
a little better."    to our lives still hanging             45
By a hair. There is nothing to stop us    we can go
Deep    deeper    into elms, and listen to traffic die
Roaring, like a football crowd from which we have
Vanished. Dead coaches live in the air, son    live

In the ear                                                                    50
Like fathers, and *urge*   and *urge*. They want you better
Than you are. When needed, they rise and curse you    they
   scream
When something must be saved. Here, under this tree,
We can sit down. You can sleep, and I can try
                                                                              55

Alive, and safe from bees: the smile of some kind

Of savior—
Of touchdowns, of fumbles, battles,
Lives. Let me sit here with you, son
As on the bench, while the first string takes back        60
Over, far away    and say with my silentest tongue, with the
man-creating bruises of my arms    with a live leaf a quick
Dead hand on my shoulder, "Coach Norton, I am your boy."

JAMES DICKEY


## *AMERICAN CHANGE*

> The first I looked on, after a long time far from home
in mid Atlantic on a summer day
> Dolphins breaking the glassy water under the blue
sky,
> a gleam of silver in my cabin, fished up out of my
jangling new pocket of coins and green dollars                  5
> —held in my palm, the head of the feathered indian,
old Buck-Rogers eagle eyed face, a gash of hunger in the
cheek
> gritted jaw of the vanished man begone like a Hebrew
with hairlock combed down the side—O Rabbi Indian
> what visionary gleam 100 years ago on Buffalo prairie  10
under the molten cloud shot sky, 'the same clear light
10000 miles in all directions'
> but now with all the violin music of Vienna, gone into
the great slot machine of Kansas City, Reno—
> The coin seemed so small after vast European coppers  15
thick francs leaden pesetas, lira endless and heavy,
> a miniature primeval memoralized in 5c. nickle candy-

store nostalgia of the redskin, dead on silver coin,
    with shaggy buffalo on reverse, hump-backed little
tail incurved, head butting against the rondure of Eternity, 20
    cock forelock below, bearded shoulder muscle folded
below muscle, head of prophet, bowed,
    vanishing beast of Time, hoar body rubbed clean of
wrinkles and shining like polished stone, bright metal in
my forefinger, ridiculous buffalo—Go to New York.    25

    Dime next I found, Minerva, sexless cold & chill,
ascending goddess of money—and was it the wife of Wallace Stevens, truly?
    and now from the locks flowing the miniature wings
of speedy thought,    30
    executive dyke, Minerva, goddess of Madison Ave-
nue, forgotten useless dime that can't buy hot dog, dead
dime—

    Then we've George Washington, less primitive, the
snub-nosed quarter, smug eyes and mouth, some idiot's
design of the sexless Father,    35
    naked down to his neck, a ribbon in his wig, high
forehead, Roman line down the nose, fat cheeked, still
showing his falsetooth ideas—O Eisenhower & Washing-
ton—O Fathers—No movie star dark beauty—O thou Big-
noses—
    Quarter, remembered quarter, 40c. in all—What'll 40
you buy me when I land—one icecream soda?—
    poor pile of coins, original reminders of the sadness,
forgotten money of America—
    nostalgia of the first touch of those coins, American
change,    45
    the memory in my aging hand, the same old silver
reflective there,
    the thin dime hidden between my thumb and fore-
finger
    All the struggles for those coins, the sadness of their
reappearance    50
    my reappearance on those fabled shores
    and the failure of that Dream, that Vision of Money

reduced to this haunting recollection
      of the gas lot in Paterson where I found half a dollar
gleaming in the grass—                                 55

      I have a $5 bill in my pocket—it's Lincoln's sour
black head moled wrinkled, forelocked too, big eared, flags
of announcement flying over the bill, stamps in green and
spiderweb black,
      long numbers in racetrack green, immense promise,
a girl, a hotel, a busride to Albany, a night of brilliant  60
drunk in some faraway corner of Manhattan
      a stick of several teas, or paper or cap of Heroin, or
a $5 strange present to the blind.
      Money money, reminder, I might as well write poems
to you—dear American money—O statue of Liberty I ride  65
enfolded in money in my mind to you—and last

      Ahhh! Washington again, on the Dollar, same poetic
black print, dark words, The United States of America,
innumerable numbers
      R956422481 One Dollar This Certificate is Legal  70
Tender (tender!) for all debts public and private
      My God My God why have you foresaken me
      Ivy Baker Priest Series 1935 F
      and over, the Eagle, wild wings outspread, halo of the
Stars encircled by puffs of smoke & flame—                  75
      a circle the Masonic Pyramid, the sacred Swedenborg-
ian Dollar America, bricked up to the top, & floating sur-
real above
      the triangle of holy outstaring Eye sectioned out of
the aire, shining
      light emitted from the eyebrowless triangle—and a  80
desert of cactus, scattered all around, clouds afar,
      this being the Great Seal of our Passion, Annuit
Coeptes, Novis Ordo Seculorum,
      the whole surrounded by green spiderwebs designed
by T-Men to prevent foul counterfeit—                   85
                         ONE

*S.S. United States, 1958*

ALLEN GINSBERG

## JACK'S BLUES

I'm going to roll up
a monkey and smoke it, put
an elephant in the pot. I'm going out
and never come back.

What's better than that.                                        5
Lying on your back, flat
on your back with your
eyes to the view.

Oh the view is blue, I saw that
too, yesterday and you,                                         10
red eyes and blue,
funked.

I'm going to roll up
a rug and smoke it, put
the car in the garage and I'm                                   15
gone, like a sad old candle.

ROBERT CREELEY

## AUTUMN BEGINS IN MARTINS FERRY, OHIO

In the Shreve High football stadium,
I think of Polacks nursing long beers in Tiltonsville,
And gray faces of Negroes in the blast furnace at Benwood,
And the ruptured night watchman of Wheeling Steel,
Dreaming of heroes.                                             5

All the proud fathers are ashamed to go home.
Their women cluck like starved pullets,
Dying for love.

Therefore,
Their sons grow suicidally beautiful                            10
At the beginning of October,
And gallop terribly against each other's bodies.

JAMES WRIGHT

264

## HAWK ROOSTING

I sit in the top of the wood, my eyes closed.
Inaction, no falsifying dream
Between my hooked head and hooked feet:
Or in sleep rehearse perfect kills and eat.

The convenience of the high trees!                    5
The air's buoyancy and the sun's ray
Are of advantage to me;
And the earth's face upward for my inspection.

My feet are locked upon the rough bark.
It took the whole of Creation                         10
To produce my foot, my each feather:
Now I hold Creation in my foot

Or fly up, and revolve it all slowly—
I kill where I please because it is all mine.
There is no sophistry in my body:                     15
My manners are tearing off heads—

The allotment of death.
For the one path of my flight is direct
Through the bones of the living.
No arguments assert my right:                         20

The sun is behind me.
Nothing has changed since I began.
My eye has permitted no change.
I am going to keep things like this.

TED HUGHES

## ALL THERE IS TO KNOW
## ABOUT ADOLPH EICHMANN

EYES: .............................. Medium

HAIR: .............................. Medium

WEIGHT: ........................... Medium

HEIGHT: ........................... Medium

DISTINGUISHING FEATURES: ................. None

NUMBER OF FINGERS: ..................... Ten          5

NUMBER OF TOES: ....................... Ten

INTELLIGENCE: ......................... Medium

What did you expect?

Talons?

Oversize incisors?                                     10

Green saliva?

Madness?

LEONARD COHEN

# Index of Poetic Terms

# Index of Authors and Titles